Saturday
Morning
Fever

Also by Timothy Burke

*Lifebuoy Men, Lux Women: Commodification, Consumption and
Cleanliness in Modern Zimbabwe* (1996)

Saturday Morning Fever

Timothy Burke
and
Kevin Burke

St. Martin's Griffin
NEW YORK

All photos are courtesy of Kevin Burke unless otherwise indicated.

ISBN 0-312-16996-5

First St. Martin's Griffin Edition: January 1999

Design by James Sinclair

10   9   8   7   6   5   4   3   2

To Mom and Dad

Contents

Secret Squirrel • Atom Ant • Dynomutt • Mighty Man and Yukk • The Secret Lives of Waldo Kitty • Ark II • Shazam! • Isis • The Ghost Busters • Space Academy • Thundarr • Tarzan • He-Man • Smurfs • Monchhichis • Snorks • The Biskitts • The Care Bears Family • The Littles • Star Trek • Emergency +4 • Dungeons & Dragons • The Real Ghostbusters • G.I. Joe

Introduction

The Kids Strike Back

Saturday morning cartoons are regarded by most American adults over the age of forty as having marginally more redeeming social value than hard-core pornography . . . but perhaps not quite as much value as an episode of a television talk show dealing with incestuous anorexic biker Rotarians. "Saturday morning" has long served as a shorthand epithet for culture judged to be juvenile, low-quality, moronic, mind-numbing, or cut-rate.

We have two words to the folks who think this way: Piss off.

It's not that we disagree with the characterization; at least, not exactly. A lot of Saturday Morning was crap. But it's *our* crap, and we're tired of smug folks twice our age telling us their crap was better than our crap and we're going to grow up and turn into demon spawn because we sat in front of the cathode god like zombies and never got any fresh air and didn't get out and make our own tree houses from scratch or didn't sell apples on the street during the Great Depression or didn't eat bark during long prairie winters or didn't get dysentery while crossing the Atlantic Ocean on the *Mayflower* or whatever.

This is our past, both personal and generational, we're talking about. We think we turned out more or less okay even though we sat mesmerized in front of the television week after week, watching cartoons ranging from *Jonny Quest* to *The Real Ghostbusters.* We think our friends turned out okay. We think most people our age turned out okay, and when they didn't, we don't think Saturday Morning had much to do with it.

In the long history of disputes over children's television, a history full of rancor and self-righteousness, there has always been one voice missing from the discussion. The parents have spoken, either as part of strident advocacy groups or as guilty individuals convinced by those same advocacy groups that they fucked up their kids by letting them watch cartoons. The experts have spoken, proclaiming time and again that they have scientifically proven that whenever a cartoon animal gets hit on the head with an anvil, children are moved to riot in the streets. The middlebrow cultural critics have spoken, extending the sneering contempt they already feel for the mass medium of television to snide new lows when forced to talk about kidvid. The executives have spoken, currying favor with hostile parents while protecting their bottom line. The kidvid producers have spoken, trying to figure out how to produce more programming at a lower price without killing the goose that lays their golden eggs.

But the kids have never spoken.

Until now.

Oh, kids spoke strongly enough by their actions, flocking again and again to the glowing screen to watch the antics of Huckleberry Hound or Sigmund the Sea Monster while fastidiously ignoring most allegedly educational programming. But the only adults who deigned to recognize that fact were the advertisers. It seemed that adults always assumed we were deranged or hypnotized, unable to control ourselves. Kids would tell any adult who cared to hear—and a wonderful few of them, having not forgotten their own childhoods, heard us—that we all knew it was make-believe when the Coyote fell off a cliff and Thundarr the Barbarian crushed some mutant sorcerer.

Now we hope all of the howling mob who moaned, whined, and pleaded for the execution of Saturday Morning will have to listen. We're all grown up. Some of us make television shows now, and those of us who do have made new cartoons and children's shows that capture the best spirit of the Saturday Morning of our youth and surpass it by a huge margin. Some of us buy kidvid memorabilia like lunch boxes or albums with contemporary bands singing cartoon theme songs. Some of us indulge in nostalgia about our favorite programs over the Internet now: our voices are heard, louder and louder, as we do so. Some of us are a target market whom advertisers hope to reach by throwing in references to Speed Racer or the Smurfs.

And some of us write books. Listen as we tell you: We're okay. Our TV shows were okay. Turn your energies toward protesting violence against baby seals or something similarly useful. If you cannot bring yourself to praise Saturday Morning, at least try to refrain from burying it.

This book is a collaboration between an academic and a journalist who also works in the film industry. As such, it's something of a hybrid. There is a lot of scholarly literature on popular culture, much of it very good, and a book certainly could be written about Saturday Morning from that perspective. This is not that book, however. Neither is this a coffee-table book, though it has pictures in it. Nor is it a comprehensive overview of children's television: that book has been written several times already, most notably with Gary Grossman's *Saturday Morning TV.* Instead, we've written a gleefully irresponsible book, largely a chronicle of our personal memories and impressions of the kidvid of our youth. It is not a dispassionate analysis of all the important issues involved. We don't cover children's television from the fifties, for example. We'll argue in chapter 1 that there are some good objective reasons for that omission, but the most important reason is simply this: we weren't alive then. There are similar omissions and gaps elsewhere in the book. We go where our own personal and generational obsessions and interests call us. Our central purpose in these pages is to tell our readers about how we experienced and remember Saturday Morning, to allow us—the kids who watched the cartoons—to speak at last for ourselves rather than be forever spoken about. This is a history, a rant, a plea, a meditation.

We've divided this book into two parts. The first section of this book is the history of Saturday Morning, its development as a distinctive cultural institution. The second part of this book, its heart and soul, is our opinionated take on Saturday morning television: the shows, the generational experience, and the conventional criticisms of kidvid.

Many people generously assisted us in the course of writing this book. First and foremost are our contemporaries. We'd rather not use the much-maligned label "Generation X," so we'll refer to them mostly as Saturday Morning veterans instead. Over the course of the past three years, we've had conversations, both in person and over the Internet, with hundreds of individuals. We have thousands of pages of archived E-mail full of stories, questions, and arguments relating to Saturday Morning. There are a few groups whom we want to thank specifically. Many students at Swarthmore College, where Tim teaches, have provided useful advice, particularly about programs from the mid-eighties that we ourselves are almost too old to remember well. More importantly, regular contributors to the Usenet newsgroup alt.society.generation-x (referred to subsequently as asg-x) and several E-mail listservers which spun off from the newsgroup have consistently proven to be the most fertile wellspring of ideas, memories, and witty observations that we encountered during the writing of this book. We have mentioned a few of the participants in these fora by name, but a great many more helped us shape this book by sharing their thoughts and memories.

Many television professionals and others involved in the history of Saturday Morning have been kind enough to share their thoughts with us or otherwise assist us: Lou Scheimer, Fred Silverman, Joseph

Barbera, Tom Minton, Victoria Fromkin, J. Michael Straczynski, Mark Evanier, Peggy Charren, Eddie Fitzgerald, Richard Pursel, Justin McCormack, Dave Burke, David Robertson, Julia Greenburg, Tim McDonnah, Tanya Laden, Jerry Beck, Gabriel Alvarez, Grace Ressler, Jon Snyder, and Mike Rex. We have also made extensive use of published interviews and other secondary materials, particularly from the *New York Times* and *Los Angeles Times,* and we're also immensely grateful for important and comprehensive reference works like *Total Television* and *Television Network Weekend Programming, 1959–1990.*

A few other people are due special thanks. Our editor at St. Martin's Press, Gordon Van Gelder, demonstrated immense patience with numerous lengthy delays in the completion of this book, and we are very grateful for all his advice and assistance along the way. Our siblings Sharon and Brendan read various drafts of the manuscript with a keen eye, as did Tim's wife, Melissa Mandos. Their combined patience, good judgment, enthusiasm, and love has sustained us both throughout our work on this book. Finally, we'd like to thank our mom and dad for all their support, guidance, and wisdom. They probably never dreamed that all those mornings watching cartoons might lead to something useful, but they nevertheless supplied the television set.

Chapter One

Weirdo Superheroes: The Origins of Saturday Morning

Eight A.M., Saturday, 1974. Children all across the United States are staring at television sets with slack jaws and glassy eyes. A mother somewhere is concerned. An advocacy group is writing a report. A congressman is denouncing the FCC. A sanctimonious intellectual is writing about the vast wasteland of television. A child psychiatrist is recording his experimental subjects smacking Bozo the clown upside the head after watching cartoons. Us? Tim is ten, Kevin is five. We're with the rest of the nation's kids, probably watching *The Bugs Bunny Show* on ABC. If we're lucky, maybe they'll show "Duck Amuck" or "Wabbit Season." If we're in a really strange mood—or maybe if Tim briefly loses his dictatorial control over the television dial—the set is tuned to *Lidsville* instead.

But how did we get there? Only ten years earlier, in 1964, there was children's television, but Saturday morning didn't really exist yet. (Neither did we.) Ten years before that—when our parents were still teenagers—children's television was in its infancy, taking baby steps with *Howdy Doody* and *Kukla, Fran and Ollie*. Radio still held a central place in American popular culture for both kids and adults.

So where did Saturday morning come from, how did it evolve, and where is it going?

Origins are always a tricky matter, and endlessly debatable. But it seems clear to us that "Saturday morning" as we refer to it in this book really began to take shape after 1960. Yes, there were numerous children's TV shows before that time. Yes, children's entertainment had some kind of association with Saturdays all the way back to radio's high-water mark and probably before that. But children's TV was much more evenly distributed throughout the week during the fifties, and, like most television between 1945 and 1958, those early children's shows also depended heavily upon their radio antecedents. The ritualistic experience of watching television, mostly cheaply animated cartoons, from dawn to noon on Saturdays didn't mature into its familiar shape until the mid-1960s.

Saturday morning was not merely a more intense version of the kidvid of the 1950s: it also became (and remains) one of the primary battlegrounds for conflicts over television and its impact on American life. Saturday morning not only became a different kind of experience for its viewers in the 1960s, it became a quintessential shorthand reference to the supposedly degraded quality of television in general. Saturday morning also became a crucial generational rite of passage for the children who consumed it, a gold mine of in-jokes and cultural reference points. In ways that are only just now being recognized, Saturday morning also changed the shape not just of television but also popular culture as a whole. Kids' cartoons nurtured new audiences, they generated new forms, they produced new ideas and attitudes. We're not just talking about television on Saturdays in this book: we're talking about a total cultural institution, capital-S capital-M Saturday Morning.

The fifties laid the groundwork, or course. Both legitimate researchers and paranoid goofballs like Frederic Wertham (a psychiatrist who led a notorious crusade against horror comics at the height of the cultural paranoia of the fifties) began to turn their attention to the relationship between children and television during the fifties. For every careful and balanced study written in this early phase, there was an equally weird and alarmist one.

For example, in the early fifties, one orthodontist claimed to have diagnosed a new dental problem, "television malocclusion," described as "an abnormal arrangement of the teeth likely to be caused by Junior's cradling his jaw in his hand as he watches television." In 1957, a British official conjured the specter of an entire generation of disfigured children who would be afflicted with "TV squint." Similar complaints were made around the same time about "TV slouch" and other syndromes.

The late fifties were also drenched with concern over a semimythical creature shambling across the front pages and the silver screen: the "juvenile delinquent." The film delinquent might be defined by Marlon Brando or James Dean, but he—or she—was a lot more likely to be played by a grade Z performer in paranoid films like *I Accuse My Parents* or *The Beatniks*. Alarmed at the spread of forms of terrifying nonconformity like Elvis records and premarital kissing, more than a few "concerned parents" followed the lead of Wertham and his peers in blaming mass media—and especially television—for spreading delinquency.

Television's general reputation was blackened further by the notorious quiz show scandals of the late fifties and other instances of bribery and corruption. It all added up to a general transformation of the public mood: television was seen increasingly as a social menace, and children appeared particularly vulnerable. From this beginning to the present day, people concerned about television's general impact on mass audiences have expressed their overall fears by talking about the impact of television on children. Children became—and remain—the perfect symbolic substitute for the mass audience as a whole. Critics could condescend to children without fear of reprisal, while they felt a bit more inhibited about voicing such opinions about adult audiences.

However, the programs which initially occupied advocates concerned with children and television were not, for the most part, programs expressly intended for children, nor were they shows airing on Saturdays. In the late fifties and early sixties, it was allegedly violent mainstream programs like *The Untouchables* that attracted the most attention. In what would later become a familiar refrain about television, some critics also alleged at the time that television news and documentaries were compromising the innocence of childhood and producing a preternaturally "adult" population of youth.

In fact, Saturday mornings in the late fifties were relatively deserted. Only about a quarter of the total network programming for children could be found on Saturdays in 1958 as compared with over 50 percent a decade later. On NBC in 1959 and 1960, one could find *The Howdy Doody Show, Ruff and Reddy, Fury,* and *Circus Boy.* ABC had *The Soupy Sales Show* at noon and nothing more. CBS had *Captain Kangaroo, Heckle and Jeckle, The Mighty Mouse Playhouse, Sky King,* and in 1960, *The Magic Land of Allakazam* and *Deputy Dawg.* Early animated characters who appeared in syndicated programs included Crusader Rabbit, Colonel Bleep, and the hilariously inept Clutch Cargo, all of whom were prone to show up on Saturday schedules at some stations. At this point, some kids' shows like *Captain Kangaroo* were praised by advocacy groups (*Howdy Doody,* in contrast, near the end of its run, was straightforwardly dismissed by one advocacy group as "monotonous or stupid"); but for the most part, television designed explicitly for children was ignored by social critics.

Some of the shows that would later be associated with Saturday viewing made their first appearances during this period between 1958 and 1961—but not on Saturday mornings. The first cartoon characters to come out of a new animation studio founded by William Hanna and Joseph Barbera were a host of anthropomorphic animals—Huckleberry Hound, Yogi Bear, Quickdraw McGraw, Snagglepuss, Augie Doggie, Dixie and Pixie. The Flintstones also made their first appearance at this point. At their inception, most of these characters were syndicated via the Kellogg's Corporation and typically appeared in the late afternoons or early evenings before mixed audiences of adults, teenagers, and children, just like the Terrytoon characters Heckle and Jeckle, who had originally appeared on television in the early evenings during the mid-1950s. Of the earliest Hanna-Barbera offerings, only *Ruff and Reddy* initially appeared as a network offering on Saturday morning.

The first Hanna-Barbera programs for television were intended to be the televisual equivalent of the animated short films that had preceded movies for many years, which is unsurprising given that both William Hanna and Joseph Barbera worked for MGM's animation department for many years. With *The Flintstones* and then, in 1961, *Top Cat,* Hanna-Barbera went even further: these animated shows were intended to air on an equal basis with other prime-time programming. Nor was Hanna-Barbera alone in this ambition. In 1961, Kayro Production's animated *Calvin and the Colonel,* a thinly disguised version of *Amos and Andy,* appeared on ABC during prime time.

And yet, when *The Jetsons* appeared on prime time in 1962, it lasted only a season there, countered by solid ratings for *Walt Disney's Wonderful World of Color* and the live-action *Dennis the Menace. The Jetsons* was moved to Saturday mornings, thus beginning the exodus of animated programming from the evening hours—an exodus that was completed when *The Flintstones* finally left prime time in 1966. There were a few appearances of prime-time cartoons between *The Jetsons* and the move of *The Flintstones*—most notably *The Adventures of Jonny Quest,* which appeared there for a season in 1964—but by the time *The Flintstones* finally moved to Saturday mornings in 1967, all three networks were airing a densely packed assortment of cartoons (and a few other types of shows) from 8 A.M. to noon. Many of these cartoons were produced by Hanna-Barbera. By 1968, this new and concentrated form of children's television—

Strange but True
Saturday Morning Facts

According to the authors of *Cerealizing America,* Frankenberry cereal initially caused the shit of anyone who ate it to turn pink.

Among the many television-related medical problems described by researchers in the fifties were:

television malocclusion, abnormal arrangement of the jaw caused by cradling your jaw with your hand while watching TV

frogitis, leg deformity caused by viewing TV in a frog-like posture

TV squint, permanent squinting expression from watching too much television

tired-child syndrome, fatigue and headache caused by too much TV watching. The cure: don't watch television.

Victoria Fromkin's invented language Pakuni on *Land of the Lost* was based on the Akan languages of present-day Ghana.

Almost all of Hanna-Barbera's early funny-animal characters wore something around the neck so that the animators didn't have to worry about keeping the appearance of their necks consistent.

Way before David Letterman made a comedic sport out of biting the network hand that fed him, Jay Ward, the creator of *The Bullwinkle Show,* was perpetually getting in trouble for making fun of his bosses at NBC. Among other jabs, he used to host picnics at the Plaza Hotel where the box lunches included "roast peacock."

Saturday morning—was becoming profitable and would likely become more so.

Other developments influenced this buildup of cartoons on Saturdays, most importantly FCC chairman Newton Minow's "vast wasteland" speech in May 1961. Minow's speech was the direct consequence of television's troubles of the late 1950s and the subsequent recasting of television as a morally troubling technology. In the speech, Minow described television as vapid and repetitious. Children entered the picture pivotally about a third of the way into the speech. Minow argued that "ratings should have little influence where children are concerned." Like many commentators in the early 1960s, Minow's first concern was with early-evening viewing by children rather than Saturday morning programming, which was still poorly developed. However, Minow did argue that "there are some fine children's shows, but they are drowned out in the massive doses of cartoons, violence and more violence."

Minow's words set the terms of debate over the impact and meaning of television for decades to come. What is striking, then, is the centrality of children to Minow's condemnation of television broadcasters. Over the long term, the most lasting impact of the speech has been on the debate over children and television. (One sign of its enduring impact came in 1995, when Minow himself published a re-examination of his speech entitled *Abandoned in the Wasteland: Children, Television and the First Amendment.*) Later, in September 1961, Minow gave more emphasis to children's programming in another speech, in which he spoke of lighting "a few million candles" to take "our children out of the darkness." In this address, Minow further suggested that the primary problem was not violence but the fact that most children's shows were simply "dull, gray and insipid." Minow's general condemnation of the emptiness of television found a ready audience—the "vast wasteland" line has been repeated many times since and mutated into such clichés as "five hundred channels and nothing on."

During 1962, what was actually happening to Saturday morning programming? ABC added *Top Cat* and *Beany and Cecil* to its late-morning schedule and picked up *The Magic Land of Allakazam* (previously on CBS). NBC began the year airing *Pip the Piper, The Shari Lewis Show, King Leonardo, Fury, Make Room for Daddy, Championship Debate,* and *1,2,3—Go!;* by the end of the year, they had added *The Bullwinkle Show* and *Ruff and Reddy.* CBS continued to air *Captain Kangaroo, The Mighty Mouse Playhouse, The Roy Rogers and Dale Evans Show,* and *Sky King* while also adding *The Adventures of Rin Tin Tin, Video Village Junior,* and *The Alvin Show.*

At first glance, these schedules hardly seem different from those characteristic of the late 1950s: an indifferent hodgepodge of animated and live-action programs—indeed, many of them, like *Sky King,* were reruns of shows produced in the fifties. But 1962 was also something of a subtle watershed. Not only did it mark the arrival of Hanna-Barbera shows originally intended to air in the evenings *(Top Cat),* it also saw a key replacement of a live-action quiz show *(Video Village Junior)* with a cartoon *(The Alvin Show).* Nineteen sixty-two also marked the appearance of Jay Ward's animated characters Rocky and Bullwinkle on Saturday mornings, though they had been on in various other time slots, including late Saturday afternoons, since

1959. Bob Clampett's puppets Beany and Cecil also made their first Saturday morning appearance, although in animated form. The density of programming on Saturday mornings increased during 1962. Shows that aired previously at other times were moved. Even more characteristically for Saturday morning, a cartoon was selected to replace a live-action show primarily for reasons of cost.

The net effect of the Minow-inspired focus on children's programming was to increase the awareness among television executives of the nature of the possible marketplace for children's shows. Executives harkened to Minow's call for programming even as they largely ignored his specific recommendations about what *type* of children's programs should be added. Each network also attempted to placate Minow by adding a self-consciously educational program to the schedule in 1962—NBC's *Exploring,* ABC's *Discovery,* and CBS's *Reading Room*—but all three shows were on life support from the outset. *Discovery* lasted the longest, until 1971, though its weekday format only lasted a year. The whole moral furor that had begun in the late fifties and culminated in Minow's speech helped to produce a rush to fill Saturday mornings with children's shows while simultaneously removing any trace of children's programming from weekday hours, where more profitable audiences could be pursued or affiliates and independent stations wished to make their own programming decisions.

———

"I cannot watch the shows. They're all cartoons, and to my mind, cartoons are not television because the figures can't really be humorous like live show characters. The kids have really become accustomed to animation, but they need live people." —Soupy Sales, quoted in Gary Grossman, *Saturday Morning TV*

———

As a consequence, from 1963 to the end of 1964, the three networks significantly expanded their offerings on Saturday mornings and decisively shifted their programming toward animation. ABC picked up *The Bullwinkle Show* during this period, and added *The Porky Pig Show, Hoppity Hooper, Shenanigans, Cartoonies,* and *Casper, the Friendly Ghost* as well as continuing to show *Beany and Cecil.* NBC and CBS similarly added shows—the first of Gerry Anderson's bizarre sci-fi shows made in "Supermarionation" appeared *(Fireball XL-5),* along with the cartoons *The Hector Heathcote Show, Linus the Lionhearted,* Total Television's *Underdog* and *Tennessee Tuxedo,* and Hanna-Barbera's *Quickdraw McGraw* and *The Jetsons.* Older programs like *Captain Kangaroo* and *Mr. Wizard* maintained a place on Saturday mornings, as did reruns of live shows like *Dennis the Menace* that had originally aired in other time slots.

In the meantime, critical assessments of the relationship between children and television continued to mount up. In the fall of 1964 a major study conducted by the American Academy of Pediatrics described a TV-caused illness known as the "tired-child syndrome." The victims of this new syndrome were primarily "sensitive" children who spent six to ten hours watching television on Saturdays and Sundays, resulting in nausea, headaches, fatigue, and appetite problems. The most crucial feature of the report was its characterization of the syndrome as a form of "addiction" to be cured by withdrawal. The notion that television represented a drug—and all of the rhetorical baggage that went with this metaphor—would develop subsequently into one of the most powerful indictments of Saturday morning.

By the mid-sixties, with the children of the baby boom clustered between the ages of fifteen and two, advertisers had a much better idea about what to do with an audience of children. The popularity of television-inspired crazes like Davy Crockett's coonskin cap had helped advertisers recognize this audience's potential. Though the relative popularity of individual Saturday morning shows—as determined by their ratings—had a significant influence on programming decisions, network competition on Saturdays was also ruled increasingly by some markedly odd forces (in comparison to normal prime time). A serious flop remained, as always, a real problem, both in terms of its ability to attract viewers and its ability to attract advertising. But a show with middling-to-poor ratings was almost as steady a producer of revenue as a popular show, simply by fact of its placement on a Saturday schedule.

The Maturation of Saturday Morning: 1965–1969

By the 1965 season, the foundations of Saturday morning programming—and thus of the Saturday morning phenomenon—had been laid. Former head of CBS daytime programming Fred Silverman told us that the introduction of the immensely popular new animated program *The Beatles* in the fall of 1965 "turned the morning upside down" and spurred all three networks to order new shows. Even before the premiere of *The Beatles,* however, Saturdays had filled up with both animation and advertising. From 1965 to 1968, the final pieces of the puzzle were assembled, creating a full schedule of network shows from early in the morning to the early afternoon on Saturday; meanwhile, the extraction of network children's shows from all other times of the week was more or less completed. Studios like Hanna-Barbera, Jay Ward Productions, and Filmation produced a host of new cartoons for television. The networks formally recognized the importance of children's television by restructuring their corporate hierarchies. Concerned critics formed new and influential organizations which focused much more centrally on Saturday morning programming. This all led in 1967–68 to protracted struggles over "violent" cartoons that served as the template for all subsequent fights regarding the Saturday morning phenomenon.

Many of the new shows were what critics derisively termed the "supers"; action-adventure programs that often centered on a super-powered character of some kind. *The Beatles* had been added just before the superhero craze, and lasted through part of that craze. A few shows from other genres, like *The Magilla Gorilla Show* and *George of the Jungle,* were added to the schedule as well during the same period, while other characters like Huckleberry Hound and Yogi Bear continued to appear in syndication. But these were the years of Space Ghost, Spider-Man, Jonny Quest (relocated from prime time), the Herculoids, Shazzan, Batman, Superman, Aquaman, and Super President. Even the funny-animal shows took on an action-adventure tilt with the addition of Hanna-Barbera's *The Atom Ant Show* and *Secret Squirrel,* while other comedic shows like *Mighty Heroes* and *Underdog* also took their basic cues from the superhero genre.

These new schedules—which represented the advent of Saturday morning in all its full-blown glory—were put into place by network executives who had been given the responsibility to develop daytime programming as a whole. The most important of these individuals early on—in many ways the prime network mind behind the creation of the Saturday morning phenomenon—was Fred Silverman. Silverman is perhaps better remembered today for his dramatic rise and fall as the chief executive of both ABC and NBC during the 1970s, but he first rose to prominence within the television industry in the late 1960s as the vice president of daytime programming at CBS. Silverman himself demurs today when asked about his role in the creation of Saturday morning—no doubt partly because he still remembers that many of his critics during the 1970s cited his previous association with children's programming as a snide form of commentary on his later tenure at ABC and NBC.

Nevertheless, press reports between 1965 and 1968 testify to Silverman's centrality. Influential producers of kidvid like Joseph Barbera and Lou Scheimer recall Silverman as the lead figure in the network expansion of Saturday schedules. They both note that it was Silverman's taste in shows, his sense of what would and would not fly, that generally determined what sort of material appeared on Saturdays. In 1966, it was Silverman's belief in the potential of superhero characters that led to their conquest of the airwaves, and it was Silverman's dictum in 1968 that the "supers" should be banished from network television that played the key role in their disappearance.

The rise of the superhero cartoons brought the new institution of Saturday morning to the attention of pundits, focusing their animus squarely on the new cartoons. At first, critics largely commented on what they saw as the low quality of the shows, echoing Minow's condemnation of children's television as "dull, gray and insipid." However, the crowd of usual suspects—newspaper critics, activist intellectuals, church and parental groups, and concerned experts—were joined in their criticism of superhero cartoons by some members of the animation business itself. The new cartoons took the technique of "limited animation" already in use and refined it to an even greater—and more cost-cutting—extent. By 1966, Hanna-Barbera's animators had become particularly notorious for their usage of the technique, but virtually all of their competitors also employed it.

Limited animation, or planned animation as William Hanna once termed it, was a polite term for cheapskate cartooning. The technique featured frequent shots of the characters with only their mouths moving, minimized action, and maximized reuse of previously animated sequences. The technique was anathema to many veterans of cinematic animation. In a 1966 *New York Times* article, the great animator Chuck Jones disparaged the new cartoons as "illustrated radio" that transformed animators into "mechanics . . . [who] have rules against creativity."

Part of the animators' anger had as much to do with the impact of the new techniques on their average wages and work conditions as it did with defending a particular artistic vision. Limited animation also changed the relative relationship between animators and writers, but the animators did not welcome the change. The new cheaper cartoons relied heavily on exposition, since it was a lot cheaper to animate two otherwise unmoving heads talking about what was happening offscreen than it was to show those events happening. This gave writers much more of a say in the making of a cartoon. The contrast between the average look and feel of a classic Warner Brothers cartoon and a Filmation-produced episode of *Aquaman* is fairly dramatic. (The defenses of limited animation offered by the producers of the new cartoons were often pretty lame. William Hanna said, ridiculously, that the old theatrical shorts were "harder to watch because of all that tedious detail.")

"Hey, kids! Pull all the knobs off your television sets. In that way, we'll be sure to be with you next week." —Bullwinkle the Moose

---

Indeed, some of the creators of Saturday morning felt disappointed with the changes the business was undergoing. In his autobiography—and in an interview with us—Joseph Barbera evinced clear signs of dismay over the migration of animation from early prime time to Saturday mornings. At the time of the original debate over the superhero cartoons, Barbera noted that the fierce competition between the producers of animation had led to "script meetings . . . [where] we talk about character analysis and motivation." He seemed astonished at the time that such steps had become necessary for the production of cartoons, suggesting a deep-seated belief in the triviality of children's television as it stood in the mid-1960s—and a frustration with the intensely competitive, indeed almost cannibalistic, concentration of programs within a five-hour period on only one day of the week. Both Hanna and Barbera frequently observed, with a certain amount of wry frustration, that their worst competition was themselves. In another instance, David DePatie, producer of *The Super 6* and *Super President and Spy Shadow,* responded to complaints about the low quality of shows by sneering, "You could animate Superman on toilet tissue and it would sell." None of this hullabaloo stemmed the tide of limited animation, with its overwhelming economic appeal.

The whole debate certainly helped solidify the image of Saturday morning as a ghetto for cut-rate schlock—an image that was aggravated by another ferocious debate, this time over allegedly violent cartoons. The standard arguments of past years that television was fostering juvenile delinquency were transported over more or less intact and with renewed vigor to indict Space Ghost, Shazzan, Aquaman, and their ilk. One particularly stupid survey claimed that Saturday mornings were as full of murder and mayhem as prime time, claiming to record the deaths of "20 monster people of various descriptions" via "shooting, vaporization or mashing" in one episode of *The Herculoids.* (This involved, among other things, a markedly odd definition of "death.") The senior editor of *Redbook* magazine wrote in a commentary that *The Herculoids* and *Shazzan!* had "a terrifying viciousness that goes beyond anything else I'm aware of on television." This statement came in the same year that the Vietnam War aired live on American television sets. In 1968, the president of the PTA issued a sweeping denunciation: "Television cartoons are worse than immoral. They are full of horror and violence and negative values."

A number of the shows in question received exceedingly good ratings, particularly *Space Ghost* and *The Herculoids,* but the emerging economic logic of Saturday morning was already making it clear that the networks' most important goal was simply to have cheap programming scheduled in a solid block for four or five hours. A property like *Space Ghost* was more valuable because of its ratings, but in financial terms it was mostly interchangeable with other animated series. In fact, as Joseph Barbera recalls it, Fred Silverman's top priority was the constant development of more programs for CBS rather than the nurturing of a single success like *Space Ghost.* Quantity overruled quality. In this environment, if particular programs proved to be serious political liabilities for the network, they were replaceable.

Moreover, by 1968, the schedules for all three networks were saturated with superhero cartoons. But what really killed the superhero cartoons was the year 1968 itself. In the aftermath of urban riots and the deaths of Robert Kennedy and Martin Luther King Jr., the pressure on the networks to scale back televisual violence grew to a fever pitch. Superhero cartoons were one of the easiest targets for the networks to give ground on. In 1968, they became the focus of an intense crusade, particularly at *TV Guide,* which issued numerous broadsides directed at the "Weirdo Superhero." One *TV Guide* author, for example, offered a semidelusional description of characters from these cartoons, including a description of a *Space Ghost* villainess who "gets her jollies slicing up people." (The author appears to have been watching television in an alternate universe. We think the author must have been talking about the Black Widow, but we never saw her gorily slice up her victims.) The same author pointed the finger at Marvel Comics' Stan Lee for introducing "ugly" superheroes with "hang-ups." Another *TV Guide* columnist, Richard Doan, often called for "routing" "cartoon monsters" and "weirdo superheroes."

Many of the leading producers of animated cartoons ended up ritually confessing their sins and promising to do penance by producing nonviolent shows for the 1969 season. Friz Freleng proclaimed that he had never liked "that kind of thing," while Norman Prescott of Filmation, who had earlier defended superhero cartoons, said, "The parents had every right to holler: I'm with them all the way." At the networks, Fred Silverman presented the shift from superhero cartoons to comedy as something which had been planned all along, both for the sake of balance and because "most children like to laugh." Silverman elaborated further in 1969: "Our fall schedule will be revolutionary. New forms. A 2½ hours comedy bloc on Saturday mornings. Road Runner, Bugs Bunny. We've bought reruns of *The Monkees* and we'll slot them there, too. Maybe a circus thing."

So the first round of superhero cartoons was banished into syndication by mid-1969. Of course, syndication hardly equaled oblivion, and many of these programs were regularly seen by children over the next two decades. But Silverman and others made it clear that the superhero—and similarly "violent" characters like Jonny Quest—was now unwelcome on the networks. Here and there, this dictum was violated rather sneakily, as on *The Banana Splits Adventure Hour,* previewing on NBC in the fall of 1968 and running to the fall of 1971. The Banana Splits, according to NBC and Hanna-Barbera, were to prove the perfect antidote for the excesses of the previous year. However, while the Banana Splits themselves were actors in costumes who ran around doing goofy little bits of slapstick, some of the serials like *Danger Island* that appeared alongside the Splits were as "violent" as any of the superheroes. Similarly, in 1969, ABC simply moved *Spider-Man* and *The Fantastic Four* to Sundays in order to finish running episodes that they had already ordered from the producers. *Superman* and *Jonny Quest* survived on CBS into 1970 and 1971, respectively. But on the whole, the exile of superheroes and action-adventure characters stuck until the advent of *Super Friends, Josie and the Pussycats,* and *Star Trek* between 1972 and 1974, and these new shows were markedly different in tone from *Space Ghost, The Herculoids,* and their peers.

The battle over the superheroes called attention to the concentration of children's programming by the networks. The dispute acted as a lightning rod, drawing the amorphous dread and anxiety about children and television that had been brewing in earnest since the quiz show scandals and Minow's speech straight down into Saturday mornings—and in the process, completed the invention of the total Saturday morning phenomenon. A 1968 article by John Leonard in the *New York Times* typified the evolving debate by taking the most venerable questions about television—for example, about television's educational potential and its effects on the socialization of children—and refocusing them on the networks' Saturday programming. Leonard's piece also heralded the birth of the Children's Television Workshop, whose shows *Sesame Street* and *The Electric Company* would often serve in the minds of critics as the good yin to Saturday morning's evil yang. Though anxieties about the impact of television

Weirdo Superheroes   **23**

on children would subsequently widen again to include prime-time programming, Saturday mornings would remain a prominent part of the debate from that point forward. And by the end of 1968, the furor gave birth to a new organization of parental critics that would prove to be one of the most important influences on the new world of Saturday morning: Action for Children's Television, or ACT.

Chapter Two

Saturday Morning Supreme: The Seventies

Saturday morning, like streaking, *Charlie's Angels,* and polyester, is at its heart a thing of the seventies. From 1969 to 1979, millions of children watched some of the programs now so closely associated with the memory of Saturday morning, including *Hong Kong Phooey, Josie and the Pussycats, Scooby-Doo, H. R. Pufnstuf, Super Friends, Fat Albert and the Cosby Kids,* and *The Archies.* The experience of watching *The Funky Phantom* or *The Harlem Globetrotters* is as evocative of the seventies as disco or Jimmy Carter. During this decade, the networks not only offered a full slate of programming on Saturdays, they also learned to manage and market Saturday morning more productively and profitably. At the same time, network executives faced a whole new slate of formidable legal, political, and social challenges from articulate and well-organized advocacy groups. These challenges built upon foundations laid down during the late 1950s and the 1960s while also introducing new issues and concerns into public debate, in particular drawing upon a growing consensus among experts about the harmful effects of children's television.

The retreat of superheroes from Saturdays in 1969 certainly did nothing to assuage various critics. Jack Gould offered a fairly typical assessment when he pronounced the new shows an "unrelenting parade of basically cheap cartoons, junk bereft of style, professional competence, touches of humor or any evidence of an inclination to raise standards of substance." A few of the new schedules were not only failures with critics, but failures with their audiences. ABC almost completely reshuffled its schedule three times between 1969 and 1972, discarding shows like *Cattanooga Cats, The Hardy Boys, Hot Wheels, The Smokey Bear Show,* and *Motormouse* in short order.

However, CBS, still under the watchful eye of Fred Silverman, assembled an enormously successful Saturday schedule that dominated the ratings in the early seventies. *The Bugs Bunny/Road Runner Show,* added by CBS in the fall of 1968, would prove to be—in one fashion or another—the stable core of Saturday schedules on one network or another from that date onward. *The Archie Show* and its various spin-offs, including *Sabrina and the Groovie Goolies,* proved equally popular. The characters of Dick Dastardly, Muttley, and Penelope Pitstop, first introduced in 1968's *The Wacky Races,* would appear on CBS in various formats through the fall of 1971, while the racing/competition format introduced in these shows would return in other Hanna-Barbera shows later in the decade. CBS also added another of the basic staples of Saturday morning in 1969 with *Scooby-Doo, Where Are You?,* and in 1971, they added the first of several Flintstones spin-offs, *Pebbles and Bamm-Bamm.* During the same period, NBC picked up *The Pink Panther Show,* another staple cartoon. More importantly, they added two live-action shows from a new source, Sid and Marty Krofft Productions: *H. R. Pufnstuf* and *The Bugaloos.*

For the rest of the decade, Saturday morning consisted mostly of reshuffled versions of the shows which premiered between 1969 and 1972. The studios often produced new characters and shows which recycled the early seventies formulas: *Scooby-Doo* and *Josie and the Pussycats* begat *Speed Buggy; H. R. Pufnstuf* begat *Lidsville.* There were a few notable new shows that offered slightly different formulas between 1972 and 1979: shows based on the Jackson Five, the Osmonds, and the Partridge Family, for example. Other important programs added later included *Dr. Doolittle, Hong Kong Phooey, Josie and the Pussycats,* and *Land of the Lost.* There were also cartoons like *Star Trek* and *Emergency +4* based on prime-time shows popular with children.

The superhero made a cautious return in *Super Friends,* though the early seasons of this show rather markedly avoided superpowered conflict, leaving Wonder Woman, Superman, Batman, and Aquaman to face natural disasters, petty crimes, and occasional mild miscreants who usually realized the error of their ways by the end of an episode. Later in the seventies, other action-oriented programs like *Tarzan, Shazam!,* and *Isis* would also appear, but even they bore the marks of the earlier banishment of superheroes: direct conflict was minimized and the characters usually stopped to deliver sanctimonious homilies throughout the show. A few programs were also periodically exiled to Sundays, which became a sort of impoverished shadow version of Saturdays.

———

"Television was a positive, peak, mythic, nontrivial, nourishing, energizing, ecstatic force in my life. And until I see a study suggesting that such a thing is even possible, I shall continue to ask the researchers unfriendly questions." —James Morrow, 1982

———

The battles fought over Saturday morning in the seventies began with the formation of the most powerful and influential of all the advocacy groups concerned with children's television, Action for Children's Television (ACT), which drove both public debate and public policy during the whole decade. They were "the mothers from Boston." Under the leadership of two strong and articulate women, Evelyn Sarson and Peggy Charren, ACT petitioned the Federal Communications Commission (FCC) and the Federal Trade Commission

(FTC), sponsored numerous studies, convened conferences, issued statements, circulated petitions, wrote handbooks for parents, and offered guidelines for advertisers.

The core membership of ACT began meeting in Boston in 1968 as the furor over "weirdo superheroes" mounted. The founders of the group later identified these "monster cartoons" as a critical factor in their original decision to organize. From the very beginning, ACT developed its own distinct perspective on children's television. ACT's primary tenet was that children were not consumers and should never be seen as such. ACT stressed that this was literally true—children did not independently purchase any of the goods advertised to them on television, but instead pressured their parents to buy products for them. However, ACT also argued that children should not even be imagined as consumers, that without the urgings of television, children would not possess the desire to consume.

ACT sent letters to the networks outlining various proposals, letters which were regarded more or less as inoffensive lunacy, though they did help add additional impetus for the appointment of network executives whose primary responsibility was to children's television rather than all daytime programming. But in May of 1970, ACT surprised both the network brass and journalists by submitting briefs to the FCC calling for the total removal of advertisements from children's television as well as stringent federal regulation of kidvid.

While pursuing the quixotic general goal of cleansing the commercial taint from children's television, ACT spent much of the seventies lobbying the FTC and the National Association of Broadcasters (NAB) for small and specific reforms to advertising practices. They frequently campaigned against exaggerations and half-truths in toy advertisements, arguing in one typical instance that ads for Hot Wheels and a doll called Dancerina falsely represented the toys' capabilities. Later in the decade, they similarly attacked potentially misleading ads for an action-figure called Bulletman. In 1971, ACT also began pressuring the networks to refuse advertising for vitamins and drugs, a move aimed in particular at Flintstones vitamins, on the grounds that Flintstones vitamins were too much like candy, and that the use of cartoon characters to advertise a medicinal product for children set a dangerous precedent. Another favorite ACT target was ads for sugar-filled products like candies and, even more typically, cereals. In a typical comment, Charren once wrote, "And what are they selling on these programs? Things they wouldn't sell, *couldn't* sell, to an adult. . . . Some of these products were created just for children's television. Take Frankenberry. This is a purple cereal, highly sugared, with purple marshmallows in it—a product which, according to some people who have opened it in their kitchens, smells funny."

ACT surveyed the frequency and placement of ads and brought considerable pressure on the networks both to reduce the number of ads and to put "bumpers" in between the ads and the programs. (Bumpers were short segments in which the network announced, "After these messages, we'll be right back.") This group's consistent concern throughout the decade was what it saw as the illegitimate combination of programming and advertising content, whether it was Fred and Barney shilling for Cocoa Pebbles (of course, Fred started off his career selling cigarettes in prime time, which was even worse), Rodney Allen Rippy selling Jack in the Box, or Captain Kangaroo personally recommending products to his viewers, which he did right up until 1971.

Advertisers could not reply that they were merely providing information for the benefit of rational and independent consumers. On Saturday morning, the diminished judgment of the audience was a given. As a consequence, the advertisers' attempts to stave off ACT and similar groups often involved a combination of minor concessions and apologies, interestingly unconventional views of children, and aggressive characterizations of capitalism as being as patriotic as Mom, Apple Pie, and the American Way.

Most advertisers involved with Saturday morning—those who managed accounts for the manufacturers of toys, cereals, games, vitamins, and the like—knew from the beginning of ACT's attack that they were going to have to police their own house, or at least be seen to be doing so, in order to stave off serious regulation by the federal government. Of course, the manufacturers of the products most criticized by the advocacy groups, like sugary cereals and Flintstones vitamins, had differing feelings about making such concessions, depending on who was on the chopping block. Toy manufacturers might argue that ads for Dancerina or Bulletman weren't particularly deceptive, but they could also afford to concede the issue and withdraw or redo the ad. General Mills, on the other hand, couldn't just nod its head and agree that the sullied name of Count Chocula should never henceforth be heard over the airwaves.

Though manufacturers and advertisers occasionally spar over the exact relationship between marketing and profit, few businessmen involved with toy manufacturing or similarly child-oriented products doubted that the placement of advertising on Saturday morning was crucial to their expansion. Companies like Kenner, Mattel, and Hasbro all achieved some of their most profitable successes by combining toys and television. As David Owen points out in his essay "The Man Who Invented Saturday Morning," "television expanded the market for new toys and made it possible for manufacturers to spend more money on new products. It also enabled retailers to cut their prices, since the increased customer traffic permitted narrower profit margins." The same pretty much went for sugared cereals and chocolate milk. The companies were certainly making immense contributions to the network coffers: in 1970, Mattel spent $8 million on television advertising; the two largest cereal advertisers spent a combined $16 million. In total, advertisers spent around $75 million on Saturday and Sunday children's shows during 1970 alone.

So when advertisers made concessions to ACT and other critics, they did so strategically and with a calculated amount of buck-passing. They passed voluntary guidelines, rules, and codes every time federal regulation seemed imminent. For example, in 1972, the

NAB amended its rules to call for 25 percent less advertising on children's shows and for the end of advertising by children's show hosts, or by animated characters *during* the broadcast of their own shows. (So Fred and Barney could go on selling Fruity Pebbles, they just couldn't do so while *The Flintstones* or one of its spin-offs was on.)[1] Later, the NAB passed code reforms suggesting that advertisements to children could not be scary or violent, nor could they "directly or by implication contend that if children have a product, they are better than their peers or lacking it will not be accepted by their peers." (That pretty much staved off the development of a marketplace for Flintstones deodorants.) The NAB further dictated that advertisements aimed at children should not distort or exaggerate the "characteristics or functions" of a product. As the leaders of ACT and other consumer rights advocates were fond of pointing out, these reforms were more evaded than obeyed, almost inherently so: how could an advertisement for toys not exaggerate in some fashion? How could an advertisement not imply that you were a better kid and more fun to be with if you had a Barbie with a kung fu action grip and a miniskirt?

Given the government's general reluctance to impose mandatory regulation on television, particularly during the Nixon and Ford administrations, minor concessions usually succeeded in staving off the critics. Another common—and often more interesting—stratagem of advertisers was to criticize directly the way that experts and advocate groups viewed children. Some of this was a pretty standard part of corporate public relations: if cornered by hostile experts, then hire your own and suggest that your opponent's findings are "controversial." The tobacco industry does it all the time. But occasionally, advertisers found themselves suggesting that children could make rational and mature judgments in a fashion more or less similar to adults. Defending the rational individuality of an adult is not a radi-

---

1. Both changes were accompanied by another reform banning advertisements for hemorrhoid remedies, which says something interesting about the connection between kidvid advertising and other alleged offenses to "good taste."

cal gesture—but seeing a child in the same fashion certainly is. James Neal Harvey, an advertising executive who frequently opposed ACT and its allies, wrote, "Children are a lot smarter about television advertising than many people think. . . . Do they like all commercials? Of course not. They favor some and hate others, even as you and I. Are they deceived or misled by commercials? Not on your cathode."

The attack on children's television was often equated with an attack on capitalism itself. Harvey, for example, complained that ACT's ambitions went "a lot deeper than . . . trying to replace Bugs Bunny with Beethoven. . . . it is that a lot of people in this country think that there is something fundamentally wrong with trying to offer a product for sale to a child, and that the functions of our free enterprise system of producing, promoting and selling goods at a profit are rather immoral facts of life from which children should be shielded." Other advertisers and broadcasters typically framed the issue by summoning the fearful specter of Big Government, painting ACT and its allies as believers in government-controlled TV.

As a whole, controversies over kidvid in the seventies forced advertisers to take an unusually public role in the kinds of disputes they typically preferred to resolve by quietly donating money to someone's campaign fund or by lobbying behind closed doors. These debates also forced advertisers to express an unorthodox confidence in the critical intelligence of children. At the same time, Saturday morning also provided a lucrative opportunity to target an extremely specific demographic group whose role as present and future consumers in the general economy was more and more important. For all the controversy over commercialism, the actual content of Saturday morning programming and advertising remained almost entirely separate during the seventies. This separation changed dramatically in the eighties with the advent of cartoons which served directly as advertisements for particular toys, thus altering the nature of the debate over commercialism.

Advertisers and advocacy groups were both pleading their case to

Cartoon Animals We'd Like to See

For some reason, the animal kingdom is reduced to a very small range of species in Saturday morning cartoons.

Dogs dominate, but that's to be expected, we suppose. Bears also head the list: Saturday morning bears include Yogi, the C.B. Bears, the Hair Bear Bunch, the Care Bears, the Hillbilly Bears on *The Wacky Races,* and Winnie the Pooh. There's a decent number of cats, mice, ducks, pigs, rabbits, wolves, apes, monkeys, and so on. There's an alligator and an octopus.

But this leaves so much of life's diversity untapped. Our proposals for cartoon animals include the following:

WOOGUMS THE NAKED MOLE RAT

You can't help but love an animated character that looks like a gopher with multiple skin grafts. And they're social animals, so you could have a whole litter of 'em.

KRUNCHY THE KOMODO DRAGON

Krunchy's little buddy Jose the Gila Monster keeps telling him, "Mr. Ranger wouldn't like it if you took a bite out of a tourist and waited for him to die from sepsis before eating his carcass," but Krunchy's bigger than the average lizard.

SMIRKY THE SILVERFISH

Nothing cuter than a book-eating invertebrate. And you could have Smirky deliver inspiring public-service announcements about the value of reading: "Go read now, before I eat your comic book collection, fanboy!"

COO-COO THE COELACANTH

Living fossil but still the life of the party. Hanna-Barbera, you've got our number, so give us a call: this character is going to make us both rich once the nation's kids get a load of his humorous adventures, particularly when he foils his enemy, Mr. Natural Selection.

UKULELE THE E. COLI

Digestive bacteria who's got a hankering to infect under-cooked fast-food hamburgers. It's a madcap race between him and Danny Dysentery straight to the small intestine.

LENNY THE LEMMING

Short episodes, because he's always throwing himself off a cliff. Hosted by his pal Dr. Jack K. Could run into trouble with the crazed zoologist lobby, though, since lemmings actually don't throw themselves off cliffs.

the federal government throughout the seventies. Congress, for example, provided a crucial forum for critics of children's television through hearings before congressional committees from the very earliest days of television. Bureaucratic institutions, particularly the Federal Communications Commission and the Federal Trade Commission, played even more important roles—during the seventies, the FCC and FTC were forced repeatedly to engage the issue of whether and how they should regulate children's television. It was the issue that wouldn't go away. Most of the time, commissioners did their best to satisfy diametrically opposed constituencies and priorities, but they usually ended up like the proverbial armadillo in the middle

If it weren't for books like these, kids would never learn how to watch TV properly (and safely)!

of the road, squashed flat by the competing claims of advocates, experts, executives, advertisers, and politicians.

The FCC was first aimed at the problem of children's television by Newton Minow's "vast wasteland" speech, but for the balance of the sixties, the FCC's official position toward children's television largely stayed confined to the bully pulpit. ACT's petition for the formal regulation of children's television changed all of that: the FCC was forced to not only critique the content of children's television but also to consider some kind of statutory response to kidvid, or at least they appeared to be doing so. At the same moment, the FCC came under intense pressure to avoid regulation from the television industry, whose power had been growing steadily since the quiz show scandals.

In the early seventies, FCC chairman Dean Burch, a former head of the Republican National Committee, reacted carefully to ACT's petition by commissioning a study of the problem. Burch's perspective on children's television was cautious and carefully calibrated. While conceding in a 1973 interview in *TV Guide* that most adults would regard kidvid as "god-awful," he noted that children themselves were "up bright and early Saturday morning, before we are, to watch the cartoons." Burch also argued that the FCC members themselves were simply not qualified to run the television industry, and for that reason alone, should refrain from interfering too closely. At the same time, Burch largely accepted ACT's more specific criticisms of abuse by advertisers and called for the advertising industry to police itself or be policed by the federal government. Some of Burch's fellow commissioners were a little less temperate in their approach. Nicholas Johnson, for example, referred to network executives as "child molesters" and "evil men."

In 1974, the FCC formally ruled on ACT's petition, following the line laid down by Burch in the preceding five years. They rejected ACT's request for the complete elimination of advertising from children's viewing hours. At the same time, the commission formally endorsed a set of voluntary guidelines regarding programming and advertising, in particular calling for a reduction of the total time devoted to advertisements during children's viewing hours, and promised to review network compliance with these guidelines at some unspecified future time. In combination with the surgeon general's report in 1972 and the Federal Trade Commission's studies of television advertising, this policy statement codified the federal government's cautious approach to the problem of children's television.

"Is Mickey Mouse running over an opponent with a steam engine and the opponent afterward puffing up to normality and running off—is that 'violence'? I don't know." —Dean Burch, chairman of the Federal Communications Commission, 1973

The election of Jimmy Carter in 1976 led to some changes, however. ACT had pressed suit against the FCC after its 1974 report, losing its appeal in 1977. However, the Carter administration was much more fundamentally sympathetic to the views of kidvid critics, particularly to ACT's antiadvertising crusade. This sympathy translated first into more aggressive pressure from both the FCC and the FTC, particularly on the subject of commercialism. In 1978, the FCC agreed to return to the subject of children's television and create a new Children's Television Task Force. Around the same time, the

FTC announced in a substantial report that it was seriously considering a ban on advertisements in children's television and followed up its announcement with major hearings during the year, continuing into 1979. By the early eighties, this situation reversed quickly under the Reagan administration, with its entrenched hostility toward regulation. That hostility not only staved off what had seemed to be imminent federal regulation of children's television, but also helped produce a favorable political climate for a new burst of commercialism in children's television.

Looking back, the common mainstream characterization of Saturday morning as a ghetto of incompetents seems particularly odd in light of the executives who played a role in its construction. If Saturday morning was the essence of ineptitude and greed, one might then expect that it would have been supervised by the inept and greedy, people who worked largely in silence and obscurity except when called forth to do battle with angry mothers, educators, politicians, and experts. The reality is almost exactly the opposite, however. From the first flowering of Saturday morning in 1965 to its apex in the mid-seventies, some of the names closely associated with children's programming included not only Fred Silverman but also figures like Chuck Jones, the famed animator; Grant Tinker, who went on to an immensely successful career as a network executive and television producer; and a moderately well known person by the name of Michael Eisner.

Executives with a strong interest in kidvid like Silverman, Eisner, and their less well known but equally capable contemporaries like George Heinemann entered the seventies with great confidence. Not only was Saturday morning flooding the network coffers with money—children's television was one of the great growth areas of the early seventies, with a high margin of profit—but the "weirdo superheroes" had been sent packing. Each network had committed to purging its schedule of violence, sometimes at considerable cost. Not only did these changes fail to provide the networks any relief, but

Saturday Morning Supreme

the networks actually found themselves fighting off vigorous new challenges on issues like commercialism. A certain amount of slack-jawed astonishment at the ingratitude of parents, experts, and educators crept into public statements by network spokesmen through the rest of the decade. For five or six years after the banishment of the sixties superheroes, executives charged with the development of children's TV continued to announce officially that their Saturday schedules had been completely purged of violence as if they were still waiting for the accolades to pour in.

Almost all efforts by the networks during the seventies failed to satisfy their critics. For example, each network attempted to develop several self-consciously "educational" or "high-quality" shows to serve as a sort of papal indulgence for their sins. Executives never tired of pointing out that sponsors for such shows were hard to come by. ABC aired the boring educational program *Curiosity Shop* and the aggressively multiracial *Kid Power* starting in 1971. More successfully, CBS also added short news segments called *In the News* and ABC launched educational segments called *Schoolhouse Rock.* CBS had *Captain Kangaroo,* now on weekdays; it also revived the venerable news show *You Are There* as a children's program early in the seventies and offered *30 Minutes,* a junior version of the program *60 Minutes,* later in the decade. CBS also added *Fat Albert and the Cosby Kids,* which it trumpeted as a special high-quality addition to its lineup. NBC offered the unusual if almost entirely unwatched show *Take a Giant Step,* later retitled *Talking with a Giant,* based on a revolving theme set each episode by a panel of children. (In the later versions, kids interviewed a guest celebrity.) NBC also briefly revived *Mr. Wizard.*

Most of these shows were canceled fairly quickly, though some, like *Captain Kangaroo,* more or less held their ground. *Schoolhouse Rock* and *In the News,* the two major exceptions, achieved an enduring place in the hearts and minds of their audience. None of these shows, successful or not, earned much credit for their networks. The leadership of ACT and other similar groups would occasionally offer carrots in the form of approval and encouragement for educational programming projects, but more often used the stick of condemnation. In particular, demanding critics frequently compared the networks' efforts to the work of their public-television counterparts and inevitably found them wanting.

Another public relations strategy pursued by the networks with the aim of rehabilitating the content of Saturday morning involved hiring expert consultants and prominent cultural figures to oversee the creation of children's programming. Chuck Jones, who had been one of the chief critics of Hanna-Barbera and other practitioners of "limited animation," was hired in such a capacity by ABC in 1970, and in 1973 Joseph Papp, the noted producer of Shakespearean drama, signed a contract with ABC to develop a variety of programs, including children's shows. And almost every show in development after 1972 could boast that it had been vetted not only by the usual gauntlet at Standards and Practices but also by various "experts" working as consultants for the networks and studios. *Fat Albert and the Cosby Kids,* for example, was not trumpeted as a "quality" show merely because of Bill Cosby's involvement: CBS also hired (and showily announced they had done so) a panel of educators to review the content of each show. After *Fat Albert,* this practice became increasingly common with all of Saturday morning: CBS employed expert advisers in the following season to supervise the content of *Valley of the Dinosaurs, Shazam!, The Harlem Globetrotters Popcorn Machine, The Hudson Brothers Razzle Dazzle Show,* and *The U.S. of Archie.* One of the advisers to *Fat Albert* said that his goal was to see that children's programs "be entertaining and at the same time, teach values and value conflicts." As a result of this trend, by the early eighties, consultants had clustered around most kidvid like flies on a corpse, particularly at ABC.

Other mollifying gestures on the part of the networks during the seventies included backing for the same various minor reforms to advertising practices that had been supported by marketers, and other efforts designed to make advertising more palatable to kidvid critics. NBC, for example, funded a series of public-service spots designed to teach young children how to be responsible consumers. (Several corporations also sponsored their own series of similar messages.) However, since advertising constituted the core of Saturday morning's profitability, the networks generally tended to strike a considerably less conciliatory tone in dealing with this issue.

ACT's proposals for the reduction or complete removal of advertising from children's television typically called for the federal government to require certain hours to be set aside for children's programming, which represented a double blow to the revenue structure of the networks and local affiliates alike. Some of the potential threat along these lines was underscored by a successful 1973 campaign in Los Angeles against the syndication of superhero cartoons on the independent channel KTTV. Pressure from advocacy groups (led by the National Association for Better Broadcasting), including a challenge to the renewal of the station's operating license, led to an agreement to remove *Superman, Batman,* and *Aquaman* altogether, and to accompany other shows like *The Man from U.N.C.L.E.* with parental discretion warnings.

Network executives regularly warned of the dire consequences of moving too far toward regulation and often threatened to abandon kidvid. In 1975, all three networks reported mournfully that the profitability of Saturday morning had shrunk to the barest margins, in part due to pressure by ACT and its allies. In the entertainment industry, accounting is a perverse art (the movie *Forrest Gump* is still said not to have made a profit after becoming one of the top-grossing films in history), but advertising revenues for kidvid did dip as the seventies wore on, a development which ultimately had dire consequences in the eighties.

In between public relations gestures, the networks had actual schedules on Saturday mornings to manage. In the first half of the seventies, CBS's schedule was the consistent ratings champ, and consequently, the most profitable. Although ratings influenced children's programming to a relatively limited extent in comparison with their effects on prime time (largely due to the minimalist economics governing the production of kidvid programs), competition between networks for hit shows from a limited number of producers remained intense, even after new studios like Sid and Marty Krofft Productions appeared on the scene. Many programs switched hands on multiple occasions. Warner Brothers cartoon characters like Bugs Bunny, Daffy Duck, and the Road Runner were the perennial vagabonds of Saturdays, migrating all over the schedule and among all three networks. *H. R. Pufnstuf,* a ratings success on NBC in the fall of 1969, found its way over to ABC in 1972. Scooby-Doo, originally developed for CBS, popped up on ABC later in the decade, while the Archies defected from CBS to NBC.

Even more notably, all three networks reran shows that had appeared as much as ten years earlier, sometimes with new framing sequences or partnered with new programming. *Space Ghost,* for example, snuck back onto network schedules in 1976 as a replacement for *Land of the Lost.* Godzilla, who was originally given his own animated show in 1978, would be variously repackaged six times over the next two years with reruns of *The Adventures of Jonny Quest, The Funky Phantom, Dynomutt,* and *Hong Kong Phooey.* Bundling programs this way was primarily the work of Fred Silverman, who decided that such combinations were more likely to prove attractive to children.

This sort of bed-hopping and déjà vu programming marked Saturday morning as being quite different from the world of prime time. On prime time, programs rejected by one network were occasionally picked up and turned into successes at another network, but such instances were rare. Similarly, though syndication has meant that few past programs ever die a final death, the networks themselves have rarely rerun older programs outside of Saturday morning. The des-

Everybody Wants to Rule the World

Saturday morning was simply bubbling with mad and misguided scientists who usually had glasses, wore lab coats, and worked in laboratories full of dripping and hissing glass containers with weird-looking chemicals in them. In the seventies, their favorite schemes were to shrink people or to control minds through technology. In the eighties, the fashion changed to ecological sabotage and pollution, but it was pretty much the same shtick.

We'd like to suggest some interesting schemes for world conquest and revenge against an uncaring world that Saturday morning's mad scientists overlooked, though we suspect the Brain on *Pinky & the Brain* will get around to some of these any day now.

1. Monopolize the world's supply of Cheez Whiz.
2. Threaten people with a ray that makes nose hair grow extremely long.
3. Promote more cartoon violence.
4. Find out the secret recipe for Scooby Snacks.
5. Start a company called "Microsoft" and buy up computer operating systems.
6. Assassinate Scrappy Doo and be crowned Emperor by a grateful populace.
7. Mix that red bubbling stuff in the flask with the green stuff in the beaker.

8. Gain mental control of the lichens of the world and send them to attack Washington, D.C.

9. Allow the rabbit to eat Trix, which breaks the Seventh Seal and begins Armageddon.

10. Crossbreed a Smurf with He-Man to create the ultimate warrior race.

perate need to reduce Saturday morning programming costs to the lowest levels possible often meant a lot of recycling. The question of the day was not "Which show is number one and which show is number ten?" but more loosely "Which shows are popular and cheap and which shows are complete flops?" The nature of the audience was such that a rerun of an older popular program would often draw bigger ratings than would a brand-new show that had met with a lukewarm response.

Networks also followed a few general rules in organizing their schedules during the seventies. Programs which had been paid for but which the network intended to discard in the near future were sometimes exiled in disgrace to Sundays, where they were watched only by serious die-hard viewers—although ABC invested a bit of effort to make viewership on Sunday mornings something more than the last resort of cartoon junkies. While many animated shows were moved around the schedule more or less at random between 8 A.M. and 11 A.M., the late mornings and early afternoons took on a more distinctive character. This time was increasingly reserved for live-action shows which acted as buffers between kidvid and afternoon sports—either shows considered to have more diverse or teenage audiences like ABC's *American Bandstand* or *The CBS Children's Film*

Festival or live-action adventures like *Shazam!, Ark II,* and *Space Academy.*

Another distinctive feature of kidvid programming added during the seventies was the preview show which aired before the beginning of every season, just before school started. Network premieres are presently dispersed more widely over the calendar year, but in the seventies and early eighties, the fall was still the sacrosanct time for the introduction of new programming. Each network offered a special program in late August that previewed upcoming prime-time shows followed by a second program for children that focused only on Saturday morning. The preview show was usually accompanied by print advertising campaigns, placed in comic books and in *TV Guide,* promoting the new season on Saturdays.

Over the course of the seventies, the networks tried to reassure critics that they were acting responsibly toward children. At the same time, they also worked hard to optimize the profit-making potential of Saturday morning. The potential contradictions of the two objectives were apparent to many, including some executives. The signs of their contradiction were visible not only in public debates, but also within Saturday schedules, in the presence of "educational" programming, in the recycling and migration of particular programs and characters, in the increasingly sophisticated understanding of children's tastes within network circles, and in changing relations between advertisements and programs. By the early eighties, such contradictions pushed the networks to the brink of abandoning children's programming altogether.

Virtually all parties to the creation of the Saturday morning phenomenon relied on expert consultants to a greater and greater degree as the seventies wore on. One of the great unacknowledged contributions of Saturday morning to the United States of America during the seventies was its immensely positive effect on the economic health of academia, psychology, and pediatric medicine. It is tempting to think that the difficult job market in some of these professions resulted from the relative drying up of federal and private funds for the study of children's relationship to television. Our conservative guess at the number of patrons who commissioned kidvid studies in the seventies would be, rounded off, slightly higher than the number of scientists who mooched off of Star Wars funding in the eighties.

The studies conducted pertained to almost every major issue raised about seventies kidvid: Can television educate children, and if so, how? Must children's television be commercial, and if not, how could it be financed instead? Are sugared cereals really bad for kids? Do children know the difference between television programs and advertising? Does television raise or lower the intelligence of children? Do children with high intelligence like television, and if so, why? What are the different needs of very young children, preteens, and teenagers? What would happen to audiences if Scooby-Doo contracted rabies and tore out Daphne's throat? and so on.

However, the relationship among violence, television, and children was always the most central concern for the experts. By the late sixties, the sort of ranting about the loss of precious bodily fluids and suchlike dangers that had been Frederic Wertham's stock in trade had largely given way to a more serious and (to outsiders) more opaque debate about competing experimental and theoretical models within the field of child psychology and sociology. This debate rested on a foundation of studies conducted in the early sixties by figures like Albert Bandura, Paul Mussen, Eldred Rutherford, O. Ivar Lovaas, and Leonard Berkowitz.

The two most comprehensive early studies of children and television, Hilde Himmelweit's 1958 report and Wilbur Schramm's 1961 work *Television in the Lives of Our Children,* were both the product of collaborative work by sizable teams of researchers examining a wide variety of issues. Both reports produced relatively complex answers about the impact of television on children, something that was in short supply later on in the debate over Saturday morning. Schramm and his coauthors sensibly concluded that "for *some* children, under *some* conditions, *some* television is harmful. For *other* children, under *other* conditions, it may be beneficial. For *most* children, under *most* conditions, *most* television is probably neither particularly harmful nor particularly beneficial."

The studies by Bandura and other psychologists, in contrast, focused specifically on aggression among children. At first, this research attracted relatively little attention outside of academic circles. However, from 1968 onward, critics of Saturday morning began to cite these studies as proof that kidvid caused children to be violent. In the broadest terms, these studies were roughly similar in their experimental design. Children were divided into experimental and control groups. Children in the experimental group watched selected segments from cartoons or other material deemed by the researcher to be violent. After watching, they (as well as the control group) were given the opportunity to express aggression in some fashion: Bandura put children in a room with dolls to punch and asked children if they wanted to see him pop a balloon, while Lovaas was looking for "rowdy" play with toys. The studies tended to show—though never with perfect consistency—that the children who had watched a "violent" cartoon would express more "aggression" when given the opportunity.

Not surprisingly, other psychologists specializing in the behavior of children were critical of the design of these experiments—and even more critical of their usage by kidvid critics. The experimenters themselves conceded that they had not demonstrated that children would be more likely to commit violent acts against other people as a result of watching cartoons. Even so, the studies did a great deal to bolster complaints about the alleged violence of Saturday morning during and after the controversy over the superhero cartoons—both by implying that cartoons caused violence and by making use of the content of many cartoons as "violent" stimuli in experiments. In fact, these experiments played a key role in broadening the definition of cartoon violence, particularly in tandem with a report written in

1972 by George Gerbner. (Gerbner would go on to issue annual "violence indexes" that assessed the content of television.)

For example, the initial critique of weirdo superheroes for their violence was transferred lock, stock, and barrel to the sorts of funny-animal "chase comedies" that were previously considered inoffensive. Warner Brothers cartoon characters like Bugs Bunny and the Road Runner and older Hanna-Barbera characters like Tom and Jerry were attacked with particular vehemence. One psychiatrist branded Bugs "TV's Mr. Violence." Sam Blum, an editor of *Redbook,* wrote in the *New York Times Magazine* that, excepting *The Archies,* all seventies cartoons used "violence as their main, if not their only, joke. . . . 'Bugs Bunny–Road Runner' involved animals dropping anvils on each other, hitting each other with hammers, firing guns at each other, attempting to poison each other, blowing each other up and tricking each other so that they fall off high places." (Such studies are clearly the general inspiration for the "Itchy and Scratchy" cartoons which appear on *The Simpsons,* with their rousing theme song, "We fight and fight and fight, fight fight fight.")

The debate over psychological research reached a fever pitch around the 1972 publication of the surgeon general's report on the effects of television violence. The report was carefully written to allow many different factions to claim some measure of satisfaction, though it was this very balancing act that led to a substantial controversy over the report. However, even in its initial sanitized version, the surgeon general's report helped to legitimize the notion that Bugs Bunny and his cartoon compatriots were "saturated" in violence at a level comparable to or exceeding the superhero cartoons. Testimony about the report (along with the question of what role the networks played behind the scenes in muting the report's critical tone) helped the progressively stronger public alliance between academics, educators, and advocacy groups like ACT and the PTA gain a lot of political capital. Not only were politicians at both the state and local levels much more willing to attack television, but more professional associ-

The Burke Brothers' Guide for Kids Whose Parents Watch Television

On August 4, 1977, *Variety* reported that a recent British study concluded that the introduction of television to the tiny island of St. Helena noticeably improved the behavior of the island's children. According to the report, "Some children, intriguingly, actually feel that their parents, not themselves, may be adversely impacted by exposure to television."

This just confirms something that most kids have known for a long time. Parents need careful, loving guidance from their children to develop good viewing habits. Kids, here are some helpful guidelines for training your parents to watch television the right way.

1. Mom and Dad may have the strange idea that watching television is bad. Parents are very impressionable, and can unconsciously imitate what they read in magazines and books or overhear from other parents. Talk with your parents and help them realize that television is good for them. Encourage them to develop good critical thinking habits about what they hear at PTA meetings. Supervise your parents when you notice them reading *Redbook*.

2. Mom and Dad may not understand television violence very well. Parents are easily frightened by ray guns, exploding robots, superheroes, giant monsters, coyotes falling off cliffs, or cartoon animals whose heads take on the shape of frying pans after being hit by one. You need

to explain carefully to them that this is not violence but entertainment. Point out that if Mom were to hit Dad with a frying pan, he would just get a big bump on his head. Let them give it a try if they want. If necessary, go find your little brother and beat the crap out of him while Mom and Dad watch in order to demonstrate violence to them.

3. Mom and Dad may get easily confused about the difference between television and reality in general. They may react poorly to animation, particularly computer animation, as a result. They may also react to fictional events as if they really happened. You can reassure them that even really important adults like former vice president Dan Quayle make this mistake fairly often, so it's quite normal. Be patient and supportive, but carefully explain the difference between fiction and reality to your parents. Teach them to turn the channel or even turn the television off for a while if they don't like what they are seeing.

4. Some programs are just not appropriate for adult viewing, although you should remember that some parents may be uncommonly mature. Go slowly in introducing them to your favorite shows and be prepared to lay down boundaries if necessary. Parents prosper in an environment where there is some structure, some rules. If your parents continue to defy you by watching inappropriate shows, then tell them to go surf the Internet for a while.

5. Parents may carelessly purchase products for themselves based on television advertisements. Be especially wary when Dad takes an interest in Rogaine or Mom goes

for the Slim-Fast plan. Parents often fall for slick advertisements for medicines, especially when they're made to look like chocolate. Also remind your parents that cars, computer chips, and beer may not work nearly as well as they do on the television. Then make them drive you to Toys "R" Us with their wallets full of cash.

ations of experts like the American Medical Association decided to join the crusade against televisual violence.

Another result of the surgeon general's report was a massive wave of new studies. A lot of the findings supported earlier work and further confirmed for many researchers a link between aggression and televised violence. Many of the new laboratory experiments attempted to use what were supposed to be less biased and more realistic tests to measure responses to violent cartoons. For example, in one study, children were asked after seeing selected violent scenes what they would do if another child hit them and were given several multiple-choice responses to choose from. In another study, children were put in front of an "aggression machine" and asked to push buttons labeled "hurt" or "help" in response to images of other children.

This new research also led to more specific suggestions about the content of kidvid. Experts began to offer advice to producers and networks about what sorts of morals, plots, and characters were good—and not good—for television. Child psychologists, sociologists, and other experts had moved into an increasingly central role in the actual production of children's television, serving as consultants and advisers to all three networks. By the mid-eighties, this development all but threatened to drown children's programming, as the range of expert opinion widened to include representatives from various political and social pressure groups seeking to bend kidvid to their own particular agendas.

This huge swirl of activity around kidvid in the seventies underscores the importance of the Saturday morning *phenomenon,* not just the cartoons themselves. But in the end, it all came down to what was on the screen. Most of the essential core programs of Saturday morning actually appeared on the television in one form or another during the seventies. The majority of seventies kidvid came from Hanna-Barbera Studios, with Filmation and Sid and Marty Krofft second and third. Consequently, Hanna-Barbera's strengths and weaknesses best illustrate the role producers played in the classic years of Saturday morning. Moreover, as a result of the 1991 merger of Ted Turner's Cartoon Network and Hanna-Barbera (and also the output of Ruby-Spears), most contemporary Saturday morning veterans are likely to see Hanna-Barbera programs when they desire to satisfy their nostalgic yearnings. Filmation's library is now split up, and the Krofft shows have generally appeared only in one-shot specials during the nineties, though they may appear regularly in syndication in the near future.

As we noted in chapter 1, William Hanna and Joseph Barbera had deep roots in theatrical animation, and their earliest contributions to television clearly reflected those roots. The various characters they developed in the fifties and sixties were cousins to more frenetic and comedically inspired Warner Brothers characters like Bugs Bunny and Daffy Duck. Yogi Bear, Huckleberry Hound, Quickdraw McGraw, Top Cat, and their peers starred in comfortable, modest, and somewhat amusing cartoons that initially had the same relationship to prime-time programming that the Warner cartoons had to movies: they were appetizers before the main show.

With *The Flintstones* and *The Jetsons,* Hanna and Barbera even aspired to put their cartoons into the big top itself, right alongside live-action programming in prime time. In the case of *The Flintstones,* they succeeded for six years. This was a bittersweet success for Joseph Barbera, treasured but never to be repeated. It was not for lack of trying: the studio attempted another prime-time animated sitcom, *Wait 'Til Your Father Gets Home,* in 1972. But without the visual gags provided by the Stone Age setting of *The Flintstones, Wait 'Til Your Father Gets Home* simply underscored the relatively pedestrian and derivative reach of the studio.

So as far as the seventies was concerned, Hanna-Barbera's business was Saturday morning cartoons. Their one live-action show, *The Banana Splits,* was canceled in 1970, leaving the live-action market to Filmation and Sid and Marty Krofft. Live-action shows were more expensive to produce and were scheduled in part because kidvid critics held to the belief that live action was somehow inherently more wholesome than animation. Hanna-Barbera Studios, ever in search of maximized profits, decided to stick to cartoons, and even economized their production. There is a marked difference between the technical quality of the first season of *Scooby-Doo, Where Are You?* and the Scooby episodes of six years later, a difference which was evident across the board in Hanna-Barbera's (and, to be fair, Filmation's) later seventies efforts. These economizing measures led to massive overproduction, to the transference of most of the actual labor of animation overseas to South Korea, to the exploitation of animators and writers, and to a growing indifference both to network priorities and kidvid audiences. Nevertheless, the studio remained capable of turning out popular programs throughout the decade, ranging from *Scooby-Doo* to *Smurfs* in the early eighties.

Hanna-Barbera's dominance of Saturday morning produced some rather curious twists on business as usual in the television industry, as we noted earlier in our discussion of the networks. One longtime writer of children's television pointed out that the studio's situation was sometimes analogous to that depicted in the Mel Brooks film *The Producers.* A flop could make as much money as a major hit; worst of all options was a show with middling ratings. Hanna-

Barbera's increasingly large library of previously produced shows could be used to replace a serious flop, and in the seventies, no other kidvid producer stood ready to provide replacements. So in this sense alone, Hanna-Barbera held an almost perfect monopoly. If shows succeeded, they provided new material for the studio's library. If they failed, the network would have to turn to the studio to provide another program.

This also meant that Hanna-Barbera was its own worst competitor. Its shows, generally made with a fairly strong "house style" and with the same group of actors providing voices, particularly Don Messick and Daws Butler, tended to blend together into one somewhat indistinguishable blur. Talent was spread thin within the studio, in part because of the sheer volume produced and because of its relatively rapid growth. Moreover, because of its relentless pressure to economize, a hectic and spasmodic work schedule, and Hanna and Barbera's tight management of the studio's output, there was little incentive or opportunity for strong individual talent to emerge. According to several former Hanna-Barbera employees, this led network executives to attempt to monopolize those individuals within Hanna-Barbera who were regarded as capable of delivering hit programs. It also led some productive Hanna-Barbera staffers to leave the company and attempt to compete with their former employers. Discontent with Hanna-Barbera's business practices, particularly the company's extensive use of overseas production, finally led to a full-blown strike against the company in 1977. Though it was settled by arbitration, it left a lot of ill will in its wake.

Sid and Marty Krofft Productions managed to compete with Hanna-Barbera by providing a relatively small number of highly rated live-action shows. Filmation, which had provided at least some competition for Hanna-Barbera in the late sixties and early seventies, stayed alive largely through producing a small number of live-action shows while economizing its cartoon operations even more stringently than Hanna-Barbera. It also managed to produce a number of reasonably popular shows based on licensed characters, particularly Tarzan and Batman. However, it was Filmation that would provide the first of many staggering blows to Hanna-Barbera's preeminence in the production of kidvid during the eighties by premiering a syndicated cartoon based on the adventures of a character who existed primarily because of a line of toys: He-Man.

The seventies were the template for Saturday morning, but by the end of the decade, the formula was in danger of failing, both because of the repeated challenges of critics and because of internal pressures. Only five years later, Saturday morning would look as if it were doomed to undergo a massive mutation, or even to die out altogether.

Chapter Three

From the Ashes: The Near-Death and Rebirth of Saturday Morning

Much as we hate to admit it, the Smurfs seem to have saved Saturday morning. That's what Fred Silverman tells us, at least, and the evidence suggests that he is right. According to Silverman, at the end of the seventies and the beginning of the eighties, the networks were pretty tired of Saturday morning. Hit shows were harder and harder to come by. The main suppliers of kidvid—Filmation, Sid and Marty Krofft, Hanna-Barbera—seemed to be tapped out, serving up retread programming like *Fred and Barney Meet the Schmoo, Jason of Star Command,* and *The Godzilla/Hong Kong Phooey Hour.* There were fewer kids watching, as baby boom gave way to baby bust. Attacks on children's television by critics, advocacy groups, experts, and so on showed no signs of abating. And more significantly, a few far-sighted people at the networks guessed that the nature of the television business might be about to change with the rising importance of syndication, cable, and videotapes. Fred Seibert, the current president of Hanna-Barbera, emphatically reminded us that for kidvid, "cable changed everything."

The question then was, Why have a network version of Saturday morning at all? Why not just give the time back to the affiliates and let them schedule kidvid however they liked? If they wanted kidvid, there was plenty in circulation, and doubtless the major producers of children's television would go ahead and produce more. Besides, given how despised Saturday morning had become in the general culture, what ambitious network executive would want to work in what Filmation's Lou Scheimer admitted was a "programming ghetto"? Even Fred Silverman, the man who rose to the top through Saturday morning, had left for greener pastures.

Silverman claims that just as these thoughts were occurring to network executives, NBC scored a major hit with *Smurfs,* which tabled all thoughts of dropping Saturday morning for a while. *Smurfs* was one of those rare programs that both kids and advocacy groups liked. Admittedly, since Silverman himself was responsible for pushing *Smurfs* into production—Bill Hanna acknowledges in his biography that he and Joseph Barbera needed a lot of convincing to develop the program—this story has more than a little self-promotion about it. Other professionals involved in the kidvid field, including writer Mark Evanier, said that as far as they knew, children's television was in fairly good shape in the early eighties. But on the whole, we think Silverman's story reflects the state of kidvid at that time. Profitability was down, the hassle factor was way up, and the television marketplace generally was changing. Papa Smurf and his posse seemed to have saved the day.

———

"Children get their sadistic tendencies from the inner actions in the family and not from external stimuli." —Psychiatrist Dr. Carl M. Grip, 1962

———

However, they brought temporary salvation at best. The cracks in the edifice of Saturday morning that had been evident as early as 1978 widened perceptibly in 1983 when Filmation's program *He-Man and the Masters of the Universe* made its syndicated debut. On the surface, there was nothing particularly startling or different about *He-Man*. It was similar to past action-adventure cartoons—indeed, it was arguably better than many on the air at that time, with fairly good stories and some reasonably interesting characters. Where it differed was in the degree and type of its success. To begin with, it was syndicated, usually airing on weekday afternoons. It did not air on a network nor did it air on Saturday mornings. Its ratings were extremely good. As a strongly rated syndicated program, it once again raised the issue of whether the networks really needed to nurture their own extensive kidvid offerings on Saturdays. And as a program which made huge amounts of money for a toy manufacturer, it also raised a whole host of additional issues and led to some very unwelcome changes in the nature of Saturday morning. As Lou Scheimer told us, "He-Man nearly destroyed the networks' Saturday schedules."

In the seventies, popular Saturday morning characters were made into toys or otherwise licensed for commercial appearances on lunch boxes and similar products, but only as an afterthought to their televisual popularity. (There were a few exceptions to this: there was an unsuccessful cartoon based on Hot Wheels toys in 1969, for example.) He-Man, however, was based on a line of toys by Mattel which had been designed *before* the cartoon ever appeared. The program's success fueled the success of the toys, which led to the development of more toys in the He-Man line, which led to the addition of characters on the show, which led ultimately to a spin-off program called *She-Ra: Princess of Power*. The content of the program was funneled directly into the commercial development of a line of products.

It was, as one might guess, a stratagem that Mattel and other toy manufacturers rushed to reproduce. Between 1983 and 1990, kidvid schedules were choked with programming whose primary purpose was to flog lines of toys like the Transformers or the Care Bears. Even long-established characters like the Superfriends went through changes designed to promote new lines of toys directly connected to their shows. Syndicated programs airing on weekday afternoons were the most prominent evidence of this shift, but the networks' weekend schedules also reflected the trend toward new forms of commercialism. The earliest commercial tie-in programs to appear on the networks were not connected directly to toy lines, as in the case of CBS's 1983 program *Saturday Supercade,* a hideously stupid anthology of cartoons about characters from arcade games. By the late eighties, despite the vehement opposition of ACT and other groups, the new commercial spirit dominated all but a small proportion of televisual kidvid.

Even when programming was not narrowly devoted to promoting a particular product, most of it was designed to shill for some other network program, some particular celebrity, or a film. This development had firm roots in the seventies, when animated versions of popular shows like *Star Trek* and *Emergency!* appeared on the networks, but by the mid-eighties, it had given way to abominations like *Hulk Hogan's Rock 'N' Wrestling!* and *Rubik the Amazing Cube.* As television writer and producer J. Michael Straczynski put it, the networks were busily "fouling their own nest."

Straczynski, who worked on both *He-Man* and *The Real Ghostbusters* (both of which were tied to a line of toys), told us that he felt some commercially motivated cartoons were misjudged by hostile critics. We tend to agree, since *He-Man* and *The Real Ghostbusters* were fairly good programs in comparison to much Saturday morning kidvid. For Straczynski, the low moments came when the alliance of toy manufacturers and cartoon producers diminished any efforts toward making a quality program. As Straczynski points out, *He-Man* helped sell toys because kids liked the show. Toy manufacturers found out later in the eighties that a really crummy syndicated cartoon based on a line of toys could not produce a major commercial success. At one point, Straczynski said, he was asked to develop a proposal for a show based on Legos. Irritated by the gold rush atmosphere then prevailing, and astonished that the makers of immobile square blocks thought a meaningful cartoon could be made about their product, Straczynski wrote up a satiric pitch for a show featuring cute kids and their "Mayan talking blocks" that they discovered in a jungle in Mexico. To his surprise, the manufacturers still seemed eager to proceed with the idea.

Another emblematic low moment unfolded in 1988, when CBS announced plans to develop a Saturday morning cartoon based on the Noid, an animated trademark character that was used briefly in television advertisements for Domino's Pizza. (This followed on the heels of a CBS attempt to develop a program based on the line of bubble-gum cards called Garbage Pail Kids.) This plan was a self-evident sign of creative bankruptcy, but in statements about the show television executives insisted on digging their own graves. One commented that the Noid "appeals to something in every adult and child," while another said that "the Noid is a very distinctive character that has endeared itself to adults and kids alike." You just might have been able to say something like this about Captain Crunch, but to say it about the Noid, a totally cipherlike and soullessly commercial invention, was the height of industry cynicism.

For Straczynski and many other professionals, the ascendancy of commercialism in eighties kidvid was a relatively minor issue compared to the total triumph of prosocial programming. However, Peggy Charren, the former head of ACT, looks back at the eighties as a moment of near defeat for the critics of children's television; as she put it, Reagan appointees saw television as nothing more than a "toaster with pictures." We're not so sure that this picture of the eighties is accurate. The critics got some of what they had been asking for: television vetted by experts, without real violence or conflict, utterly sanitized.

Given the Reagan administration's antipathy toward federal regulation, how did this happen? First, the power of ACT and similar groups was eclipsed by new and far more strident voices from the religious right. We're not exactly big fans of Peggy Charren and her fellow travelers, but we'll take them any day over the kind of censorious cultural ayatollahs who rose to prominence in the eighties, particularly the Reverend Donald Wildmon and his American Family Association. Charren and ACT at least had the virtue of rationality, along with genuinely good intentions, and, as Charren continues to point out today, ACT never approved of censorship. In our discussions with her, she was strongly critical of the recent cutting of supposedly violent scenes from Looney Tunes cartoons.

Wildmon, on the other hand, is a committee censor with a puritanical streak that would embarrass Cotton Mather. He is perhaps better known for his campaigns against the movie *The Last Temptation of Christ,* the television program *NYPD Blue,* and the National Endowment for the Arts, but he and his group also achieved notoriety with an attack on children's television, specifically, Ralph Bakshi's *Mighty Mouse: The New Adventures.* The incident in question involved a sequence in which Mighty Mouse pauses to smell a flower. Viewing it in slow motion and in extreme close-up, one arguably can see a sort of powder or dust on the flower. This almost subliminal image was enough for Wildmon to leap to the ridiculous conclusion that Mighty Mouse was sniffing cocaine and thus teaching kids to snort it too.

This is the sort of thing that dim-witted followers of the religious right have been muttering about for years, whether it's backward-masked messages in pop music or secret stealth helicopters in the basement of the United Nations. However, such sentiments were a new ingredient in the Saturday morning stew during the eighties. Suddenly right-wing culture commandos were playing Spot-the-Hidden-Satanic-Message every time a children's show came on the air, and pressuring the networks about every one of their bizarre hang-ups, ranging from the belief that wearing black clothing makes one a devotee of the occult to attacking any hint of "one-world" sentiment, which we all know is really part of a plot by the Illuminati and the Trilateral Commission to conquer the world and drain off our precious bodily fluids.

The networks did pretty much what you'd expect: concede just enough to these assembled nutcases to make almost everyone else unhappy while resisting them enough to keep them angry. In substantial measure, it was easy to incorporate the concerns of Wildmon and his allies into the process of vetting kidvid because Standards and Practices supervision of children's television had already become such a dominant force. (Standards and Practices was the title of the internal division maintained by each network to supervise the content of its programming.) Since the whole point of Standards and Practices often seems to be to keep programs from offending anyone (no matter how absurd their objections), it wasn't a big stretch to add new items to the list of no-no's. The networks were not about to allow Wildmon or his closest allies to join in this vetting, but over time, consultants who were basically sympathetic to the agenda of the religious right managed to worm their way into the process.

These censorings just added insult to injury, since the iron fist of the consultants had already gotten a firm choke hold on Saturday morning in the early eighties. It got to the point where there was effectively one and only one moral-of-the-day which was regarded as appropriately prosocial: Cooperation is good. As Mark Evanier said, "In virtually every script we did, one kid had to be portrayed as the complainer and would eventually learn to give in to the group." Like Evanier, we find that moral more than a little suspicious: appeals to cooperation are frequently used to squash individuality and idiosyncrasy.

By this time, consultants and Broadcast Standards and Practices executives interfered with virtually every aspect of the production of kidvid, from general plotting down to the tiniest minutiae. Straczynski told us about a typical incident during the time he worked on *The Real Ghostbusters.* In one episode, the script made mention of the *Necronomicon,* the fictional invention of classic horror writer H. P. Lovecraft. (In Lovecraft's stories, the *Necronomicon* is a book whose revelations are so terrifying that scholars of the occult are driven mad simply by reading it.) Straczynski was informed by a network flack that the reference to the *Necronomicon* would have to be taken out because it was a real book closely tied to Satanism. When Straczynski pointed out that this was completely wrong, the S&P executive replied that she had consulted an expert who confirmed that the book was real. As Mark Evanier describes it, the standard answer to any complaint by production staff to cuts made by ABC executives was "We hired an expert." In some cases, creators took to delivering programs late so that network censors had no time to do anything about them.

———

"In the olden days, children had no toys *per se* but played with pine cones and lumps of coal. This made them happier, smarter, and better behaved than today's children, and everyone, except today's children, would like for the olden days to return." —David Owen, *The Man Who Invented Saturday Morning*, 1986

———

It's not that Standards and Practices representatives were completely craven, or that they all hated kidvid. Many couldn't bring themselves to believe that kids might be smart. In the eighties, S&P executives routinely scrawled "KWG" for "Kids Won't Get" in the margins of cartoon scripts. Even today, some network executives are visibly uncomfortable with kidvid shows as smart and multilayered as *Freakazoid!* or *The Tick*. Mostly, S&P's tendency to give in to the least application of outside pressure was yet another result of Saturday morning's ghettoization in the larger culture, and given the copious scorn heaped upon kidvid, no network executive with career ambitions was going to plant his or her feet and fight like mad to protect the creative autonomy of kidvid producers. What kudos would you get for insisting on the artistic integrity of *The Real Ghostbusters* or *Garfield and Friends?* No one from the ACLU would rush to your defense, no television critic would crusade on your behalf.

Saturday morning's true winter of discontent stretched from 1982 until 1985, when the first glimmer of hope began to dawn. During these bleak years, kids endured programs like *Pac-Man, Monch-hichis, The New Scooby & Scrappy-Doo, Dragon's Lair, Meatballs and Spaghetti, Kissyfur, Gilligan's Planet, Benji, Zax & the Alien Prince,* and so on. There were occasional bright spots—*Thundarr the Barbarian* and *Blackstar, The Littles, Dungeons & Dragons*—but the networks were running on automatic pilot, and so were Hanna-Barbera and Ruby-Spears, the main suppliers of Saturday programming, particularly since Filmation was increasingly preoccupied with the syndicated marketplace on weekday afternoons.

"[Generation X] wants and receives a culture which is high on impact and low on significance, without any basis or need for justification. . . . their response to the imperatives of any system of values is cynical at its most energetic and usually exaggeratedly phlegmatic or insouciant. They live precisely beyond freedom and dignity, contemptuous of both the discipline of non-violence and the structures of meaning. In short, their desires correspond to the features of the Saturday morning cartoons on which they were raised." —Ben Crawford, "Saturday Morning Fever"

In many ways, cartoon production had reached an impasse in the mid-eighties. Animators complained that the long dominance of limited animation, coupled with the related centrality of overseas animating, had effectively disempowered them and handed primary creative authority over to the writers. Discontent among animators had run high since the late sixties, culminating in the 1977 strike at Hanna-Barbera. Even after the strike was settled, discontent remained a potent force among animators. Writers were also dissatisfied, often pointing out that working on Saturday morning programming got you less money, less prestige, and less protection from careless rewriting by producers and network executives than writing in any other area of television. The main producers, particularly Hanna-Barbera, were accustomed to promoting the company rather than the individual talents of their employees and had little incentive in the late seventies and early eighties to innovate or diversify their output. Individual creators were rarely allowed to take charge of a particular show, and there was usually little time to polish pilots before they aired. Network executives, according to Evanier, grew so desperate to monopolize the efforts of the best talents within Hanna-Barbera that they began putting successful studio staffers on network payrolls.

So what changed? How did we get from this dismal impasse to the relatively vibrant, exciting Saturday and weekday cartoon schedules that became available to children beginning in the early nineties? For one thing, the complacency of Hanna-Barbera and Ruby-Spears was challenged abruptly by the entry of new animation studios and distributors into the marketplace, like Nelvana, Marvel Entertainment, and the eight-hundred-pound gorilla of animation, Disney. The initial animation standards of these newcomers' programs, while not among the finest ever seen on the small screen, were significantly more exacting than the lazy limited animation that had become standard fare on Saturdays. Programs like *Droids: The Adventures of R2D2 and C3PO* (based on the *Star Wars* characters) and *Wuzzles,* both appearing in 1985, looked and felt a bit different. This coincided with the slow but perceptible arrival of a new generation of writers and animators into the business, people who did not harken back to the old world of cinematic animation. Their influence was visible in mid-eighties programs like *The Real Ghostbusters, Dungeons & Dragons,* and *Garfield and Friends,* all of which had markedly better scripts and animation styling than the late-seventies shows.

Three shows in particular played a critical role in bringing Saturday morning back to life. The first was Ralph Bakshi's 1987 *Mighty Mouse: The New Adventures,* the program which incited Donald Wildmon's wrath. Bakshi's previous work on Saturday morning—the first cartoon version of *Spider-Man* and a show called *Mighty Heroes*—had appeared two decades before the new *Mighty Mouse.* In between, Bakshi had made a number of animated movies ranging from the controversial X-rated version of *Fritz the Cat* to the dismal *Lord of the Rings.* The fact that network executives even permitted him to take a role in a new animated series was a small sign that Saturday morning was changing.

Some animators have charged that the real work of developing *Mighty Mouse* was done by John Kricfalusi, who went on to create the revolutionary *Ren & Stimpy Show,* but many of those animators who worked on the program question this claim. Eddie Fitzgerald, one of the animators on the series, told us that Bakshi "stood up for quality" on the show, and that without his constant attempts to fend off worried network executives, none of the show would have aired. Bakshi initially was determined to show the network that he could be trusted to stay within their guidelines. Fitzgerald and Tom Minton, a writer and producer on the show, told us, "Ralph made it clear at first that we should tone down the material as a compromise, but when he started seeing our ideas he said, 'Okay. I love it.'" From that point on, Fitzgerald said, "[CBS] would ask for changes in the material and Ralph would just nod and agree and afterward totally ignore their requests."

The end product was wildly entertaining, with a sense of humor which clearly harkened back to the old Warner Brothers cartoons. Like those classic works, the new *Mighty Mouse* made sly references to mainstream cultural icons, most hilariously in the episode "Pirates with Dirty Faces" by making a deranged pirate captain out of a caricature of Marlon Brando. It was the first Saturday morning show since the late sixties to appeal consciously to both adults and children, presciently understanding that this was not only the best road to making a quality program but also potentially a path to commercial success. It was also one of the first Saturday morning shows to make nostalgic references to past televisual animation, particularly in the classic episode "The Ice Goose Cometh," which brought an old animated character back to life in an animated world he no longer knew.

The second show that revitalized Saturday morning was the landmark live-action program *Pee-Wee's Playhouse*. While *Mighty Mouse* made witty use of the history of televised animation, *Pee-Wee's Playhouse* astutely mined another nostalgic mother lode: kids' variety shows with live hosts, a genre with roots stretching all the way back to the origins of television. Relatively few people caught on to *Mighty Mouse* before its premature Wildmon-influenced demise, but *Pee-Wee's Playhouse* was an invention of such staggering originality and creative genius that it quickly drew a substantial audience of adults and kids. Paul Reubens's established comic persona was amusing enough, but the show surrounded him with a remarkable set, memorable supporting characters like Miss Yvonne, the King of Cartoons, Conky the Robot, and Jambi, and clever writing that worked on many levels. The show was a subversive delight and helped break down entrenched network resistance to original, creative kidvid: it showed what could be done if creators with a distinctive vision were able to put that vision on the screen without the interference of network flacks. *Pee-Wee's Playhouse* came to a sudden end after Paul Reubens was arrested for public exposure in a Florida porno theater. From our perspective, there has never been anything in American cultural history as stupid and pointless as the reaction to Reubens's arrest. This shouldn't have made a damn bit of difference to anyone, and as far as we're concerned, *Pee-Wee's Playhouse* should still be on the air. It's perhaps *the* single greatest instance of kidvid genius, among the finest programs ever associated with Saturday morning. We could not care less what Paul Reubens did when he wasn't up on the screen as Pee-Wee.

Though far more subtle in its impact than either of these two gloriously innovative programs, *Beetlejuice,* which first aired in 1989, was a sure sign that Saturday morning had entered a new era of greatness. It was precisely the kind of cartoon that networks and studios had botched badly earlier in the eighties: as the spin-off from a popular movie, it should have been wretchedly generic and witless.

Instead, it featured distinctively individual animation and funny, intelligent scripts. While it took liberties with the film's plot in order to make it work as an ongoing cartoon series—Beetlejuice was now Lydia's gross but loyal friend, and the two of them set off in most episodes for adventures in the Netherworld—in many ways, the adaptation outshone the original movie. It was particularly telling that this program appeared on ABC, which had a reputation for being the most censorious and uptight of all the networks when it came to kidvid.

The late eighties were not quite the end of really bad commercialized kidvid on the networks, let alone on the syndicated markets, where there's still a pretty hefty number of toy tie-in programs. CBS premiered a program based on the California Raisins in 1989, for example, while NBC was showing the painful *Captain N: The Game Master*. But at last it was possible once again to produce kidvid with style, originality, and wit. The Saturday Morning Renaissance began full force when the fledgling Fox Network recognized that kidvid was an area where the relative inattentiveness of the established networks had created a major opportunity. Fox's rise from presumptive failure to major player has had a lot to do with its development of a revolutionary schedule of kidvid on both Saturdays and weekdays.

Fox executives, particularly Margaret Loesch, the head of Fox Kid's Network, understood that the path to kidvid success lay in allowing individual animators and writers to develop their own programs with less network interference than the previously established norm. They were not the only ones who grasped this principle: the cable channel Nickelodeon also commissioned a number of new animated programs like *Rugrats* and *The Ren & Stimpy Show* with the same understanding, though Nickelodeon executives later blew it by snatching *The Ren & Stimpy Show* away from its creator, John Kricfalusi, turning what had been one of the best cartoons ever made into unwatchable dreck. It took a bit of adjustment, but in fairly short order Fox developed a full lineup of children's programming that included standout shows like *The Adventures of Batman & Robin, Eek! the Cat, Animaniacs,* and *The Tick.*

Mark Evanier pointed out that Fox had some unfair advantages: as a new network, it initially could get away with looser controls by Standards and Practices than the other networks could permit, and Fox's control of its weekday afternoon schedule allowed it to make broader use of the programs it purchased. The upshot of the whole matter is that Fox's strategies briefly made Saturday morning the best it had ever been. By the mid-nineties, there was a good supply of excellent programs on Saturdays and weekday afternoons, supplied not just by Fox but by Disney, the fledgling WB Network, the standard three networks, and cable channels like the Cartoon Network and Nickelodeon. Almost all the major producers sporadically followed what we regard as the number one rule of good children's entertainment: Make programs that both adults and children like, and never, ever talk down to kids, no matter how young they are.

––––––––

"You know, pal—maybe I *should* de-wire myself. De-wiring would reconnect me to the world of natural time—sunsets and rainbows and crashing waves and Smurfs." —Ethan in Douglas Coupland's *Microserfs*

––––––––

Whether it will stay that way is another matter. As of the spring of 1997, ACT had disbanded and Donald Wildmon seemed more worried about lesbians on prime time, but the proposition that kidvid is insidious junk harming the fragile mind of the nation's kids is so firmly embedded in public culture that the wheels of censorship and self-righteousness just keep chugging steadily along. In 1991, Congress passed the Children's Television Act, which required all broadcasters to certify that their children's programming served educational and informational purposes. The response, we'd agree, was overwhelmingly cynical: broadcasters certified programs like *G.I. Joe* and *Teenage Mutant Ninja Turtles* as educational, since various characters allegedly learned the meaning of cooperation or some such thin moral. Critics of kidvid leaped all over this response, claiming that it proved once and for all that sterner controls were required. Around the same time, some of the new programming, like the extremely well written and sleekly animated *Batman* cartoon, drew fire from experts and advocates for its allegedly violent content. As we write, the Federal Communications Commission is contemplating a major new regulatory program aimed at children's television. Chilling developments like the V-chip and a new ratings system for television are already inhibiting the development of good kidvid. The last two seasons' worth of new cartoons on the networks and in syndication has also shown a marked tendency to revert to the nasty commercialism of the eighties at the same time that some of the best programming of the Saturday Morning Renaissance has been canceled or cut back.

———

"I have to say that tshe shows with 'cartoon overtones' are among the most popular television programming for adults in the whole country."
—Fred Silverman, 1977

———

It's the weirdo superheroes all over again. Charren and other critics say that they have never advocated censorship, and that they have always wanted to see quality television. And yet, they have also nurtured the demand for prosocial programming, which is precisely what turned Saturday morning into a wasteland for almost a decade. Saturday morning hit a high point in the mid-nineties. If it's going to stay that way—if the critics really mean it when they say they want quality television for kids—then they're going to have to learn how to stand back and respect their children's good taste and judgment and to give the producers of kidvid enough creative license to make the shows that kids *really* want to see.

Chapter Four

Willing Slaves of the Cathode God: Saturday Morning and "Generation X"

In June 1995, novelist Douglas Coupland proclaimed that "X" (as in Generation) was over.

Having received this tablet from the mountaintop, the mass media obediently trumpeted the death of Generation X to every marketing boardroom in the nation. Truth to tell, as a marketing strategy, X was already on life support. X didn't mark the spot: X was the kiss of death. The demographic group called "Generation X" has the inconvenient habit of reacting negatively to being treated as a target market. Small wonder. Most of the ink expended initially on defining "Generation X" came from the pens of neoconservatives and other cranks who hated the people they were describing, who saw X as the disastrous consequence of the sixties. The marketers who came next were no better, offering distorted portraits of "grunge" or "slacking."

The mass media's understanding of X, from the perspective of those named as such, has been crassly manipulative. For example, most pundits initially used the definition of X offered by William Strauss and Neil Howe in their book *13th Generation: Abort, Retry, Fail;* namely, people born between 1961 and 1981. By 1994, media observers had subtly tweaked the numbers so that Generation X consisted of people born between 1965 and 1981. Why? Because the media like to believe that generations have some kind of essential moral and social character, a kind of collective personality, and they had pegged X as a bunch of rootless, alienated, and jobless whiners who were still living at home with Mom and Dad. The problem was that to the limited extent that any of this has been true, it has been a transient by-product of being twenty-five years old in a stagnant economy. As Xers turn thirty and increasingly get jobs and kids, they mess up the stereotype.

Now X is supposedly dead, but in the interim, a lot of people who resent the label nevertheless have been provoked to think about what, if anything, they actually do share generationally. We don't think there's a lot. "Generation X" as it is typically represented in the mass media is a white and suburban construct. The real generation is naturally more diverse. When it's stacked up against things like race, class, and gender in this society, an age group is not terribly unifying or important.

But we do think that there is something of a common cultural vocabulary shared by people born after 1960 or so, a sort of hidden code. Knowledge of that code may not create something as deep and complex as an identity, but it does lend itself to a shared outlook of sorts. Of course, marketers and pundits know this, and their hunger for books and guides on X has largely been motivated by their desire to crack this code and speak to X in its own pidgin. Almost all such efforts thus far have been visible failures. A Budweiser ad campaign, for example, in which young folk ask the deathless question "Ginger? Or Mary Ann?" while playing a game of pool, met with derision among many members of the target market.

So for the advertiser who has gotten this far, we've got some bad news: You aren't going to find out how to crack the code here. In fact, we've got worse news than that: You *can't* crack the code. You'd think the "Ginger or Mary Ann" ad would have worked, after all. It's somehow not *quite* an authentic Xer conversation, but it's

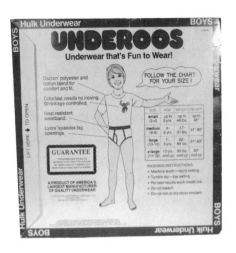

Only a child with supreme self-esteem
would admit to wearing Underoos.

pretty close. Unfortunately for Madison Avenue, the missing ingredient is one that they probably can't reproduce no matter how hard they try. When Xers talk about Saturday morning and other popular culture, they often mix deep affection, knowing cynicism, and ironic distance together in a distinctive attitudinal cocktail. It's virtually impossible to replicate this outlook within the space of an advertisement, because the cynical and mocking aspects of an Xer attitude toward popular culture are at least partially rooted in a knowledge of the conditions that have governed the making of popular culture—particularly the influence of advertising. Many Xers know perfectly well—and knew even as kids—that Saturday morning was a cut-rate cultural bargain bin made for the pleasure of advertisers. They still love it, but it's a conditional kind of love.

There may be no better defining generational experience than conversations that begin, "Do you remember this cartoon where . . ." In this chapter, we explore our collective experiences with Saturday morning, looking not only at what and how we watched, but also how we have assembled our collective memory of cartoons and cartoon watching.

Musty Basements and Strawberry Waffles: Saturday Morning Ritual

Saturdays not only featured the greatest number of cartoons but they were also a special time because they left us free from school and often free from parents. As a special time, Saturday morning demanded the observance of special rituals. The first challenge of the day: just how terrifyingly early to get up? Some kids settled in front of the cathode altar in time to see test patterns, though the programming at the crack of dawn was invariably among the worst of the whole Saturday morning bloc, as it was scheduled by local affiliates rather than the networks. (Network programming didn't begin until 7:30 or 8:00.) As one of our correspondents noted, "It sucked when you got up too early, like at five, and something like Captain Noah was on. He was a fake Captain Kangaroo just for Philly kids."

Other kids had to deal with restrictive parents and were allowed to watch only a limited amount of Saturday programming. Devious children in these households sometimes still managed to sneak in some early viewing, knowing that only a truly fanatical parent would manage to take note of a low-volume television set being on at 7 A.M. on a Saturday. And of course, some kids hated getting up early even when they were young. More than a few of our correspondents noted that all the cartoons that had traditionally aired before 8:30 or so were terra incognita for them because they preferred to sleep in. With Saturday morning, the tough got going when the clock struck five, and the whimps just had to settle for looking like ignorant dorks in the schoolyard while the rest of us talked about the Superfriends or *Emergency +4*. Such is life. Age was also a factor: virtually everyone we know got to a point in their early to mid-teens where they preferred to sleep in. As one person told us, "I remember the exact moment when I knew my childhood was over. I was eleven and I leapt out of bed to go watch the Saturday morning cartoons. [I] thought to myself, 'You know, I could just sleep instead.'"

Who could forget Kaptain Kool & the Kongs? We wish we could.

Whether you got up at the crack of dawn or not, the next potent question, beyond the issue of what show the television should be tuned to, was when to eat breakfast and what to eat. Cereal was a typical answer: not only was it relentlessly advertised between shows, but just about any kid could make it, and most importantly of all, it was highly mobile. There was a nice sort of synergy if you were gulping down your Cap'n Crunch while the good Captain himself cavorted across the screen during commercial breaks. In some households, a big breakfast was an important part of the total ritual. One person told us about how their mother used to get up about 8 A.M. and make strawberry waffles for all the kids. In our own home, our mom sometimes made this really cool coffee cake, though it was more typical for her to make it on Sunday, when kids actually came to the table to eat. Another veteran described progressing from cereal to making himself oatmeal and eventually to preparing his own breakfast with eggs, sausage, and the like. For the most part, though, Saturday morning was not about food. Sugary cereals helped audiences to develop the necessary near hyperactivity most conducive to early-morning viewing, but anything which took a kid away from the

TV set for too long was a serious problem. As one of our correspondents noted, "If you took the time to actually sit at the table and slog through pancakes and whatnot, that's at least a good ten minutes of TV time gone forever."

Where you watched television was also crucial. Saturday morning veterans consistently told us that getting everything just right in the particular room where they watched television was as important to them as actually watching the television. In households with one television, parents were more likely to interfere with Saturday morning before the full ritual could be completed, particularly for the die-hard kids who tried to make it all the way to the bitter end, since the conclusion of Saturday morning and the beginning of sports sometimes overlapped. In many households with two televisions, or with a special den or room set aside for television viewing, children were able to colonize the room for the whole of the morning, claiming it for their own. Many of our correspondents gave us lovingly detailed descriptions of their own special cartoon-watching spaces. One friend reminisced about the dank basement with peculiarly musty old furniture where the kids watched cartoons. Another person described how he carefully organized the viewing room with the proper pillows in the proper places and kept the curtains shut so the room would stay comfortingly dark. Still another person described setting out her favorite toys when she woke up so she could have them at hand when boring shows were on.

With food secured and the room properly customized to the individual preferences of the audience, Saturday morning was ready to go full speed ahead. It was at this point, regardless of when viewing began in a particular household, that the most important and difficult issues arose. What was the best way through the network schedules in order to maximize viewing of the cool shows and minimize exposure to crap? What should be done when two great shows were on at the same time? Careful planning was required. Particularly at

A typical morning schedule. Take special note of the advertisement for the wacky doughnut machine.

the beginning of each season, kids needed to experiment a lot to hit the optimum pathway. (Remember, folks, this was before VCR and, for many, remote controls.)

Take, for example, an average morning in April of 1974. At 8 A.M., it didn't take a rocket scientist to tune into *The Bugs Bunny Show* on ABC—though you always had to be wary, since the Warner Brothers cartoons switched networks and time slots every couple of years. The alternatives were *The Hair Bear Bunch,* a wretchedly generic Hanna-Barbera effort, and *Lidsville,* a Sid and Marty Krofft live-action show which was surreal even by their normal deranged standards. (In the Burke household, we'd switch to *Lidsville* if Sylvester and Tweety came on, because they were deemed boring.) Then at 8:30, most kids probably switched to *Sabrina, the Teenage Witch,* avoiding *Yogi's Gang* and *The Addams Family.* Nine o'clock belonged to the *Super Friends,* though this wasn't yet their coolest incarnation. Some might have chosen *The New Scooby-Doo Movies,* or *Emergency +4,* a cartoon adaptation of the popular live-action program about paramedics. Those who chose *Emergency* probably switched the channel at 9:30, though, when the lame Hanna-Barbera retread *Inch High, Private Eye* came on. Then came 10 A.M., a long dark interlude which tested the character of the Saturday morning audience. Those insufficiently devoted to the ritual might well have given up and done something wholesome at this point, facing a choice between *Lassie's Rescue Rangers, My Favorite Martians,* and *Sigmund and the Sea Monsters.* But for the bold and determined, there were still rewards

scattered ahead in the schedule, including *The Pink Panther Show* and the animated version of *Star Trek*.

These kinds of difficult choices faced Saturday morning audiences in the past (and still confront them today). Meticulous research and carefully tested strategies paid off in the end, reducing the time spent

78   **Saturday Morning Fever**

watching programs like *The Skatebirds* to almost nil. Or at least this was the ideal. Complications could crush any plan and leave you exposed to *Fangface.* Primary among these pitfalls were your brothers and sisters. This was nature, red in tooth and claw. Savage struggles for primacy over the channel dial, or later, the remote control, unfolded by the light of television sets on Saturdays.

As far as we can determine from our conversations with veterans, the outcome of these struggles developed along one of two lines. In the first case, an alpha sibling triumphed utterly and controlled viewing with an iron fist, subject only to parental bans on particular programs deemed to be undesirable. Often this was the eldest child. Control usually slipped from the grasp of this autocrat sometime around age thirteen to fourteen, when his or her cartoon viewing became more irregular. Many of our correspondents reported that while they still watched cartoons at this age, they were usually content to let younger siblings choose the programs, so that the elders could adopt the proper attitude of surly disinterest.

On the other hand, in some households, low-level war raged constantly on Saturdays. Fragile truces were made and broken within the space of an hour. Boys and girls in these homes struggled mightily with each other to get the television turned to "their" programs, a dilemma which became more acute in the 1980s with the rise of highly gendered programs like *My Little Pony and Friends* or *The Real Ghostbusters.* Veterans whose memories include struggles of this sort tell us that each week, a different range of programs might be seen, depending on which sibling was more wily or feral.

There were exceptions. One person described a far more cooperative approach: "My sister and I used to take turns watching a different network each week so that we could watch as many of our favorites as possible. One week we would watch the ABC shows, the next week the NBC shows." Someone else told us, "When my brother came along, I, always wanting companionship and someone to share The Cartoon Experience with and knowing how boring those damn cribs can be, would sneak into his room, undo the crib, pick him up, and carry him out to the living room. I'd shove him to the back of the sofa, surround him with the bigger pillows so he wouldn't fall off, and sit next to him after igniting the Boob Tube."

If one was forced into weekly combat with siblings, one could choose to invite parental intervention, but only the unwise or the desperate took the risk. Parents were an X-factor in Saturday morning ritual, usually to be evaded, placated, or quietly subverted. Parents were always perilously poised to intervene arbitrarily in cartoon watching if middle-class guilt or the latest report from ACT happened to seize hold of them. A quiet détente generally existed, in which parents pursued their own Saturday pleasures—gardening, fixing a nice breakfast, reading the paper, or having sex. Some kids had to deal with various restrictions—for example, that only particular programs were approved for viewing, or that they had to "earn" the right to watch cartoons by doing homework and getting good grades. One man told us that his parents used to make him read for forty-five minutes for every thirty minutes of television he watched. Almost every kid, in every household, had to cope with the inevitable intervention of a parent somewhere in the late morning at the advent of the unavoidable comment about the advantages of fresh air, exercise, and so on. A deterministically glassy-eyed expression and a few optimistic mutters to the effect that one was just about to dart out the door and frolic was usually enough to get an adult to bug off and return to his or her own pursuits, but occasionally, sulking and tantrums might also be necessary.

In a few blessed households, Saturday morning was an opportunity for parents and kids to do something special together. One friend of ours, Kathleen Hubbard, recalled, "My dad was a really early riser when I was a kid, so if I ever watched Bullwinkle, it was with him. Next earliest was Bugs Bunny. He loved that, so we often watched it together." Another person told us, "My father always woke me early, very early. . . . He carried me to the TV room, wrapped me in my beloved

Snoopy blanket, and brought me cold, sweet cereal. He adjusted the set and returned to bed. I still remember that ritual, and I think it the purest expression of love and tenderness I have ever experienced."

The fresh-air phase also usually marked the edge of a border zone where only those fully dedicated to the Saturday ritual dared to venture. Somewhere around 11 A.M., many kids fell victim to some other social activity—soccer games, dance practice, and so on—and others were unable to resist parental pressure to venture outside, blinking like a Morlock in the daylight. But the brave and the bold soldiered on into the netherworld of the late morning and early afternoon, a time dominated by crappy live-action shows like *Jason of Star Command* or programs with queasily marginal appeal to most kids, like *American Bandstand.* This was the Bataan-death-march phase of the ritual, but Saturday morning stalwarts simply gritted their teeth and stuck with it to the bitter end—signaled by the arrival of sports on all three networks. At that point, there were no more options, no more strategies. Saturday morning was over, and the television was either turned off or given over to the watching of athletic events. A few unusually dedicated acolytes report that they tried to extend the ritual into Sundays, where the pickings were truly slim in most local television markets. Of course, most TV stations also carried cartoons on weekday mornings and afternoons, but until the eighties, this was a pretty picked-over viewing experience.

The weekly ritual was punctuated by a few special ceremonies and moments. In some television markets, bad monster movies and similar fare aired in an afternoon time slot on Saturdays. Watching *Godzilla vs. the Smog Monster* or *The War of the Gargantuas* had a different subcultural logic than watching Saturday morning cartoons, but the two experiences were somewhat related. Assuming that parents did not make a bid for control of the television, this made the whole of Saturday into a kids' television festival. You could also try to carry over Saturday morning into your regularly weekday life as a kid, and many of us did in schoolyard conversations, use of toys, and after-school play with other kids. One man wrote us to describe his boyhood use of the Superfriends at play and in idle daydreaming: "All week long I acted out elaborate fantasies in which I joined ranks with the 'Friends, battling the dire evil of the Legion of Doom. In my private world I was superpowered, as were various significant real-life adults. . . . I clearly remember a visit to the wishing well at a local mall, throwing in my coin and silently wishing to be transformed into a superhero; despite prodding, I refused to tell my mother what I had wished for."

The most sacred moment in the whole year, however, came in the fall, when the networks showed their special Saturday morning preview shows. Today's youth are sadly deprived of this pleasure, since the networks allowed the fall preview to wither away over time. But in the seventies and early eighties, the preview show was an intensely exciting occasion. Siblings and friends clustered around the television, waiting eagerly for revelations about the coming season. As writer Douglas Lathrop recalled, "Those preview shows were on the Friday night before the new season started—it'd preempt whatever it was that my parents liked to watch. I was so revved up over *Hong Kong Phooey* after seeing the preview that I couldn't sleep that night." Through the annual preview, the weekly ritual was made new again, part of the general renewal of childhood life that took place every fall, at the start of a new school year.

Making Memory and Talking Back:
Saturday Morning Conversations

Most Saturday morning veterans watched cartoons with a fair amount of ironic detachment. Cartoon veterans are and have always been active readers of television, probing for hidden meanings and unanswered questions. We were all nitpickers who compared notes with each other in playgrounds and at slumber parties. We talked back to the television set. We saw things in Saturday morning programming that were never intended to be there. This is the characteristic form of generational double consciousness—watching cartoons with both affection and smart-ass sneering—that is so hard for many outsiders to reproduce.

Almost without fail, when we have mentioned this book in a group of our approximate contemporaries, whether they are friends of ours or total strangers, someone will ask a question like "Do you remember the show with a baby superhero?" or "What was the name of that weird show with a sea monster?" That invariably starts a torrential flow of reminiscence, moving from embarrassment ("Am I the only one who remembers this stuff? I know I wasn't supposed to like it.") to mutual enthusiasm ("People I didn't know had the same experiences as me, even though they lived hundreds of miles from me!"). While we were having a beer at a local pub, a bartender heard us discussing characters from *G.I. Joe* and excitedly inserted himself in the conversation and shared his own memories. Within a week of arriving at college as an undergraduate, Tim found himself sitting in the cafeteria with a bunch of people from his dorm hall. The key thing that allowed the folks at the table to break the ice and begin getting to know each other was remembering the cartoons that they watched when they were kids. Saturday morning veterans can't help themselves: when a session in cartoon nostalgia begins, people find themselves compelled to remember, and surprised by what they recall. As one frustrated law student confessed while reminiscing about *Scooby-Doo* episodes, "How come I remember all this and I can't remember the difference between a shifting executory interest and a contingent remainder in property law?" In John Javna's book *Cult TV,* he recounts the story of a couple that starting dating after they met and discovered that both of them could sing the whole theme song for "Super Chicken," clucks and all.

Such conversations, whether conducted in person or over the In-

Kevin Meisner of Arlington, Virginia, publishes this obsessive cereal zine in his spare time. We particularly liked the segments on monster cereal premiums, with the fashion layout modeling a Boo Berry Halloween costume.

ternet, turn on idiosyncratic and twisted riffing on cartoons as much as they turn on straightforward remembrances of beloved programs. We've encountered countless examples of this, ranging from (our personal favorite!) the woman who claimed to be able to sing the *Banana Splits* theme song in the voice of Alec Guinness to the person who dressed up her Barbie doll as the Saturday morning character Isis. We've heard from a woman who desperately wanted red hair like the lead character in *Josie and the Pussycats,* but settled for dressing up like her at Halloween, and from another woman who named her baby girl Josie in honor of the show. We've heard from a guy who used to perform his own perverse versions of Fat Albert episodes in his college drama group, including "It's Not Cool to Mess with Satanic Ritual" and "Weird Harold Gets AIDS."

Saturday morning veterans routinely make use of stock phrases and memorable lines from cartoons, like Snagglepuss's signature line, "Exit, stage left," or Bugs Bunny's "Of course, you know this means war" in their everyday conversation. As alt.society.generation-x regular Kelly Conlon commented, "I sometimes recite lines from cartoons like 'I keep my feathers numbered, for just such an emergency' or 'THERE ARE NO LA BREA TAR PITS IN SCOTLAND!!',

and, oddly enough, most people seem to know what I am referring to." Another asg-x participant, John Everett, talked about his use of references from the cartoon *Tarzan:* "In fact, to this day, I still earn a puzzled look here and there when I tell some kitty, 'ankh sheeta.' Of course, less frequently, I include in my vocabulary 'tantor,' 'mangani,' etc. My brother and I for years used to call any bald white guy 'phobec.'" Singing cartoon theme songs is equally common (and was even before the release of the album *Saturday Morning*). Our subjective impression is that the most remembered and recited themes are from *Josie and the Pussycats, Hong Kong Phooey, Speed Racer,* and *The Banana Splits,* but many people also take pride in their knowledge of fantastically obscure songs.

A good deal of reminiscing involves dissing hated characters and programs. If Scrappy-Doo (or, as one poster on alt.society.generation-x called him, "the demon bastard puppy") were a real person, he'd have long since been beaten to death with baseball bats by enraged Saturday morning veterans. Cartoons based on video games like "Q*Bert" or *Pac-Man,* seem universally reviled.[1] *Clutch Cargo,* an early cartoon which superimposed filmed sequences of human lips moving over nearly motionless animated faces, stands out like a beacon of cheapness and ineptitude for anyone who remembers it. People also do a lot of trash talking about genres, particularly humorous cartoons starring anthropomorphic animals versus action cartoons, either superheroic or otherwise.

In contrast, some characters and shows are beloved by almost everyone—Jay Ward's characters, particularly Rocky and Bullwinkle, the Warner Brothers characters, Pee-Wee Herman's program *Pee-Wee's Playhouse,* the Hanna-Barbera program *Hong Kong Phooey,* and Ralph Bakshi's *Mighty Mouse: The New Adventures* were the most frequently named favorites in our own informal surveys. (This

---

1. However, a lot of cartoon aficionados like the syndicated program *Sonic the Hedgehog.*

Willing Slaves of the Cathode God   **85**

is leaving aside contemporary programs like *Animaniacs* and *Gargoyles,* which have legions of devotees.)

There are also programs with equal numbers of vehement detractors and enthusiastic fans: most older cartoons from Japan—*Speed Racer, Kimba the White Lion, Voltron, G-Force,* and so on—fall into this category, as do older Hanna-Barbera characters like Yogi Bear and Huckleberry Hound. Certain obscure programs also crop up again and again on lists of shows that people remember with immense fondness, even if they haven't seen them since they were kids. The clear winner in this category is the live-action show *Lancelot Link, Secret Chimp.* This is especially remarkable considering the program's short run and its relatively limited life in syndication. Other obscure short-lived programs that we heard about frequently included *The Mighty Orbots, Dungeons & Dragons, Ark II, The Secret Lives of Waldo Kitty, Mighty Heroes, Pandamonium,* and *The Wacky Races.*

Dredging up memories of kidvid leaves us with loads of mysteries to investigate. Saturday morning was crawling with strangely inexplicable things, full of missing premises, incomprehensible motives, and unanswered questions. Why did Gargamel want to hunt down the Smurfs anyhow? Are Scooby-Doo's pals in high school or are they adults? Don't Marvin and Wendy's parents worry about them hanging around the Super Friends, what with them being taken hostage virtually every episode? Why does Witchiepoo want Freddy the Golden Flute, anyway? There were always questions to be asked about the improbabilities and inconsistencies within each program. As one person put it with regard to *G.I. Joe,* "The amazing thing here was, the bad guys could *not* aim. You'd see 500 red lasers shoot across the screen and the one blue beam from the Joes would hit 5 Cobras. That's talent!" Children in the 1960s and 1970s were left to their own devices to figure out the meaning of allusions to movies and celebrities from the 1930s and 1940s in many Bugs Bunny cartoons. The cartoon version of Bob Clampett's *Beany and Cecil,* though made with skill and subversive wit, frequently seemed to pre-

Cereals

Top Ten Cereals Sold on Saturday Morning

1. Freakies
2. Quisp
3. Cap'n Crunch
4. Count Chocula
5. Boo Berry
6. Crunchberries
7. Lucky Charms
8. Trix
9. Crispy Critters
10. Cocoa Pebbles

Five Worst Cereals Ever

1. Vanilly Crunch
2. World Federation Wrestling Stars Cereal
3. Cookie Crisp
4. Strawberry Shortcakes
5. Cinnamon Crunch

Greatest Cereal Ad Campaigns

1. Count Chocula and Franken Berry in the early seventies
2. "Cap'n Crunch is missing"
3. Voting to allow the rabbit to eat Trix
4. Jay Ward's Cap'n Crunch in the mix-sixties
5. The Freakies Song
6. Quisp ads

sume a certain amount of familiarity with the characters in their earlier puppet incarnations, a familiarity that confused kidvid audiences of the seventies did not necessarily have. Even familiar Saturday morning advertisements generate questions. One Swarthmore student, Kate Zyla, pointed out that "the commercial kids were always force-feeding Sonny the Cocoa Puffs bird in order to get him to go cuckoo, but they always refused to give the Trix rabbit any cereal. We wondered why the rabbit didn't start trying to go for the Cocoa Puffs."

Other aspects of the origin and development of cartoons also provoke discussion among kidvid viewers. The profusion of reruns, repackaging, and outright repetition that until recently prevailed on Saturday morning makes for a dizzying sense of déjà vu. Saturday morning veterans often find themselves at a loss to clarify exactly when it was that they saw a particular program. We all conflate multiple versions of the same character, or squeeze together disparate elements from different shows into our memories of a single program. Many of the questions we received via E-mail during the writing of this book concerned attempts to disentangle the torturous histories of various characters. Some examples: Did Batman ever have a partner who was a little ratlike thing? Which caveman family lived in the valley with the modern family, and was that the animated show or the live-action one with the big lizard people? Was there a wise Sleestak with different-colored skin on *Land of the Lost,* or am I imagining it? Did I really see Sonny and Cher on *Scooby-Doo,* or was that Danny Partridge? Was *Jason of Star Command* the live-action show where you shot laser guns at the screen and the bad guy had a glowing eye socket, or was that *Captain Power?* What the hell was that show with little puppets who flew around in ships and in a submarine? Was there a shark who talked like one of the Three Stooges, or am I thinking of the show where the Three Stooges were robots, or is that just the episode of *Scooby-Doo* with the Three Stooges?

One person gratefully told us that he was convinced that his memories of the show *Rocket Robin Hood* were hallucinations until we confirmed that it was a real program. Another person asked us, after rambling on about a show that appeared to be *H. R. Pufnstuf* with some details mixed in from other Sid and Marty Krofft shows, "Am I actually thinking about something that was on TV, or am I having some kind of a brain fart?" A third asked us to please sort out his dim memories of a particular show so that his wife would stop calling him crazy.

Another major type of discussion among Saturday morning viewers, both then and now, involved viewing shows in precisely the manner that kids were not supposed to look at them. You might call this "Saturday Morning Babylon" or "Sex Lives of the Superheroes." Not all of this sort of talking back to the television involved sex—for example, we've had a number of former viewers tell us about their assumptions regarding offscreen violence in shows like *Thundarr the Barbarian.* As one correspondent put it, "I always assumed that Thundarr thoroughly murdilized the bad guy after the last commercial break. He wasn't a mellow dude." And it's clear to many folks that Saturday morning was crawling with hidden drug users like Popeye (spinach), Underdog (superenergy pill), Scooby-Doo (Scooby snacks), and H. R. Pufnstuf (mostly because of his name and the generally psychedelic atmosphere on his show).

We've heard people declare their hidden lust for a remarkable range of characters, including Jan from *Space Ghost,* Race Bannon from *Jonny Quest* (a favorite with both gay men and women), Natasha from *The Bullwinkle Show,* Mandrake the Magician from *Defenders of the Earth,* Speed Racer, Casper the Ghost, the Brain from *Pinky & the Brain,* Alvin of *Alvin and the Chipmunks,* and Betty Rubble from *The Flintstones.* Our favorite profession of cartoon affection, though, is on a World Wide Web page dedicated to Velma from *Scooby-Doo,* where V-X, the author, declares, "Velma was always my favorite cartoon girl. Her name, her orange knee

We're not sure what to make of this H. R. Pufnstuf–obsessed zine. Fun for the whole family?

socks, her trademark cry of 'Jinkies!' still make me catch my breath. She was, and is, my ideal gal-pal. . . . Take it from me, do yourself a favor, brother: find yourself a Velma. Today."

There's also a lot of talk about the sexual activities of the characters themselves. Sniggering about the sex lives of characters is probably a more popular subject for boys (and men), but when contemporary stand-up comedians do routines on this subject, there's usually a pretty healthy amount of multigender laughter.

In a similar vein, many Saturday morning veterans have wondered about the activities of characters like Smurfette, the only female

Smurf in an entire village of Smurfs. If She-Ra and He-Man got it on, would their child be named She-Man? Were Bert and Ernie gay? Can Plastic Man really stretch *every* part of his body? Does the Thing have a thing, and what does it look like, anyway? Actually, the most notorious instance of such speculation doesn't involve Saturday morning directly. Science fiction writer Larry Niven's famous essay "Man of Steel—Woman of Kleenex" reveals just how unlikely—and dangerous—a sexual encounter between an invulnerable Superman and an all-too-vulnerable Lois Lane would be.

Of course, there are the poor lost souls who grew up without television. Kids in television-equipped households sometimes took pity on these culturally deprived creatures and let them taste the forbidden fruit during sleep-overs and the like, but there wasn't much one could do to help them get in touch. If you want to make your kid just a little bit weird, totally banning television is probably a pretty good way to accomplish that objective. (We hasten to add that weird kids are a-okay with us.) In any event, in our experience, kids who were deprived of Saturday morning by parental edict have still managed to pick up some knowledge of the world of kidvid, largely by careful surveillance of their friends' conversations. They're hoping to catch up without actually having to submit to the Cathode God. It's a sort of fractured knowledge, the kind in which Fred Flintstone was Jonny Quest's best pal. It'll do.

Always, these kinds of conversations—whether innocent, lewd, or satiric—are not merely about memory, but about commentary as well. Saturday morning veterans don't just habitually suffer through rosy-colored fits of nostalgia: they comment on and mischievously play with the raw material of past kidvid. Saturday morning isn't the dead hand of the past: it is a living, active part of our present.

Cracking the Code:
Saturday Morning in the Wider Culture

The living power of active memory, for the hardened veterans of Saturday morning and even for the kids who only had glancing encounters with television, is all around us in the wider skein of popular culture today, from stand-up comedy acts to the latest kidvid. Saturday morning subculture isn't as well-organized, structured, or obsessive as fan culture. We're not talking Trekkers here. Only a relatively small minority of Saturday morning veterans actively collect memorabilia, though many covet particularly cool toys, lunch boxes, and so on from their misspent youth. The most devoted fans of animation actually tend to scorn Saturday morning as pure junk. Saturday morning is a set of reference points linked by subversive allusions, guilty pleasures, and sly nostalgia. If you didn't live through it, you'll have a hard time figuring it all out. Even if you did experience it, you won't always know what's what—some Saturday morning programs were not syndicated or aired only in local markets, so sometimes the Saturday morning code can be deciphered only by a very narrow age group or people who grew up in a particular region.

Schoolhouse Rock has provided the most powerful example of Saturday morning's influence on culture, especially with the segment that featured a sing-along version of the Preamble to the U.S. Constitution. Many of the *Schoolhouse Rock* tunes have lodged firmly in the memory of those who heard them, as the healthy sales for recently released CDs of the songs, both in original form and in new versions, clearly demonstrate. In the self-consciously GenX-oriented film *Reality Bites,* one of the key attempts at generational mood involved the characters singing "Conjunction Junction." The Preamble song really stands out, though. During the writing of this book, we were repeatedly told a story which went like this (with minor variations): an unwary older teacher resignedly asks students to recite the

Preamble, expecting them to fail, and is then stunned by the entire class singing the whole Preamble in perfect unison.

Saturday morning veterans have made their youthful viewing experiences visible in the wider culture in a variety of other ways. Some of this is still pretty arcane, as in various Saturday morning–related pages on the World Wide Web. These run a pretty wide gamut. Consider, for example, the huge variety of Web pages dealing with the Smurfs: they range from "Smurf You" to "Some of the One Hundred and Some Odd Smurfs," which catalogs the little-known existence of Smurfs like Cannibal Smurf and Disgruntled Postal Smurf. There are also in-jokes about older Saturday morning icons within contemporary kidvid programs, such as the wildly funny "Toby Danger" segments on the WB cartoon *Freakazoid!* that spoof classic Jonny Quest episodes.

Some references take a real insider to spot. For example, when interviewing the creators of *Mystery Science Theater 3000* for *Film Threat* magazine, Kevin discovered that the show's original opening sequence was a subtle allusion to similar opening sequences on many Sid and Marty Krofft programs. The rap group De La Soul has a tune that samples "Three Is a Magic Number" from *Schoolhouse Rock.* The musical group Red Aunts use an image of Penelope Pitstop on posters advertising their concerts, and there are relatively obscure punk rock groups called Sleestak and Lidsville. Promotions for auto racing on ESPN have used images and theme music from *Speed Racer,* as have advertisements for Volkswagen. (As asg-x regular Maia Gemmill put it, "I don't even particularly like *Speed Racer* and they make me want to buy a VW.") Rap singer Coolio's song "Cartoon Ghetto" is full of jibes at Saturday morning programs. The popular computer quiz game *You Don't Know Jack* has numerous references to Saturday morning culture. If you don't know Saturday morning, you probably had a hard time deciphering all the references to cartoon subculture in Douglas Coupland's novel *Microserfs,* from Emmett's fears about the "subtle but massive Hello-Kittification of

North American animation" and the end of "our Hanna-Barbera her-
itage" to recurring references to cartoon holes, chipmunks trapped in
a factory, and Marvin the Martian. A song by the Replacements con-
tains the phrase "Twizzle Twazzle Twozzle Tome, Time for This One
to Come on Home," taken from "Tooter Turtle," one of the cartoon
segments in Total Television's *King Leonardo and His Short Subjects.*
The most recent issue of the fanzine *The Frostbite Falls Far-Flung
Flier,* devoted to Jay Ward's programs, includes a regular feature
called "Bullwinkle Briefs" that records almost one hundred references to Jay Ward cartoons in various pop culture venues.

Some Saturday morning references are found a long ways away
from the United States. At Swarthmore College in 1995, two Peru-
vian academics gave a talk about a new breed of radical activists who
had been giving speeches in the streets of Lima. Some of the speak-
ers, they noted, began their addresses by yelling out, "I have the
power!"—a slogan they took directly from local broadcasts of *He-
Man and the Masters of the Universe.* Still further away are the Martian rocks that the Pathfinder mission team dubbed "Scooby Doo"
and "Yogi."

These allusions are growing increasingly visible even to those who
didn't live through Saturday morning: there's an ever-increasing
number of references to older kidvid in mainstream popular culture,
particularly by stand-up comics and in sitcoms. This can sometimes
be pretty lame: there are comics who think all they have to do is say
the word "Smurf!" to get a laugh. But on the other hand, there are
truly great comics like Rosie O'Donnell for whom old television programs have become a crucial and hilarious stock-in-trade, or per-
formers like the late Andy Kaufman who have taken one small bit of
Saturday morning (in his case the theme song to *Mighty Mouse*) and
spun it into comedic gold. On the whole, such references share in the
characteristic Generation-X take on the televisual past with its mix of
affection and mockery. One scene in the film *Slacker* portrays two
conspiracy theorists sharing their observations about the sinister

hive-mind of the Smurfs and their higher agenda regarding the return of Shiva. On the NBC sitcom *Newsradio,* the running gag for one 1996 episode involved a character trying to design and market a hat that made its wearer look like a character from *Fat Albert.* (The running gag *within* the gag was that the person designing the hat thought the hat belonged to the character Mushmouth, when in fact it actually belonged to Dumb Donald.) On *Saturday Night Live* and the short-lived *Dana Carvey Show,* Robert Smigel's cartoons "The Ambiguously Gay Duo" and "The Ex-Presidents" played twisted riffs on Saturday morning cartoons like *Super Friends* and *The Archies.* These references to Saturday morning reflect and reflect back, like a hall of mirrors.

While mainstream culture now increasingly makes reference to Saturday morning, it was Saturday morning's references to mainstream culture that first introduced the wider cultural world to many of us when we were children. Several of our friends pointed out that they saw the cartoon character Underdog before they had ever encountered Superman, so rather than seeing Underdog as a humorous revision of Superman, they initially saw it the other way around. We suspect most of our contemporaries first encountered celebrities like Humphrey Bogart and Bing Crosby through their appearances in old Warner Brothers cartoons. To many Saturday morning veterans of a certain age, *The Honeymooners* probably seemed derivative of *The Flintstones* rather than the other way around. Certainly for both of us, our first acquaintance with opera, particularly *The Barber of Seville,* came from Bugs Bunny. See, cartoons *are* educational.

Saturday morning veterans don't necessarily worship the cartoons they watched when they were kids, nor are they necessarily uncritical fans of television itself. The people with whom we've corresponded while writing this book have remarkably diverse opinions about television and the time they spent watching cartoons as youngsters. Most delight in their memories, even when they are no longer avid viewers of television, but quite a few people look back with regret. As asg-x regular Brian Upton once put it, "When I hit my mid-twenties, I started to realize that most of the stories I had to tell didn't revolve around something I'd done, but something I'd seen." Some of our contemporaries feel as if the time they spent watching television is time lost forever, that it doesn't go toward making anything solid or lasting. Others don't begrudge the time they spent watching as children, but also note emphatically that they no longer see much use to television.

In fact, Peggy Charren and other crusaders against kidvid might be comforted by the sentiments we encountered. The skepticism and wry distance toward Saturday morning memories that we see as a characteristic property of Generation X is partly a result of the efforts of groups like ACT to educate children and parents about television. We all learned to be wary of television, both through our own native intelligence and because of the profusion of warnings and public service messages to which we were exposed. This is not all to the good: it's why so many of our contemporaries also hesitate at first to admit that they watched Saturday morning cartoons or that they remember them well today. Many people feel guilty about watching and liking television, then and now, particularly people who aspire to be regarded by others as thoughtful or intelligent.

"The child of the TV era is a surrogate for, and an extension of, the same conflicts that have beset adults struggling to accommodate themselves to the new technology." —Cecelia Tichi, *Electronic Hearth*

Whenever we've been part of these kinds of discussions about television with our friends and contemporaries, however, the discourse has seemed relatively measured in comparison to the shrill way in which television is characterized in mainstream culture. The distinctions that Saturday morning veterans make between good shows and bad ones, between time wasted and time gained, between television as a comfort and television as a learning experience, are often subtle shadings of a modestly shared generational viewpoint, part of a murmured, almost subliminal conversation. In contrast to the relentlessly self-promotional way that baby boomers tend to monopolize the whole of American culture in order to project their own youth as the only one worth having, Saturday morning veterans have a pretty good sense of proportionate nostalgia.

Chapter Five

The Shows Themselves

In this chapter, we offer our own biased, skewed, and idiosyncratic readings of some of the key programs of Saturday morning. This is not a comprehensive guide to all kidvid. Some shows which probably ought to be discussed in this sort of review are missing. For example, we have relatively little to say about either *The Flintstones* or *The Jetsons,* partly because we think they've been discussed comprehensively by other authors and partly because we find both shows pretty boring. Other shows that we dearly love—Jay Ward's programs *(The Bullwinkle Show, George of the Jungle)* and the classic Warner Brothers cartoons—have received ample treatment in other publications, so we've left them out of our review here. The great programs of the mid- to late eighties—*Mighty Mouse: The New Adventures, Pee-Wee's Playhouse,* and *Beetlejuice*—were discussed in chapter 3. Some shows are too ephemeral or just plain lame by even our own generous and perverse standards—*C.B. Bears* or *Rocket Robin Hood,* for example. Other shows, though worthy of discussion, substantially predate the time frame for this book or are too recent, *Crusader Rabbit* on one end and programs like *The Tick* or *Reboot* on the other.

Let us sound a cautionary note about our subversive readings of the kidvid of our misspent youth. What's the difference between our claim that Shaggy and Scooby-Doo were recreational drug users and Donald Wildmon claiming to have caught Mighty Mouse sniffing cocaine? For one, we have a sense of humor and Wildmon doesn't. Wildmon, Ralph Reed, and their ilk are deadly serious, intent on gathering their semiliterate yahoo followers into a mob carrying torches and leading them against Hollywood and the "liberal" media. We know that Hanna-Barbera didn't intend to have us think that Scooby snacks were narcotics. We know that the Children's Television Workshop didn't intend to imply that Bert and Ernie were gay. We're just kidding around. The hidden meanings we ferret out of cartoons don't outrage us. On the contrary, we're totally pleased to find them. It's all in fun, the best part of sly nostalgia. Wildmon and his fellow brownshirts fear the alleged conspiracy they glimpse behind every cartoon gesture, while we by and large welcome the subversions that we perceive.

In his book *Making Things Perfectly Queer,* Alexander Doty talks about audiences discovering or producing queer subtexts in ostensibly straight pieces of popular culture. Doty insists that such readings are neither "alternative" nor "wishful or willful misreadings," but instead "result from the recognition and articulation of the complex range of queerness that has been in popular culture texts and their audiences all along." Some of our readings of Saturday morning fit this description perfectly. We honestly do think that there's a homoerotic side to the relationship of Dr. Quest and Race Bannon or Bert and Ernie, though certainly this wasn't planned by the creators. At the same time, at least some of our readings, like those of our contemporaries, *are* willful misreadings, or consciously "alternative" interpretations. We are prepared to argue for both the pleasure and the necessity of seeing things this way. This is how we play in the sandbox of our televisual memories. This is the way that we take popular culture and make it our own.

We're spelling this out explicitly from the start of our discussion because in our experience, many kidvid producers and various concerned onlookers suffer from massive cluelessness or fragile sensitivities when they happen to overhear these kinds of discussions about Saturday morning. For example, the proposition that Bert and Ernie of *Sesame Street* are a gay couple is something that we've heard many friends and acquaintances joke about in recent years. Somehow that sort of kidding around finally burbled up from the generational depths not long ago and prompted some homophobic grandmother out in the American backwoods to write a letter to *TV Guide* declaring that she would no longer allow her grandchildren to watch *Sesame Street* if Bert and Ernie were gay. The producers of the show were forced to respond officially, saying that since Bert and Ernie were puppets, they had no sexual identity in the first place and that in any event, there was no intention to imply that they were gay.

We want people like that homophobic grandmother and other reactionaries out there to take a chill pill before they read this book—or better yet, don't bother reading it. Since various right-wingers seem to have no problem condemning movies they've never seen, we don't particularly expect anyone bothered by our analysis to read it with any care in the first place. And the same goes for the more uptight kidvid producers. We've found that some of them can play along with these kinds of subversions, and others can successfully ignore them. A few of those we contacted, however, like Sid and Marty Krofft, perceive themselves as the latest incarnation of Hans Christian Andersen and will brook no imputation that their programs could be the subject of subversive humor.

Deal with it.

The Superfriends

Many enduring Saturday morning characters grew progressively grimmer in terms of quality over their life span. Scooby-Doo degenerated from Scooby-Dum to Scrappy-Doo to *The 13 Ghosts of*

Scooby-Doo and ultimately to babyfication on *A Pup Named Scooby-Doo.* Yogi Bear, Huckleberry Hound, and other Hanna-Barbera funny animals went from their mildly amusing late-fifties shorts to the horrific antifun of *Yogi's Gang* and *Scooby's All-Star Laff-A-Lympics.* Daffy Duck descended from heights like "Duck Dodgers in the 24½ Century" and "Duck Amuck" to stupidly chasing Speedy Gonzalez in a desultory series of Friz Freleng–directed shorts. An attempt to revive Jonny Quest in the eighties almost completely mangled the show's distinctive sixties charm. The Flintstones went from their original show, derivative but often entertaining, to rerun disgraces like *Fred and Barney Meet the Thing.*

The Superfriends, on the other hand, got better and better in each of their incarnations. At the time of their first appearance, the Superfriends were a sort of stripped-down version of DC Comics' Justice League of America. Superman, Aquaman, and Batman and Robin were already old hands on Saturday morning. Wonder Woman was the only newcomer, but in comics terms, she was a long-established and fairly well known character. Even in the early seasons, a few other established DC Comics characters made brief appearances, like Green Arrow.

The Superfriends did not begin on an auspicious note. Joseph Barbera recalls in his autobiography that the pilot episode was a particularly poor piece of animation. Two things dragged the show down in its initial seasons. First, mindful of the furor over superheroes in the late sixties, the show's writers were extremely careful to create the mildest menaces and most pedestrian dilemmas for the stars to overcome. Audiences didn't get to see Superman whale on Lex Luthor or watch Wonder Woman bash the Cheetah. Instead, viewers had to be content with (at best) the occasional mad scientist armed with a shrink ray or a bossy wife who nagged her husband into getting mobile semi-intelligent plants at the center of the world to steal giant air conditioners.

Far more annoying, however, were the characters of Wendy, Marvin, and Wonder Dog. Wendy and Marvin were two kids who hung around with the Superfriends; Wonder Dog was—surprise—their dog. Wendy and Marvin were the ultimate degenerate form of the kid sidekick, about as useful to the Superfriends as a burst appendix. They existed primarily to be rescued and to help illustrate the moral message of the week. Wendy was at least mildly competent and a semibabe, but Marvin was a total geek and annoying as hell to boot. Wonder Dog was a Fred Silverman–inspired dog sidekick, part of a shameful lineage which would eventually result in a later incarnation of Spider-Man being burdened with a little white yap-yap dog. (Silverman and other kidvid producers had an idée fixe that the presence of a dog inevitably made a cartoon attractive to kids, but that's the way it often went on Saturday morning in the seventies.) The other aggravating thing about the first run of *Super Friends* was the profusion of short public-service blurbs, in which Batman would help kids to learn to cross the street properly or some kid would learn not to drink chlorine from the pool cleaner's van.

Marvin and Wendy eventually disappeared. When looking for a cheery thought to brighten our day, we sometimes imagine that they were accidentally dropped into a volcano by Superman or eaten by one of Aquaman's pet sharks. Their replacements, the Wonder Twins, were in relative terms an improvement, but they were hardly among the most beloved of Saturday morning characters. The Wonder Twins, Zan and Jayna, and their pet monkey, Gleek, were recycled versions of Space Ghost's two kid sidekicks, Jan and Jayce, and their pet monkey, Blip. Unlike Wendy and Marvin, they actually had superpowers. Hailing from an alien planet, they were able, whenever they touched hands, to take on the form of an animal and the shape of some kind of water. This hardly inspired terror in the hearts of evildoers, of course. (Oh, no: an ostrich and a swimming pool! Whatever shall I do?) But at least the Twins weren't helpless idiots like Wendy and Marvin. More importantly, these new adventures featured a bit more superheroic adventure, some reasonably interesting plots, and the occasional addition of other members of the Justice League of America, including Hawkman and Green Lantern. (Unfortunately, these new episodes also featured insulting ethnic characters like Black Vulcan and Samurai, about whom we'll have more to say in the next chapter.)

But all of this paled beside the next incarnation of the Superfriends, *Challenge of the Superfriends,* which was one of the coolest shows to grace Saturday morning in the late seventies. In these adventures, the whole lineup of the Justice League of America faced off against the Legion of Doom, a collection of DC Comics' marquee supervillains. The Legion of Doom were visually striking and exciting antagonists with an incredibly bitchin' jet-black flying headquarters, and though their confrontations with the Superfriends generally hewed to the same narrative time and time again (nefarious plot hatched, usually by Luthor; plot unfolds; Superfriends face adversity and triumph; Legion of Doom miraculously escapes at the end while one of the Superfriends stands passively watching them getting away), the stories were still far better than in the previous two versions of the show. The Legion of Doom made such seriously badass opponents that their name has been reused by a notorious group of computer hackers, by professional wrestlers, and by formidable hockey stars playing for the Philadelphia Flyers. The Legion of Doom shows also deemphasized the stupid little bits where Superman would teach kids not to be bullies or Aquaman would talk about the virtues of good nutrition.

The Superfriends had one more iteration that wasn't quite as cool as their battles with the Legion of Doom. As a supplement to a new line of toys, the core Superfriends appeared on *Super Powers Team: Galactic Guardians* in 1985–86, in which they faced off against an extremely malevolent lord of evil, Darkseid, with the assistance of Cyborg, a character from DC Comics' *The New Teen Titans,* and Firestorm, a newer DC hero. For some reason—possibly because of the overwhelming toy imperative—this show just didn't work quite as well as the Legion of Doom shows, although the quality of the animation was pretty good. No matter. We'll never forget all the iconic *Superfriends* moments: Zan and Jayna's transformations, Aquaman summoning the creatures of the deep, Batman exclaiming "Great Scott," Toyman's hysterical laugh, Luthor pulling off the latest escape of the Legion of Doom, and so on. Wondertwins powers activate! Form of a cockroach! Shape of shaved ice!

Scooby-Doo

Over its long run on CBS and ABC, the various incarnations of *Scooby-Doo* presented as many continuing mysteries as Scooby and his comrades solved. We always knew that bad guy was Mr. Cranston or Mr. Smithers or someone like that—it's amazing in the Scooby Universe how many sleazy local businessmen had never heard of a little thing called "arson" and felt obligated instead to dress up as the Ghost and Mrs. Muir—but the real enigmas of the show retain their grip on the imagination.

The top question, of course, is: What the hell are Scooby snacks and why do Shaggy and Scooby want them so badly? For that matter, why do Shaggy and Scooby always have the munchies? And if they're always eating such prodigious amounts of food, how come they're not fat?

Scooby aficionados have long speculated that Scooby snacks were . . . enhanced . . . with controlled substances of some sort or another. This proposition, of course, would explain not only Shag and Scoob's interest in scarfing them, but probably account for their munchies and their high-powered metabolisms. Joseph Barbera told us that Scooby snacks were actually based on a gimmick used previously with Quickdraw McGraw, in which Quickdraw's canine sidekick was always begging for some kind of snack food that would make him float up into the air in ecstasy. Barbera pointed out that Quickdraw once tried the snacks and had the exact same reaction.

This, of course, hardly relieves one's suspicions about the content of Scooby snacks.

This conjecture also goes a long way toward explaining some of the other chief mysteries surrounding the show. Namely, what the heck are these folks doing to support themselves as they cruise around the country in a van? The first couple of episodes of the show vaguely implied that the (teen? twenty-something?) characters all lived in the same area and had their adventures there, but in fairly short order, we saw the Scooby gang fetch up in a wide variety of locations. But if we assume that Scooby and Shaggy were basically hopped-up drug fiends, then the travels of the Mystery Machine become a bit easier to explain: Fred, Velma, and Daphne were dealers. In fact, now that we think on it, Scoob and Shag usually had to beg Fred to give them the Scooby snacks.

Some other recurring questions are not resolved by these conjectures, however. For example, most viewers seem to have assumed that Fred and Daphne, the stereotypical blond stud and cute girl, had shacked up together. After all, whenever Fred was dictatorially barking orders to everyone else, he usually sent Velma off to be with Scooby and Shaggy—which gave him and Daphne a decent amount of off-camera quality time, we presume. Equally, we've heard from a lot of our contemporaries that they assumed the stereotypically brainy and bespectacled Velma was a lesbian. But the later versions of the series sent Fred and Velma off together while Daphne remained behind, throwing these hypotheses into doubt. It also seems clear to us that Shaggy and Scooby were lovers, but some Scooby aficionados have scolded us for having dirty minds. We're not sure why it is less acceptable to speculate about Scoob and Shag. Homophobia, perhaps? Or would the appropriate term be "bestiaphobia"? We're not sure *what* to call sex between talking anthropomorphic animals and cartoon humans, let alone what word to use for an irrational fear of such practices. Sometimes a cartoon character is just a cartoon character.

Scooby-Doo first appeared in 1969, designed in part to reproduce the success of *The Archies,* which had appeared the year before. (The influence of *The Archies* on *Scooby-Doo* was particularly evident in an early episode that featured light rock-and-roll accompaniment to a chase sequence.) The show rapidly assumed its own identity with the help of its scat-inspired name, distinctive formula plot, and deft assortment of vividly differentiated characters. In its earliest drafts, the ghost-chasing theme of the show was deemed too frightening by Fred Silverman, but even after being toned down, the first season retained a reasonably good balance between genuine spookiness and silliness. A number of the ghosts tracked down and unmasked as less-mystical no-goodniks by Scooby and company were richly imagined and drawn, including "the ghost of Mr. Hyde" (why Mr. Hyde himself wasn't spooky enough, we're not quite sure), who was revealed to be a larcenous scientist with a Swedish dominatrix housekeeper, and a creepy phantom haunting a pirate's castle, controlled by a devious stage magician. In another episode, some guy dressed up as a really wicked-looking alien specter with fluorescent footprints, a chilling laugh, and a glowing skull and proceeded to haunt a deserted airport.

In fairly short order, however, *Scooby-Doo* became predictable. Scooby and the gang would arrive in some locale, often for some barely articulated reason—they went on vacation a lot—and would encounter two or three locals. One of them would mention a ghost of some kind and then Shaggy would exclaim, "Zoiks!" and want to leave while Scooby hid under the blankets and stuttered, "A gwwwost?" Said ghost would appear and a chase scene would ensue. Then one of the locals would be dangled before the audience as a red herring, the ghost would reappear, several obvious clues would turn up, and then there would be the final chase scene in which the ghost would be captured through some kind of Rube Goldberg device and ultimately unmasked. In many cases, it was hard to see why five young adults were running away like mad from one almost certainly corporeal "ghost": you have to wonder why Fred didn't just stand there and clobber the guy with a baseball bat. Anyway, the unmasked villain, usually some guy who wanted to scare people away, would often sneer, "And I would have gotten away with it, too, if it weren't for those kids!" The police would then haul the guy away—the cop who arrested the bad guy often looked like exactly the same person, which makes one wonder if the nameless cop wasn't the narc assigned to the Scooby-Doo case. The ending in particular was remarkably predictable, so much so that it formed the basis of one of the funniest jokes at the conclusion of the film *Wayne's World.*

The first change in the show's format produced some rather unpleasant but cheesily entertaining results, namely, the addition of animated celebrity "guest stars" who appeared in each episode to help the Scooby gang track down another bogus spirit. The choice of guest stars was eclectic, to stay the least: they ranged from fictional characters like the Addams Family (who one would suppose would welcome being haunted) and Batman and Robin (somehow Scooby and the gang seemed out of their league against the Joker and the Penguin) to marginal real-life celebrities like Jerry Reed, Sandy Duncan, and Sonny and Cher.

After that, the show's decline was more marked. In the following season, we saw the first of many expansions of Scooby's family with the addition of two cousins, Scooby Dum and Scooby Dee. Scooby Dum looked sort of like the mutant banjo-playing kid from the movie *Deliverance.* He was an albino dog with a harelip and a porkpie hat— and was characterized largely by—get this—acting *stupid.* Woo! It's not exactly as if Scooby had been portrayed as Einstein up to that point, of course. Irritating as Scooby Dum was—and repetitious as the program was becoming—these two new characters were only harbingers of the coming horror. Shortly thereafter, yet another version of *Scooby-Doo* was unveiled featuring yet another relative: Scrappy Doo.

In all of our research and discussions, we have yet to discover a more universally loathed character than Scrappy Doo. The Scrapster was Scooby's diminutive cousin. Unlike Scooby, he spoke in a clear, high-pitched voice. Mark Evanier, who helped write some of the

Scrappy Doo episodes, told us that it took a number of tries and several episodes to settle on the "right" voice for Scrappy. We wonder what exactly it was they were trying to perfect—the voice which most closely simulated the experience of hearing fingernails dragged across a chalkboard? Scrappy was saddled not only with an annoying voice but also with the most utterly idiotic slogan of any cartoon character: whenever he was faced with adversity, he would cry out, "Charge!" and then, "Puppy Power!"

"Do you want to be *dinosaur stew*???" —Will on *Land of the Lost*

Scrappy changed the entire dynamic of the show. Unlike cowardly Shaggy and Scooby, Scrappy was inclined to pursue the ghost or menace of the week. This approach simply didn't work. For one, it then begged the question we raised earlier: why didn't the whole gang just kick the crap out of the ghost the first moment they saw it? The writers may have recognized this, because the next change in Scooby's format was to send Fred and Velma off together while abandoning fake ghosts and introducing "real" menaces as antagonists. These bad guys tended to be bargain-basement mad scientists, supervillains, and other rejects who had failed their auditions for *Josie and the Pussycats*. The show just didn't work, even though we have to give the writers credit for trying something slightly new: it wasn't just the villains which were new, but also the plot structure. Rather than hewing to the relatively predictable formula of the early *Scooby* episodes, these adventures meandered, sometimes involving lengthy encounters with more of Scooby's relatives or other characters. Mark Evanier defends the Scrappy episodes despite their unpopularity. As he points out, the old formula was tired. Granted. But Scrappy was definitely the wrong way to go: it would have been better to cancel the show than keep Scooby alive in this sort of cartoon hell.

Scooby-Doo went through two and a half more incarnations. First, the Scooby characters were featured as one team on the program *Laff-A-Lympics,* a show we discuss elsewhere. Later, Scooby appeared in *The 13 Ghosts of Scooby-Doo,* a show which took the evolution of the character one step further by making him hunt down real ghosts. *The 13 Ghosts* had some virtues. The plots actually got relatively intricate, and the show featured Vincent Price as a regular character, which was kind of cool. But ultimately, it didn't quite work. Scrappy was still around, and to compound the problem, the producers also added an allegedly cute Dondi-like kid named Flimflam to the team. Further, the group was hounded by two goofy regular ghosts in addition to villains-of-the-week; these characters couldn't have cut it on *Casper, the Friendly Ghost.* Compared with the recurring character of Slimer on *The Real Ghostbusters* (a show which appeared around the same time as *The 13 Ghosts*), these two bumblers just seemed annoying.

Scooby's final fate, in 1988, was the same as that of many other longtime Saturday morning stalwarts. In the last gasp of burned-out seventies kidvid before the great Saturday Renaissance led by the coming of Fox Television, Scooby-Doo suffered the ultimate indignity of babyfication in the series *A Pup Named Scooby-Doo.* Personally, we'd just prefer to think that this show appeared in some alternative universe and forget about it. Like almost all babyfications, it makes us sick to our stomachs.

Still, in this unusually lengthy and varied run, *Scooby-Doo* became one of the foundation stones of Saturday morning. As such, it inspired a lot of imitators. The most direct *Scooby* rip-off was a 1973–74 program called *Goober and the Ghost Chasers,* which directly translated both the characters and plot formula of *Scooby-Doo* with a few minor variations—the gang used ghost-detecting equipment of various kinds and Goober himself could become intangible whenever he was frightened. Another show which was similar to *Scooby-Doo* in feel was *The Funky Phantom,* which featured two guys, one rather Fred-like though a bit more of a dumb jock type, the other a sort of hybrid of Velma and Shaggy, a Daphne-type blonde, a dog, and a real ghost from the Revolutionary War and his ghostly companion cat. One would think that having a real ghost on one's side would make for a rather unbeatable combination, but Jonathan Muddlemore (voiced by Daws Butler in a reiteration of his Snagglepuss voice) was given a healthy dose of Scooby's cowardice and had to be coaxed into dealing with scary situations. The villains on both shows were strictly low-rent variations on *Scooby* villains, or worse yet, as in the case of the Houndman on *The Funky Phantom,* total losers who could have had their butts whipped by the Care Bears.

Scooby's legacy is also visible across the total span of Saturday morning. Virtually any show that featured chase sequences, mysteries, or characters yelling "Let's get out of here!" owes it some debt. Certain later shows like *The Real Ghostbusters,* though not direct regurgitations of the *Scooby* formula, nevertheless showed clear signs of *Scooby*'s influence. And few shows have inspired as much slyly subversive speculation on the part of Saturday morning veterans. We still wonder how Fred and Velma are doing off in their love nest and whether Daphne, *Fatal Attraction*–style, is ever going to track them down. And if anyone has a recipe for Scooby snacks that won't get us ten to fifteen years in federal prison, let us know.

The Adventures of Jonny Quest

As was so often the case with Saturday morning, the best part of *Jonny Quest* might have been its brilliant theme music. (It helped that the theme played during a nifty montage of some exciting scenes from various episodes during the opening and closing credits.) On the recent album of covers of Saturday morning theme songs by contemporary bands, the best track by far is Reverend Horton Heat's intense version of the *Quest* theme. The 1996 revival of *Quest* by Turner productions also paid effective homage to the classic theme while making a snazzy piece of music in its own right.

But *Jonny Quest* had numerous other virtues as well. Like *Space Ghost,* it benefited from character designs and writing by creators other than Hanna and Barbera themselves, in this case, the talented Doug Wildey. For us, the original *Quest* episodes, which began appearing in prime time in 1964, are as perfect a distillation of their time as the early James Bond films, a luscious cocktail of technophilia, blithe masculinity, and charmingly innocent cold war ethnocentrism. Like James Bond, the Quest team lived off of a regular diet of evil Oriental masterminds, vaguely East Bloc no-goodniks, various supersecret gadgets, and manly derring-do, though they didn't indulge in women, martinis, or caviar.

The Adventures of Jonny Quest was also reminiscent of other action-adventure fictions: it was one part Tintin, another part *Terry and the Pirates,* with a bit of Tom Swift thrown in, the latest in a long chain of pulp entertainments. The show followed the adventures of preteen Jonny (exact age unknown, but probably between nine and eleven) and another young boy, an Indian named Hadji. Jonny and Hadji traveled around the world with the polytalented Dr. Benton Quest, Jonny's father, and Race Bannon, who was Dr. Quest's bodyguard and jack-of-all-trades assistant. Jonny also had a dog named Bandit who often featured prominently in their adventures.

———

"We're on Muttley's side. And I guess we're on Dastardly's side. Anyway, how do you know they're bad guys? Maybe they're good. In wars everybody thinks they're on the good side, so how can you say who's bad or good? It depends on which side you're on." —Eight-year-old television viewer quoted in an article by John Culhane, 1969

———

Most episodes revolved around one of four plot types: Dr. Quest is sent by some vaguely defined government agency to investigate a mystery; Dr. Quest is testing a new scientific gizmo which is coveted by the Bad Guys or otherwise leads to havoc; Dr. Quest is called to rescue a distant colleague or old friend who is in deep doo-doo; or the Quest team is traveling in some exotic part of the world and trouble develops. Early in each episode, Dr. Quest and Race Bannon typically make some pro forma gesture toward keeping the kids out of harm's way; Jonny and Hadji usually circumvent said gesture and find themselves hostages, prisoners, or otherwise threatened by the Bad Guys, and then the whole team gets itself out of trouble through a mix of the kids' cleverness, Hadji's skills as a fakir-in-training, Race Bannon's studly fighting abilities, and a bit of technological wizardry from the versatile Dr. Quest. (In at least a few cases, Jonny and Hadji rescued Race and/or Dr. Quest, in a refreshing reversal of the usual kid/adult dynamic in these kinds of programs.)

Dr. Quest's base of operations in the original episodes was set in Palm Key, though he had access to military research and development facilities all around the globe. Various episodes found the Quest team in India, Egypt, the North Pole, the Andes, unnamed jungles full of hostile natives, the South Seas, and so on. The team faced one regular adversary, the extremely stereotypical and Fu Manchu–esque Dr. Zin. One other recurring character, Jezebel Jade, appeared in two episodes: she was a femme fatale, an amoral mercenary who was also Race Bannon's (former?) girlfriend.

The Adventures of Jonny Quest was, we'd be the first to admit, not always the most original or sophisticated example of its particular genre. Various episodes dug down deep into the store of stock pulp clichés, ranging from Dr. Quest's attempt to convince unruly natives that he was a god (the twist is that he failed, though Race later succeeded) to a land of lost dinosaurs. Somehow, however, it all clicked. The general competence of the animation, good writing and vocal acting, and a coherent creative vision all distinguished *Quest* from much of the rest of Saturday morning, though this was also partially due to the fact that Hanna-Barbera originally had aired *Jonny Quest* in prime time and thus had higher aspirations for it.

In the years after the first run of *Jonny Quest,* some kidvid professionals blamed the program for the long absence of good action-adventure cartoons from Saturday morning, due to controversies over the show's allegedly violent tone. (Mark Evanier said that in one ABC retrospective on Saturday morning, producers were told to leave out *Jonny Quest* because it had "ruined everything" with its violent content.) In comparison with insipidly prosocial cartoons, *Quest* was, we'll admit, pretty strong stuff. Some of the claims made by advocacy groups about "violence" in cartoons were silly, but there's no getting around the fact that bad guys in *Jonny Quest* got blown to smithereens, smashed by flying power boats, and so on. You didn't see them die in gory detail, but it's pretty clear that there were villainous fatalities in some episodes. This is part of what made it—and still makes it—such a good show. Unlike so many other cartoons, *The Adventures of Jonny Quest* was not lobotomized or otherwise ridiculously disconnected from the genre which gave it life. In earlier action-adventure fiction, or pulp novels, or radio serials (including those intended for young audiences) people sometimes died or were otherwise injured in the course of the adventure. That's the stuff that makes the genre work. It's not as if we got to watch Race rip off Dr. Zin's head, *Mortal Kombat* style. (Though come to think of it . . .)

And because it was so directly connected to its cultural wellspring, it was also mercifully free of the absurdly cute or "educational" touches that marred later adventure-oriented cartoons. Jonny was not the kind of helpless moron kid that so often fetched up in the company of adults in cartoons like *The Godzilla Power Hour.* Jonny and Hadji—especially Hadji, who had a store of perilously-close-to-offensive "Indian" talents, like hypnotism—could hold their own against all sorts of villains, even though they did get into trouble with some frequency. Bandit, though cute, wasn't grotesquely so, and he was actually a genuine asset to the Quest team, unlike his later canine counterparts. Most of the kids on Saturday morning were so annoying or useless that we rarely identified with them, but Jonny and Hadji seemed to be having so much fun on their adventures that we often wished we could be in their place.

"I'm gonna make mincemeat out of that mouse!" —Klondike Kat

Moreover, Dr. Benton Quest and Race Bannon were the coolest parents on the planet: Race taught the kids judo and Dr. Quest let them help him build death rays and crush nefarious spies. The Quest family lived on their own island base in the Caribbean. Race and Benton had everything covered—they were Mom, Dad, and your Really Hip Weird Uncle all wrapped up in one. Jonny's real mother was never mentioned in the original series, which is just as well, since many devoted Quest fans have noticed that Jonny resembles Race a *lot* more than he looks like Dr. Quest. We've always assumed that Race and Benton sowed their heterosexual oats at an earlier point in their lives, with Jezebel Jade or whomever, one of the two of them fathering Jonny along the way, and then they shacked up with each other to live happily ever after as America's most attractive and stable gay couple.

We're not the only ones to have noticed Race and Dr. Quest's exclusive preference for each other's company: some nervous prudes at Turner decided to give Jonny a mother in one of their attempts to revive the program. Worse yet, they implied that Dr. Quest had been married all along, and that Mrs. Quest was also a scientist who simply stayed back at home and never went adventuring. Yuck. Why didn't they just draft Aunt Harriet from the live-action *Batman* series if they needed a female character to keep a watchful eye on Benton and Race?

The latest Turner revival of the franchise, entitled *The Real Adventures of Jonny Quest,* is a bit better, on the whole, but still lacks a sense of why the original was so successful. They've added a new character, Race's daughter Jesse, who actually fits in pretty well. (We hasten to add that she sort of resembles Dr. Quest, which just makes the domestic situation at Quest Compound even more intricate.) There were some stupid things in the early episodes of this latest version: Race originally alternated between having a weeny-boy voice or a faux Southern accent, they moved the Quest team to Maine, and they briefly took away Dr. Quest's red hair. Some of this has been fixed in the more recent episodes, which have featured the return of Dr. Zin and Jezebel Jade, as well as Dr. Zin's twin daughters. As Hadji used to say, Sim Sim Salabeem! No matter what Ted Turner's folks elect to do with the Quest family in the future, Race and Benton will always have Palm Key.

Space Ghost

We know the readers of this book are reliable sorts who don't eat oysters in months with no *r*, who would never, ever cheat on their taxes, who go to church every day of the week, and who sent care packages of Twinkies to Mother Teresa on a regular basis. We know we can trust you all with a deep and terrible secret. We've seen the Cartoon Network's faux talk show *Space Ghost: Coast to Coast,* and we think it's really great. Honest. It's extremely funny and very innovative, unlike anything else on television. Any program where the main character is allowed to boast that he can open a can of spinach using his butt muscles is a-okay with us.

But—promise you won't tell anyone—we wish they'd picked somebody else to do the show. Like Dino Boy. Or Inch High, Private Eye. Or maybe Birdman, he was geeky enough.[1] 'Cause, see, we thought that the original Space Ghost was groovy. Sure, he was so straight that he makes Anita Bryant look like a member of Queer Nation. Sure, he was so stiff that his pals had to check him for rigor mortis if he ever went for more than five minutes without saying something. Yes, he had nostrils the size of asteroids. Okay, his goofy power bands made Batman's utility belt look like something you bought at the Wal-Mart: they had settings like "Puree," "Downsize,"

---

1. There have been some rumors that the Cartoon Network has considered Birdman for another *Space Ghost: Coast to Coast*–style talk show.

and "Leave an Almost Empty Carton of Milk in the Refrigerator." Indeed, he had two dorky kid sidekicks who had their own dorky sidekick, a pet monkey—and granted, he had to be rescued by the pet monkey all the time. Verily, Space Ghost bad guys Lurker and Brak looked like a reptilian Billy Barty and an addled orange wombat.

But *Space Ghost* still kicked butt. In the *Space Ghost: Coast to Coast* era, admitting that you still like the original *Space Ghost* adventures *as* superheroic adventure, rather than seeing them as the chronicle of a parody foretold, feels weird. But we're not totally alone in our liking for the original series. Steve Rude, one of the best graphic artists working today, outlined his own passion for the look and feel of the original *Space Ghost* series in a one-shot comic book which pitted the character against his entire rogues' gallery of villains. During its original run in the late sixties, *Space Ghost and Dino Boy* was one of the most popular shows on Saturday morning, so a nation of kids agreed with us, at least once upon a time.

Space Ghost as envisioned by comic book artist Alex Toth was, if nothing else, an impressive piece of design work. Clad in a white costume with a black-and-yellow hood and cape, and a red belt and wristbands, he had a clean and impressively powerful look about him. His deep and authoritative voice was provided by omnipresent vocal talent Gary Owens. We know Mr. Ghost looks dorky now, but trust us, before *Coast to Coast* and *Cartoon Planet* appeared, he cut a pretty formidable swath through his neck of the woods. If *we* had been the Black Widow or Moltar back in those days, we sure wouldn't have messed with the guy. Well, not unless we managed to take his kid sidekicks Jan and Jayce hostage while violently disposing of Blip the space monkey.

Space Ghost and his assistants had a host of groovy gadgets. His multipurpose power bands and power belt allowed him to fly, turn invisible, create force fields, zap bad guys with the appropriate ray (he had the blow-'em-to-smithereens ray when he was zapping robots or other mechanical devices, and the knock-'em-out ray when he was fighting an organic foe, for example). He had his own nifty-looking spaceship called the *Phantom Cruiser,* a planet-sized version of the Batcave called the Ghost Planet, and so on. His villains were a distinctive bunch, a cross between the cantina scene in *Star Wars* and Dick Tracy's rogues' gallery, ranging from the insect mastermind Zorak to the formidable-looking Metallis. Space Ghost's adventures unfolded in a surreal vision of outer space full of weird plant creatures and spooky wasteland planetscapes.

The plots of individual *Space Ghost* episodes didn't exactly brim over with interesting ideas or challenging narrative twists. It was pretty much a "get the call from galactic authorities to come save the day, deal with nefarious plot of today's villain, rescue Jan and Jayce, get rescued by Blip" kind of thing with most episodes. There are ones we remember slightly better, like the one where Zorak almost managed to get Space Ghost crushed by his robot monster after exchanging his power bands for fakes, or the one where a spy from another galaxy turned into an evil duplicate of Space Ghost. The appeal of *Space Ghost* always lay in the look and feel of the show, in its total atmosphere, and not in individual episodes.

"The *Herculoids* . . . holds records for the sheer number of ingenious deaths per sequence." —*Redbook* editor Sam Blum, 1968

This is equally true of another early Hanna-Barbera adventure series, *The Herculoids.* A lot of Saturday morning veterans remember this show well, though they remember the details only dimly, partly because it wasn't syndicated as extensively as *Space Ghost.* It was part of the original craze for "weirdo superheroes" in the late sixties, commissioned after the big ratings success of *Space Ghost and Dino Boy.* Much of what made *The Herculoids* a big success was the sheer strangeness of the central characters, a team of do-gooders who lived on an unnamed alien planet someplace. At the heart of the team was, unusually for Saturday morning, a nuclear family: Tandor, Zara, and their boy, Dorno, who were Aryan-looking Tarzan-and-Jane types. Tandor was the head honcho, clearly accustomed to commanding those around him. The family had a bunch of alien pals who seemed simultaneously to be allies, friends, and pets. Gloop and Gleep were the superheroic equivalent of the Shmoo, glowing yellow protoplasmic amoebas that could stretch, change shape, or even split into smaller globs. Tandor usually rode around on Zok, a dragon who could shoot energy beams from his eyes and tail, while Zara and Dorno often hitched a ride on Tundro, a sort of alien rhinoceros festooned with armor and with a hollow horn that launched big alien space loogies at bad guys. There was also Igoo, a giant ape who appeared to be made out of stone. Each of these creatures had its own distinctive sound: Gloop and Gleep had a weird guttural ululation, Zok a high-pitched eagle's cry, Igoo a rocky mumble, and Tundro the generic Hanna-Barbera roaring noise.

If the plots and visuals of *The Herculoids* seemed somewhat reminiscent of *Space Ghost,* it is probably because the show was commissioned in an attempt to repeat *Space Ghost*'s success, and because Alex Toth was involved in the design of both programs. The stars of *The Herculoids* mattered more than the stories: each member of the team was so imaginatively conceived and drawn that they stuck in your head long after you had forgotten anything about the setting, the plot, or even the villains, who were the generic robot/lizardman/mutant variety.

Another Alex Toth–inspired adventure show of the same era worth mentioning is *Shazzan!,* a Hanna-Barberized version of the Arabian Nights. Two teenagers named Chuck and Nancy each had one half of a magical ring which, once joined, summoned a pretty-damn-close-to-omnipotent giant genie named Shazzan, who had an irritatingly smug way of laughing, "Ho ho *ho,* little one!" whenever he talked to people. Chuck and Nancy flew around a generic deserts-and-big-vaguely-Arabian-cities dimension on a flying camel, embarrassingly named Kaboobie, looking to make trouble whenever they ran across evil sultans, viziers, and wizards, as they seemed to do regularly. We don't recall why they were in this setting (we dimly remember that there was some kind of overall quest or something they were supposed to accomplish), but most episodes revolved around the teens losing their rings temporarily, or managing to tork Shazzan off enough that he had to be coaxed into helping them kick ass, or being tied up so they couldn't touch rings. Since Shazzan always made quick if rather imaginative work of the bad guy (he had a touch for showy gimmicks like creating a mountain and dropping it on a monster's head, that sort of thing), the only way to take up more than about two minutes of screen time was to somehow delay Shazzan's entry onto the scene. The various evil sultan types, while torn straight out of the central casting office of orientalist ethnocentrism, were at least colorfully wicked, even a little kinky.

There were other shows less worthy of mention that fell into this genre, including the painfully forgettable *Birdman and the Galaxy Trio,* the excruciatingly bad *Three Musketeers,* and the rather odd *Moby Dick and the Mighty Mightor.* Compared to some of the great new adventure-oriented kidvid of the nineties, these early Hanna-Barbera efforts look lame: they're all atmosphere and visual design, with almost no plot. They're repetitious when viewed in sequence. But atmosphere counts for a lot, particularly in terms of what is memorable and what is not. It may be hard for anyone under the age of eighteen to believe that Space Ghost was ever a cool, competent, impressive superhero after seeing that dorky fat guy dressed in his costume dance around in the opening sequence of *Cartoon Planet.* Well, believe it, you little punks.

Josie and the Pussycats

There are five great couplets in English-language poetry. One of them is the opening of the theme song for *Josie and the Pussycats:* "Josie and the Pussycats / Long tails and ears for hats." Beat that, Shakespeare.

Josie and the Pussycats was Hanna-Barbera's 1970 reentry into the action-adventure genre after the late-sixties hue and cry about cartoon violence and weirdo superheroes. As such, it was hampered by a lot of derivative slapstick humor, hopelessly inept second-string villains, stock "Let's get out of here!" chase sequences, and other less than impressive features, all designed to assure the critics that the new adventure cartoons were anything but violent. But *Josie* represented a significant variation on earlier Hanna-Barbera adventure cartoons; it had a loopy, amusing charm of its own. In its original run, it was a strange hybrid of *Scooby-Doo, Space Ghost,* and *Jonny Quest.*

———

"Cartoons are predictable. From *Josie and the Pussycats* to *Goober and the Ghost Chasers,* they provide an undemanding blur of mediocre animation and unreal voices, undistinguishable from most of the commercials." —Television reviewer John J. O'Connor, 1973

———

The central characters were an all-girl rock band—Josie, Melody, and Valerie—and their odd entourage, made up of their friend, studly Alan, their manager, Alexander Cabot III, and Alexander's bitchy sister, Alexandra. Alexandra also had a cat named Sebastian who resembled her in both mood and physical appearance. The title character, Josie, was bland but fairly competent, as was Valerie, who was one of the first African American characters on Saturday morning. Melody, on the other hand, was a supposedly humorous and witless blonde whose ears wiggled at the approach of anything dangerous. (Her ears? We thought this was pretty stupid even when we were kids. There must be a double entendre lurking in there somewhere.) Alan was basically Fred from *Scooby-Doo,* bulked up on steroids, while Alexander had Shaggy's mannerisms and demeanor (if not his unkempt appearance), including his voice—both characters were performed by Casey Kasem.

Alexandra, on the other hand, was the straw that stirred the drink. She was a complete bitch, with a Cruella De Vil–style haircut to match, and though the show was clearly set up to make her look like a fool every time (the group always got in trouble because Alexandra, due to her lust for Alan, did something insanely stupid or selfish), we loved her. She had spunk, and her cat was a wicked little beast. She was the Dr. Smith to the show's Robinson family, though without a robot crying "Danger! Danger!" to bedevil her.

The villains were your average garden-variety mad scientists and world conquerors, not the most successful or imaginative of their breed, but not quite as pointlessly obsessed as some of their peers, like Sid and Marty Krofft's Dr. Shrinker. Unlike the Quest family or Space Ghost, the Pussycats always crossed the villain's path by accident, either witnessing something they shouldn't or incidentally possessing something of value to the bad guy. Once in a while, a memorable villain showed up, like the Sydney Greenstreet–imitating mad scientist who was growing carnivorous plants in his weird greenhouses, the evil blimp pilot who wanted to extract a scientific secret that Melody had accidentally sucked into her brain, and the superspy Mastermind.

Like the characters of *Jonny Quest,* the Pussycats and their entourage often found themselves in exotic locations, usually to give a concert. Most episodes also strove consciously to reproduce the formula that seemed to fuel the startling success of *The Archies* by mixing musical numbers into the action. (Alexandra was clearly based on Veronica, the rich bitch on *The Archies,* though we'd argue that Alexandra ultimately had more character.) On the whole, *Josie and the Pussycats* was a major success for Hanna-Barbera. In fact, in an attempt to keep *Josie* alive after its initial run, the studio commissioned a new set of episodes that launched the team into outer space, a tried-and-true Saturday morning format change.

The other success of the *Josie/Scooby-Doo* formula—lighthearted and nonthreatening adventure stories—was that it quieted the complaints of most Saturday morning critics back down to the usual dull roar. As a result, Hanna-Barbera reused the same formula for show after show, with a perceptible decline in charm and distinctiveness. For example, *Speed Buggy* featured the adventures of three young adults and their talking car, had the standard Alan/Fred stud, the pretty Daphne/Josie woman, and the Shaggy/Alex goofball. *Jabberjaw* featured the adventures of some young adults and their talking shark with a similarly derivative mix of characters. The same kind of villains— mostly mad scientists with increasingly goofy schemes to conquer the world—continued to serve as adversaries. When the *Scooby-Doo* gang actually teamed up with the Josie team or, in another instance, with the *Speed Buggy* characters, it was like seeing double. Curiously enough, the one character unique to *Josie* was the most interesting one: Alexandra. None of these other shows featured a scheming, conniving, sex-crazed bitch; it would have livened up the proceedings a good deal if they had. We assume that Alexandra just changed her name and got a job in soap operas after the cancellation of *Josie and the Pussycats in Outer Space.* Has she moved in yet on *Melrose Place?*

Land of the Lost

Victoria Fromkin, a senior professor in the Department of Linguistics at the University of California at Los Angeles, casually mentioned to her Introduction to Linguistics class that she had once written a language for a television show. When she mentioned that the language was called Pakuni and the show was *Land of the Lost,* the entire lecture hall applauded.

Land of the Lost, one of the many flowerings of the Sid and Marty Krofft Kulture Tree, is a show which somehow added up to far more than the sum of its parts. While many of its individual elements (plot, dialogue, special effects, acting) were cheap or goofy, the whole product worked well. Rick, Will, and Holly Marshall, the protagonists, were first thrust into the Land of the Lost in 1974 while on a camping trip. The extremely literal theme song told the audience, "Till the greatest earthquake ever known. High on a rapid, it struck their tiny raft and plunged them down a thousand feet below." (Cue images of the Marshall family on a raft, superimposed onto a crude miniature set in a trickle of water that is supposed to be a raging river in a deep canyon.) The Marshalls fell directly into a time door that transported them to a strange world, complete with dinosaurs and various alien-like creatures, including the Sleestaks. The Sleestaks served as regular adversaries for the marooned family: they were a bunch of big-eyed lizard people carrying around crossbows strung with rubber bands, fired with a sense of aim that made the average Imperial Stormtrooper from *Star Wars* look like a deadly sharpshooter.

Luckily, the Marshall family retained some of their camping gear. They retreated to a mountainous cave as protection from their other eternal enemy, Grumpy, a fitfully irritated but inept Tyrannosaurus rex. (Well, dinosaurs *did* have small brains, but even by saurian standards Grumpy seemed like a relative dunce.) Among them, the Marshalls had one change of clothes, one Bic lighter, some bowie knives, and three sleeping bags. Of course, like a combination of Fred Flintstone and MacGyver, former park ranger Rick Marshall could make just about anything the family needed. Bowls, cups, plates, utensils, washing machines: all that was missing was a coconut-powered radio from *Gilligan's Island*.

The adventures of the Marshalls fell into two categories: outdoor survival episodes and spooky, subterranean Sleestak episodes. The first category, the more pedestrian of the two, often featured the Marshalls' pals Dopey (a baby brontosaur who was their pet) or Cha-Ka, a Pakuni (one of the hairy monkey people who spoke Pakuni). Such stories usually led up, in standard Saturday morning fashion, to some simplistic moral. In one episode, Cha-Ka stole a Bic lighter from the Marshalls and they had to negotiate its return from Cha-Ka's elders Sa and Ta. In another episode, Holly returned Dopey to his mother in the swamps with much sobbing and good uplifting lessons all around. Moreover, these episodes were standard "lost world of dinosaurs" fare, staple story lines on Saturday morning. By contrast, the episodes in which the Marshalls explored the secrets of their new home, either in the Lost City of the Sleestaks or in the mysterious "pylons" which had powers over space and time, seemed a good deal more intriguing and imaginative than the norm. (With good reason: some of the early episodes were written by noted science fiction authors David Gerrold, Larry Niven, D. C. Fontana, Ben Bova, and Norman Spinrad.)

Land of the Lost remained in production for three seasons. The first season was relatively exciting, introducing the various characters, dinosaurs, Sleestaks, and otherworldly devices like the pylons. Fromkin claimed that a few of these episodes were also structured around Pakuni grammar to provide a small lesson in linguistics. At least one exercise designed by Fromkin alarmed the Kroffts, however. Fromkin told us, "In one of the scripts Cha-Ka got very angry and was swearing, and so I wrote all of these swear words. When I sent it to them [the Kroffts] I gave them a translation for 'Fuck' and 'Shit' and they wrote back and said, 'We can't use those words!' and I said, 'What do you mean? Nobody is going to understand them!'" This made us watch certain early episodes with a new sense of respect and admiration: Cha-Ka suddenly looks like a character from a Quentin Tarantino film.

The second season continued in similar fashion to the first, with minor breakdowns and plot redundancies. The character of Enik, a wise and intelligent Sleestak from the distant past, was used, and a new character called The Zarn was introduced. The Zarn looked a lot like Peter Gabriel at the end of the music video for "Sledgehammer" and made a wind-chime sound whenever he moved. Cha-Ka, played by Philip Paley, also became more prominent. Then the show, never exactly blessed with great acting or production values, took a noticeable downturn. Spencer Milligan, playing the father, left *Land of the Lost* and was replaced by a new actor playing Jack Marshall, Will and Holly's uncle. It was never clearly defined what happened to the dad, it simply just happened between seasons, and suddenly there

This _Land of the Lost_ game reminds us of a lame version of Smess. It's a cool picture line around the edges of the board, though.

was a new credit sequence that began with the lyric "Will and Holly Marshall . . ." and went on with ". . . as their father fell through the door of time . . ." and later with "Uncle Jack went searching . . ." The new family moved their digs to a temple near the Lost City after another earthquake destroyed the cave. Cha-Ka's hair grew longer and he no longer spoke Pakuni, Will mysteriously started wearing a new shirt, and the Sleestaks stopped hissing and started speaking perfect English. The third season was generally abysmal and _Land of the Lost_ was canceled.

Question: How do you keep a Bic lighter working for three years? Answer: Move to the _Land of the Lost_. The same logic applies to clothing and hairdos. The family should have looked like refugees from _Lord of the Flies_ by their third year, given that they were running around in a swampy, humid climate being chased by dinosaurs and lizard people. However, everything stayed neat and clean, including the characters' psyches. You'd think by year three that the main human characters would be going a bit bugshit, particularly given that the son was right smack-dab in the middle of adolescence and was probably giving some thought to putting the moves on a female Sleestak once he could figure out which ones were female. The Kroffts recently produced a new version of _Land of the Lost_. This version chose to tighten the screws on the two male characters still further by introducing a skimpily clad young woman who joined the family in the course of their adventures. Can you spell Oedipus?

Like the other Krofft shows, *Land of the Lost* poses enduring mysteries. For the other shows the main mystery is trying to figure out just what the hell the Kroffts were thinking when they made the show. Some of the lasting questions to come out of *Land of the Lost* actually deal with the show itself. It was a goofy, cheap, and crude-looking program, but we still want to know where Father Marshall went. We still want to know how to operate a pylon. We still are curious about whether the Marshall family ever got home. And more than anything else, we want to know how to say "Fuck!" in Pakuni.

H. R. Pufnstuf and the World of Sid and Marty Krofft

In 1988, an article in *Spy* described an omnipresent American cultural institution that it aptly christened "American Kabuki," namely, the costumes worn by sports mascots and theme-park characters, ranging from the San Diego Chicken to Mickey Mouse. American Kabuki had its place on Saturday morning as well, in the programs of Sid and Marty Krofft. *Land of the Lost* was actually something of an exception to their general oeuvre, in that the main characters were human beings and the goings-on—replete with dinosaurs, strange lizard-people, and foulmouthed ape-men—were relatively straightforward. The typical Krofft show was a surreal, dreamy affair in which weird giant puppet-people cavorted across the TV screen and got involved in marginally coherent shenanigans that managed to be vaguely disturbing and queerly entertaining at the same time.

The Kroffts got their start with a smaller breed of puppets. In 1960, their risqué puppet review *Les Poupees de Paris* appeared first in nightclubs, and then in a slightly less risqué incarnation on *The Dean Martin Show*. When the live-action show *The Banana Splits* first appeared on television and on Kellogg's cereal boxes in 1968, its producers were Hanna-Barbera, but behind the scenes lurked Sid and Marty Krofft, having moved from *Les Poupees de Paris* to the big time of children's television. The Kroffts never looked back, which is probably for the best as far as American culture is concerned. The market for unamusing puppet acts has been saturated for decades by the existence of Shari Lewis.

H. R. Pufnstuf, the Kroffts' first solo effort, premiered September 6, 1968, on NBC, and did well enough in the ratings during its first year to spawn a feature film of the same name. The basic plot of the series, which owed more than a little to *The Wizard of Oz,* revolved around a boy named Jimmy (Jack Wild) and his magic talking golden flute, Freddie. Jimmy and Freddie were shanghaied to Living Island (where, unsurprisingly, everything is alive) by Witchiepoo (Billie Hayes). There Jimmy and Freddie were befriended by a mutant yellow dragon, the mayor of Living Island, H. R. Pufnstuf. Most weeks, Witchiepoo schemed, with the help of her dimwit assistants, Seymour, Orson, and Stupid Bat, to gain possession of Freddie the flute.

This setup posed innumerable mind-bogglers. How the hell did Jimmy get a hold of a magic talking golden flute, anyway? More importantly, why was Witchiepoo's main ambition in life to grab Freddie? No one really knows. The usual motivations of witches and their ilk—global domination, alliance with Satan, worshiping Gaea, what have you—seemed to be conspicuously lacking. On those rare occasions when Witchiepoo would gain temporary custody of Freddie she wouldn't do much besides throw him in the dungeon (like you need to imprison a flute) or threaten to drop him in boiling oil (he did sort of look like an uncooked French fry . . . maybe Witchiepoo was just hungry and nearsighted). Perhaps Freddie, with his wincing falsetto, managed to irritate Witchiepoo as much he annoyed the average viewer. If her main goal was just to melt the little creep, then we were with her all the way. Who knows? Maybe she was just acting out her repressed anger at her parents for naming her Witchiepoo.

Sid and Marty Krofft Television v. McDonald's Corporation

FROM THE JUDGES' OPINION, UNITED STATES
COURT OF APPEALS, NINTH CIRCUIT.
OCTOBER 12, 1977. 562 F.2D 1157.

"Even a dissection of the two works reveals their similarities. The 'Living Island' locale of Pufnstuf and 'McDonaldland' are both imaginary worlds inhabited by anthropomorphic plants and animals and other fanciful creatures. The dominant topographical features of the locales are the same: trees, caves, a pond, a road, and a castle. Both works feature a forest with talking trees that have human faces and characteristics.

"The characters are also similar. Both lands are governed by mayors who have disproportionately large round heads dominated by long wide mouths. They are assisted by 'Keystone cop' characters. Both lands feature strikingly similar crazy scientists and a multi-armed evil creature."

As is par for the course in this kind of show, Witchiepoo's schemes were invariably foiled by her own miscalculations or, even more typically, by her bumbling henchmen, who looked unusually vivid even for a Krofft show. Orson was a four-armed orange gorilla with crystal eyes. Seymour was a bipedal vulture who looked like he had mange. Stupid Bat was—well, a big stupid bat. Their crowning achievement came in the episode where they served as Witchiepoo's band while Witchiepoo sang a song that observed that "there ain't no rhyme for oranges!" Now *that's* talent. The good guys weren't exactly models for *GQ,* though, including a hippie tree, a spastic owl who served as Living Island's doctor, and some weird little orange newt guys who worked as Pufnstuf's deputies. They all looked a bit like the characters of McDonaldland as they appeared in advertisements for McDonald's—Mayor McCheese, the Hamburgler, and so on. (This, apparently, was no accident: the Kroffts had been approached to develop advertisements for McDonald's, and when the deal fell through, McDonald's went ahead and did similar advertisements anyway. The Kroffts responded with a successful lawsuit.)

The general setting and goings-on in *H. R. Pufnstuf* were so oddly psychedelic that people have joked that "H. R." stood for "hand rolled." When the cable channel Nickelodeon showed a retrospective of Krofft shows recently, they played up this angle, making jokes about psychedelic culture in almost every bumper segment during the station breaks. This aura has helped make the show an icon of general weirdness: one fanzine, for example, envisions Pufnstuf as a Nazi figure, a modern-day religious icon, and a hippie. As writer and alt.society.generation-x regular Douglas Lathrop commented, "I think about them [the Krofft shows] now and I wonder how much acid these people were dropping. Still, I have fond memories of them."

Weirdly memorable theme songs were also something of a Krofft specialty: even when the show itself was eminently dismissable, the song stuck to you like glue. This trait in Krofft works was evident from the beginning: *The Banana Splits* is a show mostly known among Saturday morning veterans for its haunting theme song. The Kroffts' next show after *H. R. Pufnstuf* revolved around music. *The Bugaloos* (1970) followed the exploits of a quasi-British rock band who also happened to be flying insect-people living in a psychedelic living forest. The Bugaloos, named Courage, Harmony, I.Q., and Joy, were accompanied by their firefly pal, Sparky (Sparky looked like a particularly geeky example of a Killer Bee from *Saturday Night Live*). They were constantly being hassled by their nemesis, the envious Benita Bizarre

(Martha Raye), who made Witchiepoo resemble Calvin Coolidge on a quiet day. *The Bugaloos,* while easily being as disturbingly phantasmagorical as *Pufnstuf* and *The Banana Splits,* didn't achieve the same level of pop culture popularity: it's the kind of show that most people remember in a queasy, hallucinogenic way, kind of like a piece of food stuck between their teeth that they've forgotten about.

———

"I play a vicious witch but not really. I live in a jukebox, wear a turkey-feather boa, and want to make a record even though I can't sing. What more could a girl ask?" —Martha Raye on her character Benita Bizarre in *The Bugaloos*

———

The next Krofft show, *Lidsville,* followed past convention by featuring a cast of costumed characters, a single human protagonist, and a disturbingly whacked-out villain. The plot turned on a boy named Mark (Butch Patrick) who fell into a "magician's hat" after a magic show and landed in a "world full of hats" and, of course, an evil villainous magician, Whoo Doo (Charles Nelson Reilly in a role that made his appearances on *Match Game 74* seem sedate by comparison). *Lidsville* also featured Witchiepoo's "good" cousin, Weenie the Geenie (also played by Billie Hayes), locked up in a magic ring owned by Whoo Doo. Said ring was stolen by Mark in the opening episode and subsequently became *Lidsville*'s McGuffin. Even though Weenie was thoroughly incompetent and incapable of performing magic with any sort of accuracy, Whoo Doo inexplicably pursued Mark for stealing the Weenie and the ring. In the meantime, Mark tried to find his way back to the normal world. Though the basic *H. R. Pufnstuf* formula was adhered to rigorously in *Lidsville,* the show was distinguished by possibly the weirdest of the Kroffts' many weird premises. A world full of living hats? What was in the dimension next door? A world of living Fruit of the Looms? (Hey—there's an idea for a commercial!)

A bit later, the Kroffts produced *Sigmund and the Sea Monsters,* a tale of two boys and their friend Sigmund, a "friendly sea monster." As Sid Krofft told Kevin in an interview for *Film Threat* magazine, he thought of *Sigmund and the Sea Monsters* when he was at the beach and saw an interesting pile of seaweed, and he thought to himself, "What if that was a sea monster?" Thank God Sid wasn't walking the dog or having dental surgery when creative lightning struck. As a testament to the human imagination, the honesty of his account is refreshing, considering that a similar account of the creative goings-on at Hanna-Barbera circa 1976 probably would have involved a debate about how many frames to cut, but the story doesn't exactly reassure us about the coherency of the Kroffts' thought processes. The most interesting aspects of *Sigmund* included the weird mix of *All in the Family* and *Cinderella* that held sway in Sigmund's home, a bejeweled cave with a "shellevision" inhabited by an aggressive sea-monster father, naggingly destructive sea-monster mother (whose resemblance to Martha Raye was scary), and brutally moronic sea-monster siblings. We mustn't forget the fabulous Rip Taylor as Sheldon the Sea Genie, whom Sigmund and the boys would often invoke to magically save them from trouble. (The Kroffts seemed stuck in a queenie groove with their genies and wizards.) *Sigmund* definitely featured some plot lines that made us wonder if the

A confusing yet paradoxically simple board game based on *Sigmund and the Sea Monsters*.

title character wasn't named for Sigmund Freud. In one episode, Sigmund—basically an ambulatory pile of green crud—falls in love with a dog, while his bullying brother tries to lure him back to his mean sea-monster family by dressing up as a female monster and putting the moves on Sigmund.

The Kroffts' genie obsession materialized again in "Magic Mongo." "Mongo" revolved around "three nice kids," Donald, Kristy, and Lorraine, who were constantly plagued by bullies named Ace and Duncey until Magic Mongo, a traditional genie from a bottle, would employ his magical powers to save them. "Magic Mongo" was one of many segments in an anthology series called *The Krofft Supershow* or *The Krofft Superstar Hour.* Originally hosted by the alleged "band" Kaptain Kool & the Kongs, the series included other segments such as "Electra-Woman and Dynagirl," a thinly disguised version of the campy Batman and Robin television show, only with female protagonists and starring soap opera actress Deidre Hall. This particular show is, like *Land of the Lost* and *H. R. Pufnstuf,* one of the more intensely remembered and discussed Krofft shows. It may be that "Electra-Woman" was so far beyond even other Krofft shows in terms of raw camp that it imprinted itself violently on the memory of anyone who had seen it even once, making it the ultimate in insider references. If you didn't live through Saturday morning, you'll never have heard of it. But if you sat in front of the television at the right time, you may never forget it.

"Dr. Shrinker," "Wonderbug," and "Bigfoot and Wildboy" were the other three series hosted by Kaptain Kool. "Dr. Shrinker" told the tale of a mad scientist, played by Jay Robinson, who wants to shrink teenagers. Very original, Doc; you and all the other mad scientists should compare notes. Assisted by his servant, played by Billy Barty, Dr. Shrinker intended to dominate the world via shrinkage and began by experimenting on some hapless teens marooned on an island, whom he then spent the rest of the series chasing. As for "Bigfoot and Wildboy," we can't really improve on our friend Andrew Ross's

summary, so we reprint it here. Andrew writes,

The Legendary Bigfoot, who resembles a wookie, apparently rescued a boy who had been abandoned in the forests of the Great Northwest. Although Bigfoot speaks only in loud grunts and roars, the Wild Boy speaks perfect English, wears a costume of leather and green cloth, and is friends with a wholesome ranch girl who resembles Judy Garland in *The Wizard of Oz.* Bigfoot's special abilities include roaring, jumping great distances in slow motion, and super-strength.

The typical Bigfoot adventure involves battling evil, misguided scientists who dabble in Secrets Man Was Not Meant To Know™, or supernatural beings intent on plundering the Earth's resources. Also in most episodes, our heroes get trapped in the same cave, in an accident using the same avalanche footage, and are left to suffocate until next week's continuing episode, at which point Bigfoot remembers that he's, like, real strong and can knock enough boulders loose to make a way out of the cave.

Thanks, Andrew.

There were other less interesting Krofft shows, like *The Lost Saucer* (featuring Jim Nabors and Ruth Buzzi in a nearly lethal combination) or the aforementioned "Wonderbug." We should probably move on and close with a discussion of the memorable 1975 series *Far Out Space Nuts,* which starred Bob Denver and Chuck McCann as two marooned NASA workers. In the opening credit sequence, we find that the two lead characters were sent into space by accident

Three Krofft Haiku

After Nickelodeon aired its "Puffapalooza" marathon of some Sid and Marty Krofft shows, the Internet was buzzing with Saturday morning veterans whose memories had been awakened. R. Noyes, using the cybernym "TV's Spatch," posted some haiku inspired by the event to the Usenet newsgroup alt.society.generation-x, haiku that can still be found on his Web pages. He gave us permission to reprint some of them, so we thought we'd share these brilliant little gems with the nonwired world.

H. R. PUFNSTUF

H. R. Pufnstuf
He's your friend when things get rough
His head scares me, though

LAND OF THE LOST

Marshall, Will and Holly
Must fight the evil Sleestaks
Why not kill Chaka?

ELECTRA-WOMAN AND DYNAGIRL

Viva la Spandex!
Wonder why I feel funny
Watching Deidre Hall.

while loading food into a NASA rocket. Bob "Gilligan for the Rest of His Life" Denver accidentally pressed a launch button in the rocket, prompting his partner to roar "I said *lunch,* not *launch!*" Somehow ignoring the fact that NASA doesn't usually equip its rockets with faster-than-light drive (sheesh, at least Moonbase Alpha needed a nuclear explosion to start zooming through the universe), the two Earthmen found themselves landing in a distant star-system, where they adopted a pet named Honk, named, in the Kroffts' typically literal style, for the big car horn protruding from its face. Over the course of the series, Honk and his dumb Earthmen pals found themselves landing on various alien planets, getting hassled by the local weirdos, and searching for a way to escape their ~~uncharted desert isle~~, uh, make that lost-in-space sort of predicament. No doubt you're thinking, so *that's* where the producers of *Star Trek: Voyager* got the idea for their series. It's only an homage, we're sure.

By the late seventies, Krofft shows, which were always more expensive than their cartoon equivalents, trickled to a halt. The Kroffts did try again eventually, with the kidvid program *The New Land of the Lost* and their terrifyingly weak knockoff of the British puppet satire *Spitting Image,* entitled *D.C. Follies,* airing from 1987 to 1989. The Cartoon Network is keeping a lot of the good—and bad—output of Hanna-Barbera in circulation so that future generations will know what we speak of when we talk about *Scooby-Doo* or *Space Ghost.* But tomorrow's kids may never know the mind-numbing pleasure of the Kroffts' oeuvre unless some quick-minded television executive sees fit to rush their material into syndication. If and when this happens, we're not sure if tomorrow's kids will damn us or praise us for passing this twisted legacy on to them, but members of the Liberace fan club will doubtless thank us for reviving the most enchanting performances of Charles Nelson Reilly and Rip Taylor.

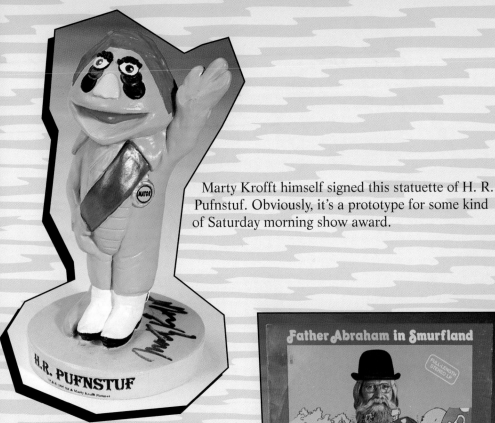

Marty Krofft himself signed this statuette of H. R. Pufnstuf. Obviously, it's a prototype for some kind of Saturday morning show award.

This record jacket presents a mystery. Is Father Abraham an Orthodox rabbi or a funky Bavarian padre? Is Father Abraham actually Gargamel in disguise? As if the cover itself weren't enough, there's the confusing chorus to track number 3, which is entitled "Smurfing Beer."

Ren & Stimpy creator John Kricfalusi produced this amusing cereal-box parody as a free gift to anyone purchasing a Spumco "Paint by Numbers" set.

The best part of
this game is screaming "Captain
Caeaeaeave Maaaan!" real loud when you win.

Another Krofft board game that's
more fun to look at than to play.

These should have been called
"Iron-Offs" since they generally
washed off a shirt after a few
laundry cycles.

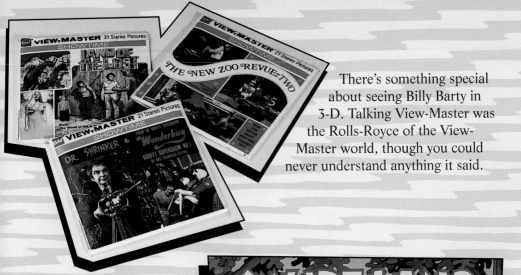

There's something special about seeing Billy Barty in 3-D. Talking View-Master was the Rolls-Royce of the View-Master world, though you could never understand anything it said.

Smurf Colorform sets allow you to stage very Smurfy versions of the Jim Jones Guyana massacre and the Donner Party's party.

Yes, kids could finally satisfy Gargamel's evil culinary urges by baking Smurfette at 350 degrees.

With this dandy little machine, as well as the Fisher-Price Movie Viewer, you could watch your favorite shows on 8mm. You could play them forward, backward, in slow-mo, or superfast. This particular one came with a nifty *Josie and the Pussycats in Outer Space* cassette.

It's surely a good thing that he wasn't "Inch High, Private Dick."

The "other" Scooby-Doo wasn't quite popular enough to get its own lunch box. It had to be bundled with another show.

This box could make anyone the number one super guy at school.

The box for *The Krofft Supershow* always gets a reaction when Kevin carries his lunch to work in it.

Future Trivial Pursuit question: Mr. T introduces a Saturday morning lineup.

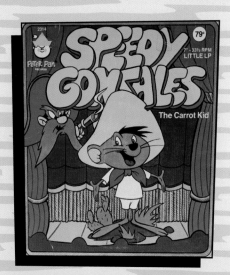

"Arriba this, yanqui imperialist."

Yet another tantalizing comic book preview of an upcoming Saturday morning season.

Look out for the eagerly anticipated second album from Father Abraham and the Smurfs containing the hit single, "Smurfing DUI."

Let's see Deep Blue win this!

More Krofft iron-ons.

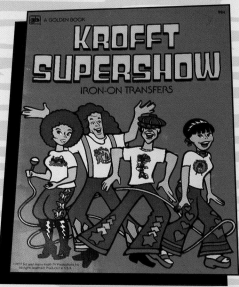

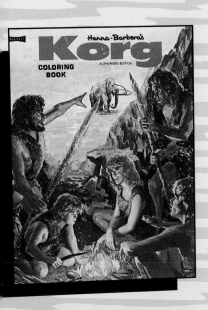

Sorry, kids—no drawings of Raquel Welch.

Sleestak beauty tips inside!

Number one Crayola guy.

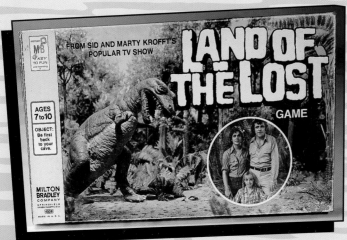

Grumpy decapitates
Chaka—lose one turn

Punishment Shows: *Davey and Goliath*

There was a class of kidvid reserved as torment for the kids who woke up too early on Saturdays, before the networks began their schedule, or worse yet, for those kids who dared venture into the cartoon netherworld that was Sunday. *Davey and Goliath* is probably the most painful example of a Punishment Show. We're not sure which was worse, the Indian-head test pattern or *Davey and Goliath.* Hell, we're not sure which would be worse: getting our heads squashed in an industrial press or watching *Davey and Goliath.* But television is a harsh mistress and the Saturday morning ritual was not for wimps. If you woke up early, called by the kidvid siren, you might just have to endure those various lame syndicated programs.

First produced in 1962 with the backing of religious leaders, *Davey and Goliath* was a sickening concoction of moralizing gibberish, full of witless piety. The show was about the escapades of a bunch of puppets, most centrally Davey, a little boy, and his mutant hellbeast dog, Goliath. (Okay, he was just a dog, but he had the disturbing habit of talking aloud to Davey.) In each episode, Davey had to deal with some minor moral conflict, along the lines of "Should I admit I threw a rock through the storekeeper's window on Halloween?" or "Am I right to hate the new kid on the block because he wears polka-dot ties all the time?" (Of course, there are the classic "lost" episodes in which Davey wondered, "Should I participate in a drive-by shooting?" and "Is cannibalism wrong?") Goliath was the omniscient interpreter, acting as Davey's conscience. Every time Davey was about to commit a sin, Goliath reminded him, in dolorous tones, "God wouldn't like that, Davey." Usually Davey didn't obey the first time, got into mild trouble, and then apologized, realizing that Goliath was right about God's wishes.

Calling the show sickly, pompous, and boring is like pointing out that cotton candy has sugar in it.

We're more than a little curious about the names of the two main characters. As far as we recall from Sunday school, Davey *killed* Goliath. Hey, maybe the show had a hidden satanic message like those backward-masked things on some music albums—maybe the creators were suggesting that Davey should overthrow Goliath's evil divine tyranny by bashing him over the head with a rock. In any event, a kid's show built around a talking dog who is apparently hearing the voice of God in his head strikes us as being just a wee bit on the creepy side. Not to mention that every adult puppet character featured on the show was straight out of the Village of the Stepford People: they made Mr. Rogers look like Pee-Wee Herman. Naturally, this was the kind of show favored by many of Saturday morning's harshest critics, which just suggests to us how infernal the world would be if they had their way. *Davey and Goliath* was bad enough when we encountered it infrequently; imagining it as the be-all and end-all of kidvid is enough to make us be afraid, be very afraid.

———

"Both *Garfield and Friends* and *Muppet Babies* (as well as other shows on Saturday morning television) create the impression that watching TV can be an empowering, humanizing interactive experience that combines watching with *playing*. . . . While such strategies can be read as merely another example of television's deceptive manipulation of young consumers, one might also argue that they encourage the kind of negotiated readings posited by Stuart Hall and the Birmingham School, where generational subgroups actively appropriate images from mass culture." —Marsha Kinder, *Playing with Power in Movies, Television, and Video Games*

———

There were many other self-consciously "educational" programs which lurked perniciously around the edges of Saturday morning. Recalling *New Zoo Revue,* for example, is sort of like a GenX version of delayed stress syndrome: you wake up in the middle of the night in a cold sweat surrounded by a giant mutant frog in a beige turtleneck sweater, a pink hippo carrying a parasol, and a guy in glasses wearing comfortable shoes playing a guitar and singing. Then the sing-along begins and before you know it, you're screaming at the top of your lungs. *New Zoo Revue* was sort of like the John the Baptist to Barney's Jesus, a prophetic warning of kidvid apocalypse. Created by Barbara Atlas and Douglas Momary, it featured a bunch of people in frightening animal suits doing wholesome things for the presumed edification and entertainment of small kids. *Revue,* we'll admit, was not strictly a phenomenon of Saturday morning. It, like *Sesame Street,* also appeared in many markets during the week.

Educational programs weren't the only evil presence at the wee hours of Saturday morning. In the seventies, a bunch of pirates, cowboys, and clowns made their desperate last stand. Having dominated kidvid in the fifties, these costumed actors had been gradually exiled to the unused backwaters of Saturday morning as the hosts of various local programs for kids. These programs were an indigestible melange of bad jokes, marginally educational segments, cartoons that no one else would show, deranged sidekicks, and live audiences of kids who usually looked like they'd just been shanghaied and enlisted as cabin boys on the HMS *Bounty.* However, these shows were better than *Davey and Goliath* because there was at least a chance they'd show a cartoon or something. And you can't completely loathe pro-

Exercise, exercise, come on, everybody, get your exercise!

The Shows Themselves

grams whose hosts had names like Ranger Hal, Sheriff John, Hobo Kelly, Captain Noah, and so on.

It also all depended on where you lived. In Los Angeles, for example, we had to cope with *That's Cat,* a half-hour educational local program hosted by Whitman Mayo, who played Grady on *Sanford and Son,* and featuring Alice Playten (who played Alice the baby-sitter on Sid and Marty Krofft's program *The Lost Saucer*). The show featured film segments about how milk is made or what happens in a factory, the kind normally inflicted on you at school in some sleep-inducing filmstrip. At the end of each episode, Alice would look directly into the camera and ask for advice on some sort of very general personal decision, like whether to burn her bra or how to whip inflation now. Cut to Whitman Mayo, who would look directly into the camera and give Alice some kind of typically geriatric advice.

Local programming of this kind died largely because live-action shows, even cheap ones, usually cost more to make than the animated shows that became widely available in the eighties through syndication. Various hosts protested their inexorable elimination, appealing to boomers who grew up on *Howdy Doody* and its ilk. But we were the audience, not the boomers, and we'd generally take *He-Man* over some salty pirate gibbering about the importance of homework and showing crappy cartoons. The few nationally syndicated shows of this sort, like *Wonderama,* survived a bit longer than many of the locally hosted programs, but we can't say that we mourn them, either. *Wonderama* was mostly a creepy viewing experience, with kids in the audience forced to come up and do jumping jacks to the tune of "Exercise, Exercise, Come On, Everybody Get Your Exercise!" Kids at home ate Fritos while watching the pasty victims from the audience perform sullen calisthenics.

Occasionally PBS kidvid would show up on Saturday morning, though it was more likely to surface in the empty spaces of Sunday. Because of their superior production values and genuinely entertaining content, such programs were always far more welcome than the terrifyingly bogus goings-on in *Davey and Goliath.* Growing up in Los Angeles, we particularly found ourselves enjoying *Villa Allegre,* a bilingual Spanish and English educational program which was strongly reminiscent of *Sesame Street.*

One other educational program which sometimes showed up on Saturday morning but was much more than a form of esoteric punishment was *Captain Kangaroo.* Bob Keeshan—the Captain—isn't necessarily our favorite person in the history of Saturday morning. He has had a habit of currying favor with parents' groups by bashing commercial kidvid while conveniently forgetting that his own program was supported by commercials, including, at one point, advertisements that he did himself during the show. (We grant that Keeshan was one of the first people in kidvid to show concern about the impact of commercials on kids, but we're cynical enough to think that had a lot to do with currying favor with kidvid critics.) The show itself, however, was often memorably entertaining, with its cast of richly imagined characters like Mr. Green Jeans and Mr. Moose. If it was on, we'd definitely watch it, sometimes even preferring it to cartoons. For that alone, Keeshan deserves our thanks. There were many times when *Captain Kangaroo* was the only raft in the painful earliest hours of Saturday morning. The good Captain helped keep you afloat until the real entertainment came on, saving you from drowning in fetid Punishment Shows with a preachy mutant hound pulling you under.

Schoolhouse Rock

Though *Schoolhouse Rock* was most assuredly an educational program—possibly the most usefully educational program ever produced for television—it was so rewarding and enjoyable an experience that it deserves to be covered entirely separate from the Punishment Shows. We've already pointed out, for example, that our entire generation knows the Preamble to the Constitution by heart due to *Schoolhouse*

The Shows Themselves   **141**

Rock. But that's not all we learned. We also discovered that nine is a naughty number, that the function of a conjunction is to be a junction, and that American women were suffering until suffrage (not to be confused with Sylvester the Cat's suffering succotash, of course).

Schoolhouse Rock was a series of animated shorts that appeared on ABC sandwiched between regular children's programming on Saturdays. The brainchild of current Disney CEO Michael Eisner, the educational shorts were, almost alone of all their breed, hugely entertaining and deeply memorable—so much so that the latest bit of successful commercial nostalgia making the rounds is a theatrical show called *Schoolhouse Rock Live!*

The shorts were divided into four types: "Grammar Rock," "Multiplication Rock," "History Rock," and "Science Rock." The grammar and multiplication segments were the best of the lot, on the whole. Each "Grammar Rock" used a musical number to describe a specific part of speech, including nouns, verbs, conjunctions, and adverbs. "Multiplication Rock" focused on single numbers and used songs to illustrate the multiplication table for that particular number. It may sound boring, but it wasn't: the songs were usually as vivid and catchy as the most memorable commercial jingles and the stylized animation kept the audience focused on the song with a good dose of visual imagination and wit. "History Rock" was a more mixed bag of tricks: the segments dealing with the workings of U.S. government were decent, but those touching on American history oversimplified things just a wee bit (one celebrated Manifest Destiny without showing any American Indians, for example, and another showed King George as a drooling syphilitic pervert rubbing his hands in fiendish glee as American tax dollars piled up under his throne). "Science Rock," oddly enough, was almost wholly forgettable: most of our contemporaries don't even remember it existed. "Science Rock" segments dealt with the functioning of the human body (including a gingerly animated sequence dealing with digestion and waste removal), forms of energy, and the solar system.

The *Schoolhouse Rock* format of short educational segments sand-wiched between regular Saturday morning programs was reproduced by several other nifty programs. One, called *In the News,* packaged news stories from the previous week into digestible little portions which were aimed at children without being condescendingly simple-minded. Another set of shorts which appeared on ABC alongside *Schoolhouse Rock* featured Timer, a little yellow blob creature with a watch who sang about health and nutrition issues. The most memo-rable of these showed kids how to make popsicles out of fruit juice and toothpicks, presumably because these would be more healthy than chocolate ice cream. Other segments suggested healthy snacks or warned kids not to "drown" their food with cheese or dressing. A different series of health-related shorts encouraged kids to practice good dental hygiene and fight off "Yuck Mouth."

Kidvid producers also tried to introduce educational segments into the body of the programs, ultimately leading to the so-called prosocial programs that dominated the eighties. These sidebars were invariably less entertaining and less educational than *Schoolhouse Rock* at its worst. The most complicated educational programming to air on Saturdays, alternating between being one of the worst exam-ples of a Punishment Show and being highly entertaining kidvid, was *The ABC Afterschool Special,* which showed both on weekdays and on Saturdays, where it was called the *ABC Weekend Special.* These varied from an entertainingly odd outing in which characters from various newspaper comic strips teamed up (unfortunately, Hagar the Horrible didn't get to put an ax through Ziggy's head) to condescend-ing kidvidized versions of the usual dreary "TV Movie of the Week," dealing with diseases, bullies, puberty, drugs, and other things we were supposed to learn how to deal with.

Schoolhouse Rock demonstrated in convincing fashion that educa-tion and entertainment are not necessarily diametrically opposed. We happen to think that kids also learn a lot from shows like *Jonny Quest*: Mr. Wizard never showed us how to build giant robotic monsters, after all. But we'd grant that there's a difference between that and learning how to multiply four by six or finding out how a bill becomes a law, lessons *Schoolhouse Rock* taught with remarkable poise. Any program that can turn the Preamble into a catchy tune deserves a place among the legends of television.

The Archies, Sabrina the Teenage Witch, The Groovie Goolies

In 1969, Las Vegas nightclubs wanted to contract the services of a pop music group called the Archies, hoping to cash in on the success of their hit song "Sugar, Sugar." They couldn't because of a small technicality: the Archies were cartoons. The Archies took the process that created the Monkees to its next logical step, going from the Prefab Four to the Fictional Five.

The Archies was one of the most dependable staples of Saturday morning, appearing for the first time in 1968 and lasting in some form or another until 1978, with a brief reappearance in the late eighties. The initial impetus for the cartoon, much as in the case of *The Monkees,* can be traced back to the Beatles—in this case, their successful 1964 cartoon incarnation. However, the characters of *The Archies* didn't just come out of the ether, but were already pop culture staples familiar to millions of Americans through comic books. As Fred Silverman put it, the cartoon version of *The Archies* came "presold with the comics." As it turns out, it also came presold with music due to the hit song "Sugar, Sugar," played by unnamed studio musicians.

The Archies had a huge influence on most subsequent Saturday morning programs in the seventies. Musical numbers sung by the band (composed of the main characters) were interspersed with the regular action. While on some later shows this had pathetically out-of-touch results, as aging executives desperately tried to appeal to the Youth of Today with that newfangled rock music, on *The Archies* it worked exceedingly well. The music was inoffensively catchy and the characters were comfortingly familiar, taken straight from the kind of comic book we read when we were on a camping trip up in the mountains somewhere because they were the only thing the local drugstore carried.

Archie Andrews, Reggie Mantle, Jughead Jones, Veronica Lodge, and Betty Cooper: they're such cultural archetypes at this point that they hardly need any further discussion. Ultimately, of course, this familiarity made the cartoon both comforting and boring. Archie was sort of like Charlie Brown as a teenager, a wimpy good kid who usually came out morally ahead in some vague manner but never quite got what he wanted, either. Reggie and Veronica were sometimes portrayed as nasty rich kids who got some mild if impermanent comeuppance, but often they were just members of the gang. (The Archie comics and the various versions of the animated program generally refrained from portraying anyone in a seriously negative light.) Betty was the good girl, like Mary Ann on *Gilligan's Island.* Jughead was the only character we still really like: he was a sort of sardonic protoslacker, the spiritual father of Jeff Spicoli.

Far more interesting than the various shows devoted to the Archies themselves were the spin-off programs they generated. Following a tradition begun in 1930s cinema, when various Universal movie monsters like Frankenstein and the Wolf Man appeared in each other's films, television in the sixties and seventies delighted in programs which put all the classic monsters together in a single setting, in part because kids eagerly flocked to see such team-ups. This became almost a stock plot device on sixties television, serving as the basis for *The Munsters* and *The Addams Family.* It also became a staple on Saturday morning from the seventies onward, appearing in shows like the live-action *Monster Squad* and the animated *Drak Pack,* as well as a one-shot Rankin-Bass special with monster puppets called *Mad Monster Party* that was often shown on Saturday afternoons. The most memorable Saturday morning monster team-up show, however, was a spin-off from *The Archies* called *The Groovie Goolies*. Actually, it was a two-for-one spin-off, since the Goolies were originally coupled with Sabrina, the Teenage Witch, who also eventually got her own animated program (and reappeared in the fall of 1996 in a prime-time live-action show).

The theme would sing out, "It's time for the Goolies get-together" and then famous horror characters Dracula, Frankenstein, the Mummy, and the Wolf Man would go cruising through Horrible Hall with an Archie-fied appearance. The show tossed together musical numbers, short tales, and little filler bits modeled on *Laugh-In* in a somewhat appealing mix. Horrible Hall was inhabited by a nest of hangers-on including Lovesick Loveseat (a small sofa with the hots for Drak), Hagatha (Drak's chubby witch-bride), Bella La Ghostly (Horrible Hall's switchboard operator), the skeletal Bonapart, and his pal the Mummy. Between bland surf tunes, the hep horrors would spew endless one-liners followed by one of the most ridiculously overenthusiastic laugh tracks in the history of Saturday morning. Sabrina was also part of the happening scene at Horrible Hall, but she had an independent appeal and was often found at Riverdale High doing vaguely amusing teenlike things with the rest of the Archie cast. Actually, because Sabrina wasn't involved in the whole "which girl does Archie really lust after" shenanigans, she was a more interesting character than either Veronica or Betty.

On all three shows, episodes were indistinguishable. Only the characters and the general feel of the show are really memorable to-day, but Archie, Jughead, Sabrina, and the whole Riverdale High gang have oozed into pop culture. Everywhere there's a teen hanging out at the drugstore sipping ice-cream sodas, everywhere two girls are inches away from a massive catfight over some geekwad boy, everywhere teenage angst means nothing more than figuring out how to explain to a boy you like that your relatives are hideous creatures of the night, everywhere kids drop spontaneously into inoffensive pop numbers at the drop of a hat, Archie will be there.

Hanna-Barbera Potpourri: *The Wacky Races, The Perils of Penelope Pitstop, Dastardly and Muttley, Laff-A-Lympics, Yogi's Gang, Yogi's Space Race*

We haven't talked much about various Hanna-Barbera characters like Snagglepuss and Yogi Bear. This is partly because we find them a bit boring, because they were more a fixture of afternoon programming than Saturday morning schedules when we were kids, and mostly because some Saturday morning shows provide us an opportunity to discuss them all at once.

Hanna-Barbera recycled previously used formulas adeptly. One of the most popular of these was the "potpourri" program, which assembled a huge cast of characters and involved them in some kind of repetitive activity like racing, general sports competition, or cleaning up the environment.

The original Hanna-Barbera potpourri was a show called *The Wacky Races,* which premiered in 1968 and ran until 1970. If you've seen one episode, you've seen them all, since they rigidly followed the same plot each time: a whole bunch of animated "theme" automobiles raced across the planet amid manic antics. There was a log-car driven by a lumberjack and a beaver, a spooky-mansion car driven by monsters, an Appalachian backporch car driven by hillbilly

bears, a car with a big engine driven by some strapping young stud, a dainty pink car driven by Penelope Pitstop, a roadster driven by the Ant Hill Mob, and so on.

Each episode followed the recipe: first one car was ahead, then the other, various cars would use their special tricks to catch up, and so on. The straw that stirred the drink was the duo of Dastardly and Muttley, who drove a big black car with a rocket on the end. All the drivers were trying to beat each other, but Dick Dastardly, an absolutely archetypal wax-mustache-and-beady-eyes villain, would habitually cheat. This being Saturday morning, his cheating always failed and left him in the dust, whereupon Muttley, his dog, would let loose with his characteristic snicker. Even when Saturday morning veterans remember nothing else about *The Wacky Races,* they tend to remember Muttley and his snicker.

Hanna-Barbera made a spin-off series entitled *Dastardly and Muttley* which featured these two characters as part of a squad of villainous World War I flying aces who flew a single four-seater plane. (The other two pilots had weird speech impediments as their character shtick.) The pilots were given the job of stopping a heroic carrier pigeon, and just as in *The Wacky Races,* the same plot was repeated ad nauseam. The pilots would go up, try to "stop that pigeon!" and then suffer a mishap of some kind. It was basically the Coyote and the Road Runner, but not nearly as clever visually.

Another *Wacky Races* spin-off, *The Perils of Penelope Pitstop,* differed a bit. In fact, it was one of the weirder shows ever to appear on Saturday morning, a combination of the old serial *The Perils of Pauline* and Snow White. It took the characters of Penelope Pitstop and the Ant Hill Mob from *The Wacky Races* and made the Ant Hill Mob—seven dwarves in twenties-style suits—her protectors. She ended up needing a lot of protection, since she was pursued by her evil guardian, Sylvester Sneekly, who perpetually ensnared her in death traps while disguised as the villainous Hooded Claw. (The Hooded Claw's voice was done by Paul Lynde, who gave him the perfect sneering tone.) The Ant Hill Mob was always riding to her rescue, though she usually managed to extricate herself by the time they got there. The death traps were Rube Goldberg devices: the Hooded Claw spent about as much time setting up each elaborate scheme as he did actually attempting to eliminate Penelope. There was also a strange undercurrent to the whole thing, since Penelope spent large proportions of each episode tied up or otherwise in bondage.

The general format proved a successful way to make use of Hanna-Barbera's large reservoir of spare and somewhat interchangeable characters. A slight variation on the potpourri format was pursued in the 1973 series *Yogi's Gang,* which took all the Hanna-Barbera funny-animal characters, from the Big Three of Yogi, Huckleberry Hound, and Quickdraw McGraw to total third-rate losers like Wally Gator, Magilla Gorilla, and Squiggly the Octopus, and put them all on a flying ark. The premise for the show was that Jellystone Park had become too polluted, so Yogi rounded up every cartoon beastie he could find to go off and fight various and sundry cartoon polluters. We found the crying Indian and Woodsy the Owl more effective ways to campaign for the environment. Anyway, eventually Captain Planet came along and filed an injunction against them for regulatory ineptitude and Yogi and his pals went back to swilling beer and ripping off picnic baskets in a dioxin-filled national park somewhere . . .

. . . Until Hanna-Barbera had need of them again for a potpourri show. In 1977, the studio produced *Scooby's All-Star Laff-A-Lympics,* which pitted three teams against each other: the Yogi-Yahooeys, consisting of funny-animal characters like Yogi, Boo Boo, Huckleberry Hound, and Quickdraw McGraw; the Scooby-Doobys, consisting of Scooby and his pals plus the Blue Falcon and Dyno-mutt; and the Really Rottens, consisting of a renamed Dick Dastardly and Muttley and various other bad guys. Snagglepuss and Mildew (an obscure wolf character voiced by Paul Lynde) served as the announcers. The teams raced against each other in a variety of events in various settings, and it was generally a colossal bore, particularly because none of these cartoon characters had the entertaining jiggle-tude that live actresses displayed on the show's prime-time counterpart, *Battle of the Network Stars.* Boo Boo ain't much to talk about as far as wet T-shirts go. The same setup was followed in the 1978 show *Yogi's Space Race,* except the setting was outer space.

We suppose that for anyone who really loved Hanna-Barbera's various late-fifties animal characters, these shows were sort of the ultimate team-up. As far as we're concerned, most of those characters were interchangeable: putting twenty of them together on one show was like Dawn of the Stepford Cartoons. As for the basic format, whether it was *The Wacky Races* or *The Laff-A-Lympics,* it was mildly amusing to see once, and past that, it was much more enjoyable to pull out a couple of Hot Wheels and stage your own imaginary races.

I Am Not a Man, I Am an Animal: *Hong Kong Phooey; Underdog; Lancelot Link; Secret Chimp; Secret Squirrel; Atom Ant; Dynomutt; Mighty Man and Yukk; The Secret Lives of Waldo Kitty*

As we said, we're not too fond of Hanna-Barbera's generic animal characters, whether they're on their own or racing each other in freaky sports contests. But there is another species of Saturday morning creature that we often liked a lot more: hybrid animal superheroes.

The kings of this genre were clearly *Hong Kong Phooey* and *Underdog.* From a quick viewing, you might be hard-pressed to figure out why *Hong Kong Phooey* is such an object of cult worship among Saturday morning veterans. It looks at first like pedestrian Hanna-Barbera fare, the adventures of an inept superheroic cartoon dog and his cat assistant. Part of the secret is simply repeated exposure: the original episodes were recycled three times during the seventies. Much of it was the totally bitching theme song, one of the all-time Saturday morning greats. More of it was Scatman Crothers's warm and humorous performance as Hong Kong Phooey's voice. And don't forget that the show appeared in the middle of a major cultural craze for Asian martial arts, when everybody was kung fu fighting. And then it turns out the show sported genuinely funny writing, ranging from gags centered on Phooey's secret identity as a janitor in a police station to his use of a book of marital arts instructions in the middle of a fight with a supervillain.

Underdog also spoofed superheroic adventure with a canine protagonist, though in this case the central reference point was clearly the Superman mythos. (Underdog's secret identity was a mild-mannered shoeshine boy in love with Polly Purebred, a TV reporter.) It was a different kind of show than *Hong Kong Phooey,* though: the jokes often involved wordplay or subtle references to the grown-up world. Underdog himself habitually spoke in rhymes, sometimes faced considerable difficulties in finding a suitable phone booth in which to change into his costume, and faced regular adversaries like Riff Raff and the cleverly named Simon bar Sinister. Small wonder that many Saturday morning veterans habitually mistook the program for one of Jay Ward's shows, since it both looked and sounded like *The Bullwinkle Show* at times. It was actually produced by Total Television, whose other clever animated programs included *Tennessee Tuxedo* and "The World of Commander McBragg." (They also made a program called *Go-Go Gophers* that was pretty rigorously unamusing, as well as grievously politically incorrect by contemporary standards.)

———

"Not plane, nor bird nor even frog, it's just little ole me, Underdog!"
—Underdog

———

A third cult favorite in this category was actually a live-action show starring a bunch of apes called *Lancelot Link, Secret Chimp.* It only aired for two years, from 1970 to 1972, and as far as we know, has never appeared since. It was a spoof of James Bond/Man from U.N.C.L.E.–style spy adventures using a bunch of chimps and an orangutan. Now, mind you, this was back when television producers still thought the very sight of chimpanzees was inherently hilarious, with the memory of J. Fred Muggs hovering somewhere in the background. So you'd think *Lancelot Link* probably would have been no more than some routine monkey business. In actuality, the writing was funny. Even with human actors, it would have been fairly amusing, and in fact it was, since some of the writers for *Lancelot Link* also worked on *Get Smart.* There were a lot of excruciating but amusing puns: Lancelot worked for Commander Darwin and his sexy chimp partner was Mata Hairi, for example.

Then again, spy parody wasn't exactly much of a reach in the late sixties and seventies, on Saturday morning, on television generally, or even in the movies. It was everywhere. Which means, of course, that Hanna-Barbera had their own spy parody: they didn't often miss the opportunity to hop on a passing trend. Their best funny-animal superhero/spy character, Secret Squirrel, predated *Lancelot Link* by several years. *Secret Squirrel* could get pretty amusing, particularly because of the title character's assistant, Morocco Mole, a dumpy little guy with a fez and dark glasses. The gags on this show were nevertheless the standard spy-gadget-in-the-shoe sort of thing. Secret Squirrel was paired with another mid-sixties Hanna-Barbera creation, Atom Ant, who was a superstrong ant wearing a football helmet, and about whom little need be said: he was a one-joke character.

However, by comparison to some late–seventies Hanna-Barbera animal superheroes, both Secret Squirrel and Atom Ant were pretty watchable. One of these later characters was a malfunctioning robot dog named Dynomutt who was paired with a human superhero called Blue Falcon. (Blue Falcon, or BF as Dynomutt called him, was basically Birdman in a new outfit.) We suppose there's someone somewhere who found Dynomutt's repeated bumblings amusing, but as far as we're concerned, we could never figure out why the Blue Falcon didn't just trade him in for a used Batmobile or use him as a shield from gunfire. *Mighty Man and Yukk* was an even slimmer premise, showcasing the adventures of a generic human superhero who could shrink and his dog sidekick, whose main gimmick was—get this—that he was so ugly that no one could stand to look at him. (He went around with a doghouse on his head.) Nurse, urgent imagination transfusion needed over here!

One funny-animal show that wasn't lacking in imagination was *The Secret Lives of Waldo Kitty*. In fact, its central theme was imagination. *Waldo Kitty,* which aired in the late seventies, took its inspiration from James Thurber's famous character Walter Mitty and followed a cat's heroic daydreams, much like the current live-action series *Wishbone* does with a dog. What made the show such a special treat was its adroit parodies of various pop culture staples like Tarzan, Batman, *Star Trek,* and Robin Hood. For many of us, Waldo was the first version of the meek daydreamer we ever encountered: the Thurber version came later. And there's no more perfect a character for kids to empathize with than a shy dreamer who lives out a thousand adventures in his or her head. *Waldo Kitty* perfectly illustrated the cardinal rule of funny-animal superheroes: it wasn't enough just to give an animal some superpowers and expect kids to lap it up. We had to relate to the animal as a person.

Filmation Live Action: *Ark II, Shazam!, Isis, The Ghost Busters, Space Academy*

It is nearing the noon hour. There's a buzzing in your head and your mouth feels pasty. Your eyes are about to drip out of their sockets. The air is bright and shiny: no matter how hard you've tried to keep the searing sun out of the room, you can't stay in the soothing darkness. You've already had to throw at least three temper tantrums to keep your mother from making you go out. Bugs Bunny has been over for what feels like a lifetime. *Soul Train* and football players are beginning to dominate the television. What do you do? What *do* you do? Will you cave in and play outside? Read a book? Clean your room? Get started on homework for Monday?

Nope, not if you're a true and loyal scion of Saturday morning. You figure if you hang out a little longer your ship will come in.

Or maybe it'll be an ark. Well, not exactly an ark. More like a Winnebago. Well, actually like two Winnebagos sewn together with some cheap nylon, thus becoming an allegedly futuristic "super vehicle" that some teenage scientists and a talking chimp in spandex uniforms drove around in while trying to rebuild a postapocalyptic world full of mutants. Yeah, that's the ticket. Nothing like a talking chimp and some mutants to keep you afloat during a long morning's journey into afternoon.

Filmation's *Ark II* featured the characters Jonah, Ruth, Samuel, and Adam the talking chimp as "scientists" repairing a world ravaged by world war and ecological disaster. As in many cheap seventies programs, the postapocalypse world looked remarkably like the foothills of Southern California. Man, those California live oaks sure looked like futuristic radioactive mutant plants to us! Unless, of course, the same outdoor set was functioning as the Planet of the Apes or another alien world, when those trees looked like the kind of freaky alien plants we would expect in those environments. Occasionally, the same landscape also got to be a tropical jungle in *The Six Million Dollar Man,* so we think it ought to win some kind of Academy Award for best performance by an outdoor environment.

After Sid and Marty Krofft Productions, Filmation was the biggest producer of live-action Saturday morning programming, providing numerous shows like *Ark II,* all of which aired at the tail end of Saturday kidvid schedules. After the success of the early Krofft shows, Filmation responded to the networks' call for more live action by introducing *Shazam!* on CBS. Based on the venerable comics character Captain Marvel, the show focused on a young man named Billy Batson who could yell the word "Shazam!" and become endowed with the strengths and powers of ancient heroes and gods. Unlike in the comics, where Billy was a young boy who worked as a radio announcer, the older television Billy traveled around in a Winnebago with a feeble old dude who dispensed appropriately geriatric wisdom and got taken hostage every once in a while just for a spot of variety. (Filmation seems to have had a bit of a Winnebago fetish, given how often they featured in their shows.)

Shazam! ran for one season before it was joined in 1975 by *Isis* to make the *Shazam!/Isis Hour.* Isis, like many superheroines, started off as a female version of a male counterpart: when she cried out "O Mighty Isis," she transformed into a sort of ancient Egyptian-style heroine. Both Isis and Shazam spent most of their time figuring out how to stop criminals—usually misguided souls who could be reformed—without hurting them. Isis actually turned out to be a more interesting character, though: her alter ego was a high school teacher, which in combination with the Egyptian trappings sometimes gave the show a bit more character than the fairly lifeless *Shazam!* (Isis stayed on the air when *Shazam!* was canceled, so we guess kids at the time agreed with our assessment.)

Both shows were vastly superior to the terrifyingly painful Filmation program *The Ghost Busters,* not to be confused with the later cartoon *The Real Ghostbusters* or the movie *Ghostbusters,* though it was the legal basis for the later cartoon *The Ghostbusters,* a tangle of titles which conclusively demonstrates that intellectual property lawyers are a low species of life. Starring Larry Storch and Forrest Tucker—a pair of actors who make Bob Denver and Allan Hale look like Laurence Olivier and Robert De Niro—and a guy named Bob Burns dressed in a really, really bad ape costume with a beanie on top, the show featured the adventures (if we can generously call them that) of a team of ghost-eradicators. *The Ghost Busters* mostly triumphed through repetitious idiocy. For example, in every single episode, Tracy the gorilla would have to go pick up some ordinary everyday object—say a tuba or something—and then the Ghost Busters would receive a message about their next case from the object, à la *Mission: Impossible.* Invariably, at the end of the message the voice would say, "This message will self-destruct in . . . five . . . four . . . three . . . two . . . one." The gorilla would give a big *que será será* shrug and begin counting down from five on his fingers with the message. Then he would be caught in an explosion and usually end up with the tuba (or whatever) wrapped around his neck.

Oh well, at least he was the best monkey for the job. Filmation executive Lou Scheimer told us, "On *Ghost Busters,* when we auditioned for the role of the gorilla, we didn't have a very large budget so our casting call was for actors who already had their own gorilla suits. On the morning of our casting call, I knew I had found the right actor when I found a gorilla sitting in our waiting room reading a copy of *Variety.*" At least the gorilla had a magazine to read while enduring the ordeal of filming the show.

Later Filmation live-action programs eventually moved into outer space, around the same time that *Star Wars* appeared. The first of these was a program called *Space Academy,* which premiered in late 1977 at 11:30 on CBS and ran for two years. Set in the year 3732, the Academy was a training school for "teenage space explorers" like Laura, Paul, and Chris, taught by a three-hundred-year-old alien dude named "Gampu," which sounds more like the name of a futuristic space disease to us. More importantly, we're a little concerned about the abundance of teenagers in the distant future as envisioned generally on Saturday morning. The final frontier isn't space, apparently: it's angst and pimples. *Space Academy* was canceled in 1979 but not before it spawned another "space show," *Jason of Star Command,* which had originally appeared as a segment in the mostly animated program *Tarzan and the Super 7.* James Doohan, painfully illustrating the dangers of being typecast, found himself playing the commander of—you guessed it—teenage space cadets. We're pretty sure he was wishing someone would beam him up and away from future cheesy sci-fi stuff. Our contemporaries primarily remember the villain from *Jason,* Dragos. He actually was mildly threatening, a swarthily piratical sort of fellow sporting a glowing mechanical eye on one side of his head who looked like he might have been at home on the television show *Buck Rogers.*

Many of these Filmation shows were repackaged and sent to the eternal void of what our brother Brendan calls Sunday Sickness Time, along with locally hosted Punishment Shows, *The Little Rascals,* and endless episodes of *The Three Stooges.* Unlike the Krofft shows, Filmation live-action programs don't have much enduring appeal. They just weren't deranged enough. For the most part, these programs are memorable merely because they represented the boundary between the experience of Saturday morning and the return to a normal kid life for the rest of the day. Once Dragos was sneering at teenage space pilots or Adam the talking chimp was cruising around postapocalyptic Southern California looking for a friendly mutant or two, you knew the end was nigh.

Bare-Chested Barbarians:
Thundarr, Tarzan, He-Man

It's one thing for the end of the world to look like a sunny day at Vasquez Rocks or Bronson Canyon, and something else altogether for it to resemble the world of *Thundarr the Barbarian.* If it's going to turn out like it does in *Thundarr,* then make out our tickets for the apocalypse. *Thundarr*'s Earth, having barely survived the close pass of a comet, brimmed with sorcery, evil masterminds, ruined cities, and ferocious mutants, all under the light of a crumbled Moon.

———

"Television has become a school for violence. In this school young people are never, literally never, taught that violence is in itself reprehensible. The lesson they do get is that violence is the great adventure and the sure solution, and he who is best at it wins." —Dr. Frederick Wertham

———

Thundarr himself was your run-of-the-mill half-naked deep-voiced barbarian with a magical sword, but his pal Ookla the Mok was one of the more memorable adventure heroes to appear on Saturday morning. Ookla was a big mutant something-or-other, a combination of a Wookie and a lion, and he rode an economy-sized mutant horse to match. They were joined by the sorceress Ariel, who was clearly getting it on with Thundarr, on a series of adventures across the ruined Earth. Produced by Ruby-Spears Enterprises, *Thundarr the Barbarian* ran from 1980 to 1984 and was remarkable not only for its exciting stories and interesting visuals but also because it represented the slow return of the weirdo superhero from seventies exile. Appropriately, Alex Toth assisted with the show's visual design, but the main artistic work was done by the great comic-book artist Jack Kirby.

Thundarr clearly drew on all sorts of cultural sources, ranging from the DC comic book *Kamandi* to the classic Robert E. Howard fantasy hero Conan the Barbarian. The title character wielded a Sun Sword, a kind of lightsaber, which one might expect would neatly cleave any evil mutant in two. This being Saturday morning, it usually just knocked them down or otherwise defeated them bloodlessly. The same bloodlessness applied to Ookla, who specialized in hurling bad guys off the edge of the screen, and to Ariel, who used magic ray beams and shields to defeat her foes. They didn't face a single recurring nemesis, but some of their enemies were impressive, particularly an evil mutant sorcerer with two faces. Kirby's work on the show gave both the protagonists and their adversaries the kind of visual heft that Saturday action-adventure lacked through most of the seventies.

An even earlier program which also helped bring action-adventure back from its semiexile was the animated version of *Tarzan* made by Filmation, which appeared in various formats between 1976 and 1982. It was distinguished partly by astonishingly cheap limited animation, far worse than the Saturday morning norm: each episode repeatedly featured the same shots of Tarzan running, jumping, landing, and looking stoically masculine. Somewhere in the middle of all that, however, it managed to evoke faithfully the feel of the original Edgar Rice Burroughs novels, particularly the later ones. Tarzan came across lost cities, races of beast-men, bitchy evil queens, nasty white hunters looking for elephants' graveyards, and so on with great regularity, accompanied by his hip little monkey pal Nkima and summoning the beasts of the jungle whenever he needed help. As with *Thundarr,* the imagination that went into depicting Tarzan's surroundings often made up for the weak animation and good but sketchily executed story lines. The relative success of *Tarzan* led Filmation to develop an animated version of *Flash Gordon,* which aired from 1979 to 1980 and again from 1982 to 1983. Like *Tarzan,* Filmation's *Flash Gordon* was surprisingly faithful to its source material, with good scripting and brutal cannibalization of the actual animation.

This is a lesson which was carried over into one of the biggest successes of the eighties, *He-Man and the Masters of the Universe.* (We were surprised to find out that only about two and a half seasons of *He-Man* were completed, but the show ran in syndication for five or six years. Its impact far outstripped the actual number of episodes produced.) Though not technically a Saturday morning cartoon—it aired mostly on afternoons—it nevertheless had a huge influence on subsequent Saturday morning programs. He-Man could have been Thundarr's cousin: they both had massive chests and liked to go running around in nothing but their shorts, they both were fond of deep-voiced declarations like "I have the *power!*" and they both wielded magical swords which somehow never actually did any damage to anyone. (And they both looked like they could be sons of Tandor from *The Herculoids.*)

He-Man lived on the planet of Eternia, which was a mixed sword-and-sorcery and sci-fi setting. The show was always a mélange of interesting elements like the supreme bad guy, Skeletor, who was definitely one of kidvid's most ominous villains ever, and painfully dumb stuff, like He-Man's "secret identity," Prince Adam. Unlike Clark Kent, Prince Adam didn't even put on a pair of glasses or comb his hair differently. It was occasionally implied that his mother, Queen Marlena, knew who he really was, but honestly, anyone who couldn't figure out the secret was in need of emergency brain surgery. He-Man's allies were an interesting bunch, though the oddly literal nomenclature of Eternia stuck them with dopey handles like Man-at-Arms and Battlecat. In other episodes, viewers encountered equally literally named characters like Sticky Fingers, Strongarm, Ram Man, Trap Jaw, and Roboto. We're not sure why some people on Eternia had relatively normal names like Teela, Marlena, and Randor, nor do we know why they didn't go all the way and have characters like Heaving Bosom, Tall Guy, and Fallen Arches. However, the only character we really couldn't stand was Orko, a little floating Smurf-like wizard whose "comic relief" mostly served as grating annoyance. Episodes varied in quality, with some major stinkers, but a few, particularly "Teela's Quest," which developed the mysterious backstory of He-Man's pal Teela (her mother was the enigmatic Sorceress, who was bound not to reveal the secret of her relationship to Teela), were very well written.

He-Man's spin-off show, *She-Ra: Princess of Power*, was intended for girls—she was the Xena of the eighties—but quite a few boys watched as well. It was also set on Eternia, but She-Ra had to deal with a different villain, Hordak, who was—to be honest—kind of a geek. Otherwise, the show was very similar to *He-Man* in its overall tone, with some self-consciously "female" touches thrown in. She-Ra was much more likely to rehabilitate or outwit her foes, for example.

Both shows also stuck preachy morals on the ends of episodes, largely to get kidvid critics off their backs: the morals were actually delivered in more or less literal form, and never got any deeper than "Learn from others" or "Don't judge a book by its cover." In some cases, the morals actively contradicted the events of the episode. In "Like Father, Like Daughter," Teela finds a loophole in her father's order not to follow him and He-Man—and manages to save her father and He-Man as a result. The moral of the episode, according to

the conclusion? "Obey Your Parents." Huh? Morals were the price you had to pay for action-adventure in the eighties. More recent "weirdo superhero" programs like the latest version of *Batman* and Disney's *Gargoyles* take far more subtle tacks, thankfully.

Something Cute This Way Comes: *Smurfs, Monchhichis, Snorks, The Biskitts, The Care Bears Family, The Littles*

Praise the Lord and pass the insulin! We're talking here about a group of shows from the eighties that can induce a diabetic coma at forty paces. Furry, fuzzy, cute, or otherwise unpleasantly wholesome, these creatures left a trail of sweetness oozing behind them as they went on their merry way through Saturday morning, sickly-sugary enough to make Chocolate Cookie Crisp seem like Spoon-Size Shredded Wheat.

The key show here is *Smurfs*. As we noted in chapter 3, this show's impressive ratings following its debut in 1981 helped make NBC a dominant force on Saturday morning. *Smurfs* was adapted from a Belgian comic strip by Peyo Culliford that was created in 1958. By the time Fred Silverman encountered the Smurfs in the late

1970s, they had become a pop culture fixture across Europe and Smurf dolls had just started to appear in the United States.

Smurfs are little blue elflike things with a painfully cheery disposition and an unfortunate tendency to frolic about, singing happy little songs. Smurfs were not independent autonomous individuals, but instead were specialized units of a greater Smurf whole, like army ants. There was "Handy Smurf," who took care of all the building and repairing in the village, "Vanity Smurf," who was only concerned with the image of Smurf, "Brainy Smurf," who was responsible for endless pontificating and number crunching, and so on. There were two exceptions: the implicit leader of the village (and the only Smurf with facial hair) was Papa Smurf, who looked like a smurfy Hemingway. And there was one female Smurf, Smurfette, who was originally created by Gargamel. (There was also a character named Grandpa Smurf, but he only appeared briefly.) Both Smurf fans and Smurf haters have wondered what this suggests about Smurf sexuality. Our theory is that Papa Smurf retired to some hidden inner chamber every once in a while and produced some new specialized Smurf through asexual budding, but there's no way to be sure. The characters in the movie *Slacker* are right: the Smurf hive-mind is pretty chilling once you look at it closely. Smurfs had other irritating habits, like using their own names as an all-purpose verb, noun, and adjective. A typical Smurf utterance might go something like this: "Papa Smurf is very smurfy today, he said he's going to smurf and then he'll use a smurf to smurf some more."

Life in the Smurf village would probably have been just peachy except for the repeated threat posed by Gargamel, a human sorcerer who loathed the Smurfs, and Gargamel's cat, Azrael. As far as we can tell, Gargamel's main motivation for pursuing the Smurfs was that he wanted them for some kind of magic formula or maybe just to eat. It's hard to make much sense out of Gargamel: he dressed like a peasant and hung out in a hovel, but he had all sorts of magical powers. Maybe he was humanity's last, best hope, stationed in this lonely post to fight a never-ending struggle against the Smurf menace. Without Gargamel, maybe we would have been overwhelmed by Commando Smurf, Serial Killer Smurf, or some similarly chilling Smurf mutant created by Papa Smurf. If it was just about hunger, though, then we can only hope that someone would get Gargamel some Spam or canned tuna, since everyone knows that eating blue food is always a bad idea.

A lot of kids liked *Smurfs,* and so did some of Saturday morning's most persistent critics, largely because the show was cloyingly prosocial. Smurfs always learned, by the end of the episode, that cooperation was good and rugged individuality was bad. However, *Smurfs* is also deeply loathed by many Saturday morning veterans, including us. We'll concede that the program had a more distinctive visual style than usual for Hanna-Barbera at the time, and that the vocal characterizations were well done, particularly Paul Winchell's performance as Gargamel. This is part of what made the show so annoying, in fact. At one point, *Smurfs* ran for ninety minutes, an unprecedented span of time on Saturday morning. You couldn't really avoid it, and it was just good enough in technical terms that you could watch it without suffering too greatly. But the Smurfs themselves were so malevolently cute that we kept hoping Gargamel would manage to boil them down into their component atoms.

Their most smurfy crime, however, was simply that their success spawned legions of imitators. In the eighties, Saturday morning was overwhelmed with syrupy demonspawn of various sorts. These little evil happiness creatures came in the form of brightly colored emotion leeches in ursine guise, pastel-hued underwater things with long breathing tubes, tree-dwelling mutants, and miniature dog beasts. Maybe the Smurfs even invaded the mind of George Lucas and induced him to put Ewoks in *Return of the Jedi.* Anything's possible. The Smurfs also helped insure that even action-adventure shows would have an avowedly cute character of some kind, like He-Man's irritating pal Orko. Certainly the success of many of these programs

The Shows Themselves **163**

led cartoon producers to the ultimate Saturday morning evil: the babyfication of established characters like Scooby-Doo and the Muppets.

Some of these saccharine shows, like *Snorks, Monchhichis,* and *The Biskitts,* were completely forgettable imitations of *Smurfs,* but others, like *The Care Bears Family,* achieved new heights of vomitrocious cuteness. Okay, we *know* we're being total guys here, singing the praises of macho characters like Thundarr the Barbarian while sneering at cute little things like the Care Bears that were very consciously aimed at female audiences. Maybe it's luck by design, having more to do with the noxiously sexist assumptions of kidvid producers than the real tastes of boys and girls, since many women we talked with in the course of writing this book had few fond memories of the Care Bears and their ilk.

Each Care Bear represented a particular emotion, though there weren't any Care Bears assigned to Insouciance, Lust, or Psychosis. Like empathic vampires, the Bears scoured the world for little children from whom they could suckle, operating with the cover story that they were just trying to "help" the kids learn about their emotions. The poor children were hypnotized into accepting this supposed assistance. (Any kid in full possession of his faculties would certainly have run screaming if a pastel-colored bear suddenly materialized and offered to help him feel love.) On their home ground, the Care Bears pursued a queasily authoritarian existence, living in total conformity while practicing for eventual world conquest with regular drills like "tummy symbol practice." They had a regular foe called No Heart. We were rooting for him.

Ellen Seiter argues in *Sold Separately* that preferring *The Care Bears Family* and similar programs was a rational viewing choice for little girls, given the overtly masculine bent of most other Saturday morning programming in the eighties. We agree that one of the worst aspects of mid-eighties kidvid is the extremely self-conscious division of cartoon audiences by gender, driven by the marketing logic of the toy industry rather than by past precedent on Saturday morning itself. But much of the best kidvid of the nineties has shown that this was anything but inevitable, that good kidvid can appeal to both girls and boys. There is one "cute" eighties show that demonstrated this as well, and that's *The Littles*. While undoubtedly inspired by the success of *Smurfs, The Littles* was ultimately a much better show, with independent roots in a series of children's books by John Peterson. The protagonists were a race of tiny humans who had tails and lived unseen among their larger cousins, with the exception of one teenager, who befriended and defended them. Besides the fact that the various Littles were actual *characters* (as opposed to the embodiment of emotions or some hive-mind specialization), the show managed to showcase some clever adaptation of human civilization and its tools by the Littles in almost every episode. Cute doesn't have to be repulsive, nor does it have to be gender-exclusive.

Haven't I Seen You Somewhere Before? *Star Trek, Emergency +4, Dungeons & Dragons*

Lots of Saturday morning programs were based on other television shows, movies, or other licensed properties. Most of them were massively forgettable, like *The Amazing Chan and the Chan Clan* or *The Fonz and the Happy Days Gang.* Some were actively painful, like *Hammerman* or *Gilligan's Planet.* In chapter 3, we mentioned the program *Beetlejuice,* which was among the best of these adaptations. There are three other shows that fit this category that are worth discussing.

The first was the animated *Star Trek,* made by Filmation in the early seventies, which some contemporary *Trek* fans disdain and others praise. We're in the latter camp, because we think it had some of the best writing ever on Saturday morning, though the animation was cut-rate. What made the show work more than anything else was the use of the entire original cast's voices. Even a single substitution would have ruined the mood. However, the show's producers also took ample advantage of the unique benefits of animation. In the live-action *Trek,* makeup was both expensive and unconvincing, but animated *Trek* characters could be totally alien without costing anything extra. Two crew members were therefore added to the regular mix, Lieutenants Arex and M'ress. Arex was the more impressively imagined of the two, a wizened three-armed alien with bright red skin. M'ress was a feline alien, complete with long tail and mane.

———

"I said lunch, not *launch!*" —Barney on *Far Out Space Nuts*

———

The plots also synced very well with the mood of the original series. Quite a few episodes were sequels to or otherwise directly connected with events from the original program. Again, in a few instances, the producers of the show seized the opportunity to portray events which would have been prohibitively expensive to film as live-action scripts, particularly one episode which featured Mr. Spock's return to Vulcan via time travel. In a few instances, the animated series even anticipated plot elements from *Star Trek: The Next Generation,* like the Holodeck. Debate has raged among Trekkers about whether the cartoon series can be considered "canon," that is, part of the official continuity of *Star Trek.* Gene Roddenberry apparently didn't think so, but given the wild plot inconsistencies between various components of the *Trek* franchise, it really doesn't matter whether the show was "canon" or not.[2] They had to leave *some* things out, of course. Captain Kirk didn't get to screw every vaguely female alien in the galaxy. And of course, as with *Tarzan* and other Filmation shows, the same sequences of the main characters running around stiffly and of the *Enterprise* orbiting a planet were reused

---

2. *Trek* fans even have a name for these kinds of contradictions: they call them YATI, for Yet Another Trek Inconsistency.

again and again, which made the cartoon more like the original live-action show in this particular case. As an adaptation of an existing property for Saturday morning, it was both hugely entertaining and faithful to the spirit of the original.

Emergency +4 was perhaps a little less successful in capturing the feel of its source, the live-action medical drama *Emergency!*, partly because the creators of the animated show insisted on mucking it up with the addition of four kids who were supposed to help paramedics Johnny Gage and Roy DeSoto. (And worse yet, they were accompanied by a veritable menagerie of pets—not just a cute dog but also a bird and a monkey!) Presumably kids could project themselves into the action this way, but we were doing that anyway—the prime audience for the regular *Emergency!* was kids aged two to eleven. We could identify perfectly well with Johnny and Roy, thank you very much. (The producers of the live-action show got the same stupid idea in their heads eventually and started having Johnny and Roy save increasingly large numbers of obnoxious kids in later seasons of the show.) The kids scored high on the "Marvin and Wendy Uselessness Scale": it would have been sweet to see them get zapped with the cardiac paddles week after week or quarantined after contracting Ebola. The cartoon unfortunately didn't feature the full staff at Rampart Hospital nor the whole happening scene at Station 51 with Chet, Captain Stanley, Marco, and Mike. Still, it wasn't too bad to get a double dose of *Emergency*. For once, the lessons about first aid and other helpful hints were a natural part of the cartoon. A lot of the rescues were similar to the prime-time action—including the bizarrely frequent encounters with poisonous snakes that appeared on the live-action show—making the show a palatable cartoon translation of its original inspiration.

Dungeons & Dragons was an adaptation of a different sort. Rather than taking its cues from a previously established television show or film, it was loosely based on the popular role-playing game of the same name. D&D is hard to explain to people who've never played it, but it basically entails guiding imaginary characters through a generic fantasy medieval setting, complete with sorcerers, spells, armor, sword fighting, and so on. The creators of the show chose to avoid portraying typical role-playing adventures with typical characters and instead went the Sid and Marty Krofft route, dropping a bunch of kids into an animated world they never made and then following their attempts to return home to Earth. Each kid took on the role of a particular type of D&D character, from a "cavalier" (a warrior of sorts) to a magician. They were assisted by a helpful mentor named Dungeonmaster.

Given that Dungeons & Dragons was high on the religious right's shit list, it's not surprising that the creators watered down the game, and in any event, since a typical session of D&D involved slaying numerous monsters, it would have been hard to get away with a close re-creation of the actual game on Saturday morning under any circumstances. It probably wasn't the smartest licensed property to develop for children's television, but in the end, it wasn't too terrible a show. Over time, it has developed a substantial following. The characters were retreads of earlier Saturday morning archetypes—Cavalier, for example, was more or less Reggie Mantle from *The Archies* in armor, with a touch of Alexandra. The program also suffered from a serious dose of eighties prosocial indoctrination, as each episode involved a simplistic moral delivered with a painful lack of subtlety, usually a paean to the virtues of cooperation. The actual setting was interesting enough, with lots of magic and weird creatures of various sorts, and the kids' recurring adversary, Venjor, was a sinister character, though he had a really goofy-looking lopsided head.

The charm of all three of these adaptations, as well as the later *Beetlejuice,* turns on two facts: (1) they were adapting properties which were genuinely popular with many kids, as opposed to "adaptations" of Hulk Hogan or M C Hammer, and (2) they really weren't trying very hard to "sell" the audience the property in question. *Star Trek* aired well after the live-action show had been canceled and well before *Trek* grew into the kind of commercial franchise it is today. *Emergency +4* aired simultaneously with its live-action parent, but the mainstream show hardly needed any extra promotion with children to be successful. *Dungeons & Dragons* bore almost no resemblance to its inspiration and probably never helped to sell a single copy of the game. If this is what all kidvid based on licensed properties looked like, there wouldn't be any problem with it.

Boys and Their Toys: *The Real Ghostbusters* and *G.I. Joe*

For all that members of "Generation X" scorn the label, it can get pretty ugly pretty fast if you try to tell someone who regards himself as a member that he doesn't belong. If you tell older Xers that they're really boomers, check your life insurance policy. If you tell younger Xers—those born after 1972 or so—that they're something else besides Generation X, start running the moment you finish saying it. Still, most of our approximate contemporaries recognize some internal distinctions between younger and older members of the generation, what some pundit has labeled "Atari-Wave" and "Nintendo-Wave" Xers. As far as Saturday morning goes, one real test of this internal division is the programs *The Real Ghostbusters* and *G.I. Joe.* You might call the older GenXers the "Herculoids Wave" or "Wacky Races Wave" and the Younger Xers the "Ghostbusters Wave" or "Joe Wave."

The Real Ghostbusters got a bad rap from the critics, who saw it strictly as a commercial for a line of toys. Granted, it wasn't quite as funny as the marvelous first movie, but many episodes of the cartoon definitely were funnier than the second film. (Then again, herpes simplex is funnier than the second film.) Granted, several of the characters were perilously close to offensive stereotypes, though J. Michael Straczynski, a writer and producer of the series, assured us that was more the doing of the network than it was the creative staff's intention. Yes, there were a lot of sequences thrown in to sell the toys. True, the show was saddled with that dreaded Saturday morning inevitability, the cute add-on character who mostly annoyed rather than amused (in this instance, a hungry ghost named Slimer).

All that doesn't obscure the fact that the show represented an important turning point for Saturday morning. It was the first televisual cartoon since the programs produced by Jay Ward and Total Television to display a truly *self-referential* sense of humor: its irreverent mastery of the ins and outs of various genres, ranging from horror to science fiction to children's stories, distinguished it from purely commercial toy-based programming. In the course of well over a hundred episodes, a large staff of inventive writers crafted scripts that drew on all sorts of sources and characters, including *A Christmas Carol,* Japanese monster movies, the Bigfoot legend, H. P. Lovecraft stories (*Necronomicon* and all), Sherlock Holmes, and Geraldo Rivera's live broadcast from Al Capone's secret vault. (Ooo, scary!) It also featured some of the wittiest cartoon dialogue seen on Saturday morning up to that point. The essential cleverness of the writing won the show many devoted followers: a search of the World Wide Web today will turn up a lot of fan fiction based on the series.

By contrast, *G.I. Joe* didn't have much to recommend it except for the fact that it took up time which might otherwise have had to go to something productive like homework. A syndicated show, it typically aired in the afternoons. Like *He-Man,* it was designed primarily to promote a line of toys. (However, the redesigned G.I. Joes were puny little midgets compared to the full-size muscular he-man toy of the seventies.) The Joes, a crack team of commandos, found themselves pitted week after week against the evil forces of Cobra, led by Destro (a metal-faced mad scientist) and Cobra Commander, who was eventually revealed to be a humanoid snake underneath his faceless mask.

Joe watchers repeatedly witnessed Joes and Cobras using gadgets based on the toys while battling each other, followed in almost every episode by the last-minute escape of Destro and Cobra Commander after their headquarters was blown to smithereens. No one ever died,

The Missing G.I. Joes

Neutron. Neutron comes with a tactical nuclear warhead, fired by his trusty Fission Blaster. Neutron helps you explain what really happened to all those melted Joes in your collection.

Militia. Militia comes with his own Ryder truck.

Procurement. Comes with a $500 screwdriver. Use his deadly power of Cost Overruns!

Tailhook. Cobra women, look out! Use his Action Grope Grip and speedy Double Standard Bo Stick to menace your female toys.

Chomper. Don't mess with this cannibalistic boxer! Press the button on his back and watch him try to bite off a Cobra agent's ears. Get him to attack his fellow ex-boxer Joe, Roadshow.

Talk Show. Fill him up with soapy water and then watch his amazing Rabid Spew power go to work.

despite tens of thousands of rounds of laser fire. Cobra soldiers always bailed out of exploding vehicles, escaped from crumbling buildings, or got knocked out by a punch. Cobra was back week after week and it never lost a minion. Cobra Commander, like Lex Luthor, always had an escape planned, and like the Super Friends, the Joes usually just watched him get away—and then vowed to really whup him next time. No wonder Cobra always lost: their leader spent most of the time planning his next escape.

There are other reasons why Cobra habitually lost. It is generally considered a no-no to build your secret headquarters in the shape of a twenty-story gold-colored cobra head, for example. Guess I. M. Pei was really addicted to that design in the Joe Universe. At least Cobra Commander had the presence of mind to build his soon-to-be-destroyed hideouts in remote areas of the world. (*G. I. Joe* might as well have been called *Where in the World Is Cobra Commander?* because the plot of most episodes involved the Joes searching various exotic locations for Cobra's headquarters, its agents, or a gadget of some kind.) Cobra also had the advantage of an unlimited money supply, like all mysterious secret organizations plotting to conquer the world.

On the other side of the fence, the Joes had the advantage of limitless tolerance from their government backers despite their persistent inability to finish off Cobra. The Joes all had one-note personalities. The leader was an upstanding Aryan fellow named Duke, whose character shtick was simply that he was the most stalwart Joe of them all. This trait made him the closest thing to a fully rounded personality that the show had to offer. There were a number of female Joes (and nary a Tailhook scandal in sight, though Duke did seem to have the hots for Scarlet, the most prominent female Joe). Some male Joes included Roadblock (a poor man's Muhammad Ali, complete with bad rhymes), Shipwreck (a buff sailor who looked like the old seventies toys, beard and all), and Gung Ho, who appeared to be a gay policeman in leather. Sometimes *G.I. Joe* looked more like *The Adventures of the Village People.* Cobra eventually added more individualized bad guys to its ranks as well. These ranged from a formidably silent ninja to Zartan, a pathetic shape-shifting geek who liked to brag about how he "ruled the swamps."

In battle, the Joes relied on brilliant tactics like abandoning heavily armed vehicles in order to engage in fistfights on top of rapidly moving objects or infiltrating enemy bases by strolling around in plain sight. After years of training, U.S. military leaders still can't get Navy SEALs to emulate those maneuvers successfully. Cobra had its own favorite moves. Captured Joes were always put in unguarded death traps which were conveniently close to the master control console for that particular secret base. Destro always abandoned his current invention at the end of each episode, even though it had brought his organization to the edge of world conquest. Whatever happened to Try, try again? The Joes wouldn't have won the Oscar Wilde Prize for witty repartee, either. Their battle cry—"Yo, Joe!"—was a monument to macho simplemindedness, and individual Joes never got more clever than scolding Cobra soldiers with phrases like, "Snake is sneak spelled sideways" and "Eat hot knuckle, snakeface!" Of course, Cobra's battle cry was nothing more than "Coooobra!" so even on the repartee front, the Joes won by default.

After Destro and Cobra Commander had teleported away, one of the Joes would deliver the moral of the episode. Joe morals were even less connected to the preceding story than in comparable eighties cartoons: "Remember, kids, amphibians are your friends," or "Never pour sulfuric acid on your eyeballs," that kind of thing. We think we'll follow *G.I. Joe*'s lead by tacking on a moral at the end of our impressionistic review of some of the good, bad, and ugly of Saturday morning. The only difference is, our concluding moral is a whole chapter rather than a one-liner. It's the thought that counts.

Chapter Six

Of Course You Know This Means War: A Defense of Saturday Morning

From fears about "television malocclusion" right up to the policies of Reed Hundt, the Clinton administration's head of the FCC, the same old boring stuff keeps being said about Saturday morning. As Cecilia Tichi notes in her book *Electronic Hearth,* "No aspect of the acculturation of television has remained at once so vigorous and so static as the debate over the relation of children to television."

ACT once accused children's television of five deadly sins: greed, sloth, envy, anger, and omission. We think ACT accurately captured the tone of the debate with its biblical finger-pointing. However, we are not here to bury Saturday morning—though not quite to praise it straightforwardly, either. We confess on behalf of Saturday morning to some of its sins. Here now is a plea for this sinner, and a few stones right back at its pious and prissy tormentors.

Quality

This is a real issue. We accept neither blanket dismissals of kidvid nor the increasingly common avoidance of the issue of quality in academic studies of popular culture. People who dismiss all kidvid not only arrogantly mistake their own peculiar tastes for something universal, but also display a lot of contempt for children themselves. By contrast, many current academic studies of popular culture, trying to undercut distinctions between "high" and "popular" culture, often avoid the issue of whether some works of popular culture are better than others. The possibility that "quality" is a meaningful concept is not actively denied in such accounts, but it becomes a sort of crazy old aunt locked in the attic. So we accept that some kidvid was by any measure really stinky. But we also disagree strongly with the legions of stuck-up prigs who claimed that Saturday morning as a whole was irredeemably bad.

Much of the attack on the low quality of Saturday morning conceals the real motives of many of its critics. By lodging accusations about low quality, older people seek to inflict their own particular tastes and desires, usually established by their own childhood experience with children's entertainment, upon all subsequent generations. Much contempt for Saturday morning expressed from the mid-1960s onward can ultimately be traced back to rhapsodizing about the superiority of earlier forms of children's television, or even children's radio and movie serials.

———

"Kids are kids and a blue dog is a blue dog. Nobody's going to say Huckleberry Hound is too American." —Turner Broadcasting executive David Levy, 1995

———

Take the Steven Spielberg film *Close Encounters of the Third Kind.* The suburban protagonist, Roy Neary, prefers the enchantment of Disney movies and Disneyland, but his annoying children would rather watch Saturday morning cartoons and go to Goofy Golf. Spielberg sides with Roy, eventually allowing him to discard his Disney-dissing children while flying off into space to the tune of an inverted version of "When You Wish upon a Star." Again and again this type of cultural prioritizing appears in attacks on Saturday morning, except that the critics unfortunately don't fly off into space at the end. In a 1969 article, John Culhane, a writer specializing in animation and film, said that "it is a safe bet that no cartoon on Saturday morning today is going to enchant a child the way Hanna and Barbera charmed this writer 25 years ago by letting King Jerry learn from Gene Kelly." In an assessment of Gary Grossman's *Saturday Morning TV,* a *TV Guide* reviewer got all misty about his own childhood television shows, which he claimed "bind us together as members of the same video family. . . . our sense of humor comes from Soupy Sales, our sense of what's right from Sky King." We suppose it's okay for the reviewer to reflect on his own generation's experiences, but then he continues, "Today's kids are missing out on something important on Saturday-morning network TV. There are no hosts any more—no role models, no sense of participation, no laughs, no *fun.* Just those square-jawed, animated disco superheroes." This baby boomer's childhood shows were better than anyone else's and by gum, all we need is Buffalo Bob and Pinky Lee to come ambling onto the small screen again.

Well, thanks for caring, but as far as we're concerned, Jonny Quest, Scooby-Doo, and Thundarr could kick Howdy Doody's ass all the way back to the woodpile. What bugs us is not that people have dissed contemporary kidvid in favor of their own memories. Everyone does that. Lots of our own contemporaries seem to think that current kidvid is much worse than the stuff they used to watch. Personally, we think it's vastly better. A lot of the programs that have appeared since 1988—*The Ren & Stimpy Show, The Adventures of Batman, The Tick, Gargoyles, X-Men, Reboot, Freakazoid!, Pinky & the Brain, Phantom 2040, Dexter's Laboratory, Animaniacs, Superman, Eek! the Cat,* and others—are at least equal to and more often far superior to the classic Saturday morning fare of our own youth.

These kinds of comparative judgments are fine as long as you're aware that that's what you're doing. The problem with kidvid critics is that they frequently have lacked such self-awareness. Rather than talking honestly about their own subjective preferences, many critics have claimed that their crusade against kidvid follows some objectively defined Natural Law of Good Taste. As a result, they have been afflicted with the presumption that nothing can ever be as good as their own (mostly) imaginary childhoods.

The critics also have pretty lame ideas about what good kidvid might be. If Saturday morning is self-evidently a load of televisual diarrhea, then what would represent the kidvid equivalent of fiber? Many of the critics—particularly groups of parents, educators, and academic experts—have tended to look to shows like *Mr. Wizard, Curiosity Shop, Mister Rogers' Neighborhood, The ABC Afterschool Special,* or, worst of all, *Davey and Goliath.* What this suggests is that production standards, artistic accomplishment, and sheer entertainment value have never mattered much to a certain class of kidvid critic. For these critics, the only thing that counts is the delivery of a moral message in a particular show. It matters little to them whether that message is delivered with all the subtlety of a nuclear warhead.

From our perspective, these critically acclaimed shows were often as grotesque as *Fred and Barney Meet the Thing* or the Scrappy-Doo episodes of *Scooby-Doo. Mister Rogers' Neighborhood,* some (though not all!) of *The ABC Afterschool Special,* and *Davey and Goliath* were sanctimonious, mewling, patently unreal, and full of big lies. We'd rather watch *The Three Robonic Stooges* any day. Much of what was made for our "improvement" was at the very least boring and often as screwed-up in terms of the messages it sought to convey as the very worst of Saturday morning. There are bright exceptions—*Sesame Street, The Electric Company, Captain Kangaroo, In the News,* some of *Schoolhouse Rock,* and more recently, *Beakman's World* and *Bill Nye, the Science Guy*—but they are exceptions, just as *The Herculoids, Star Trek, Bugs Bunny, Jonny Quest,* and other staples of Saturday morning stood above its dreck.

Not even the best of the "quality" children's shows have been good enough for the experts, who often presume television to be inherently and almost universally bad for children. A panel of experts

Saturday Morning of the Apes

Saturday morning was swarming with apes and monkeys. We'd like to outline a Simian Hall of Fame to which future animated primates may aspire—and point to a few more contemptible examples of Saturday morning monkeys and apes.

SIMIAN HALL OF FAME

Nkima. Yeah, we know Tarzan condescended to him, calling him "little one" all the time and swaggering around with him on his shoulder like he was a pirate's parrot or something. Yeah, he looked more like a bearded stoat than a monkey. But he had spunk and he was pretty useful in the crunch.

Igoo. Would have kicked any other gorilla's ass in a matter of seconds. Not only was he a giant, he was made of rocks. The secret overlord of *The Herculoids,* we think.

Gorilla Grodd. He may have sounded like he had a fatal case of laryngitis, but you don't want to mess with an evil gorilla genius who hails from a secret jungle city full of gorilla scientists.

Lancelot Link, Secret Chimp. He's Link, *Lancelot* Link, and he likes his banana daiquiris shaken, not stirred. We wonder if Lance held up as well as Sean Connery has.

Adam. The real brains of the *Ark II* team.

Ape. George of the Jungle's pal and a very fine and refined gentleman.

SHOULD NEVER HAVE EVOLVED PAST LEMURS

Grape Ape. He was big and purple. So what, big deal.

Bingo. Gorilla who was kind of the Zeppo Marx of the Banana Splits. Still, he did play the bongo drum, so that's worth something.

Bananas the Monkey. Like the kids on *Emergency +4* weren't annoying enough, they also had to travel around with this stupid monkey all the time. Too bad we never got to see an episode where he bit one of the kids and Johnny and Roy had to treat the kid for rabies.

Chim-Chim. Sorry, anime fans, but he sucked. Besides, he always looked like Spridal had been beating him up or something, and we're against monkey abuse on principle.

asked to assess quality shows by *TV Guide* in 1980 threw accolades to the *ABC Afterschool Special* and *Mister Rogers* but pronounced *Sesame Street* "too fast, too frenetic, too arousing." Translation: *Sesame Street* is just too damn *interesting!* Make it boring and make it promote a lot of values that we ourselves personally don't adhere to in our own adult lives, and we experts will eat it up with a spoon and ask for more.

Perhaps the worst thing that ever happened to kidvid is that from the mid-seventies onward, a bunch of psychologists and sociologists convinced the networks, the advocacy groups, and themselves that they had some kind of legitimate role in the actual production of children's programming. People with limited creative skills and no training suddenly played a major role in the creation of children's television. Prosocial programming, while typically fueled by the best of intentions, created shows that were thoroughly boring to watch. The only consciously prosocial shows to escape this fate were those backed by strong creative individuals who could override the experts. *Fat Albert,* for example, was worth watching primarily because its characters, drawn from Bill Cosby's imagination, were quirky and distinctive enough to override the predictable moralizing of most episodes. Other shows had no such protection. In the immediate wake of *Fat Albert,* shows like *Isis* and *Shazam!* fell victim to expert advice. The story lines of both shows were at their very best tolerably boring and were always predictably self-righteous, even when the characters had a glimmer of genuine promise.

The situation worsened in the eighties. The imagination of most consultants seemed to shrink while their total influence over kidvid dramatically increased. Efforts to make any program prosocial usually boiled down to one thing: a stuffy moral tacked onto the end of a blandly neutral story, whether it was Plastic Man delivering "Consumer Tips" or Darkseid reminding us to chew our food before swallowing. No kid ever learned anything of value from these messages. The moral, whether it was the value of cooperation, saving the environment, obeying your parents, or being honest, always stood out like a sore thumb, an alien and awkward intrusion into the program. Kids can smell hypocrisy and manipulation a mile away. We all knew to ignore it, just like today's kids will know to ignore the current transparent, phony, and simpleminded cartoon series based on William Bennett's *Book of Virtues.*[1]

A great many of the advocates of "better quality" would probably run screaming in terror if *real* quality kidvid aired on television. What children really need is fuel for their rich imaginative lives, and

---

1. Just to give one example from the cartoon *Book of Virtues:* One episode retells the story of Icarus, which is certainly a cautionary tale. Rather than let kids decide exactly what the story is telling them—and it offers several possibilities, ranging from "Don't overestimate your own abilities" to "Don't be boastful" to "Young people are stupid"—the cartoon sums it up for kids. The story of Icarus means "Always obey your parents" and that's that.

that fuel consists of the same things that drive adults: sadness, loss, violence, ambiguity, desire, love, and death. Kids aren't robots who will learn "values" merely because some Pod Person radiating unreality out of every pore stiffly voices such values.

Many of the children's books and movies which have mostly indelibly marked both of us, for example, are anything but sweet and inoffensive, qualities that advocates concerned with kidvid have generally demanded. Lloyd Alexander's Newbery Medal–winning Prydain books, for example, focus on the difficult growth and maturation of a boy into a king. Along the way, he suffers embarrassment, ethical confusion, the death and loss of friends, and awkward love for a female companion. His lessons are full of pain, violence, and hardship. It's not always certain that he's made the right choices, not even at the end of the saga. Or how about the Great Brain series, in which the central character is a young con man, cheat, and liar? Yes, he often gets his comeuppance, and his relatively innocent younger brother provides a contrast; nevertheless, many youthful readers have ended up admiring the mischievous Great Brain precisely because he's such a cunning schemer and cheat. Doubtless in a prosocial version, the Great Brain would have to learn from his mistakes and honestly confess to his crimes, rather than engage in the many mock reforms that he pulls off in the books. How about *Harriet the Spy?* Would that pass muster? Try the climax of the movie *Old Yeller,* or the death of Beth in *Little Women.*

The mothers from Boston probably would have cried bloody murder if any material like this had fetched up on Saturdays. Though they and other critics often protested that the sanitization of children's television was not their goal, it has often been the effect of their crusade. There's no room in the hearts of kidvid critics for stories without a simple moral, for likable characters who are also rascals or scoundrels, for tragedy and defeat, for violence and struggle. Mischief and danger would be banished from sight if they had their way. And yet, all of these things lie at the heart of the most meaningfully educational parts of childhood.

Children possess a critical intelligence of their own and the imaginative universe of children is complex. This is a point that Ellen Seiter makes effectively in *Sold Separately,* though she's not the only one to make the argument. The concept of childhood innocence, which survives long after it should have lost all credibility, continues to blind many well-meaning adults to the facts of childhood. We have consistently found that Saturday morning veterans have made their childhood viewing habits a meaningful part of their adult lives, with irony and grace. Critical intelligence and skepticism aren't just adult superimpositions upon the victimized innocence of our lost childhoods: they were part of our childhoods and ourselves from the very beginning.

Children's advocates often complained that superheroes, chase comedies, and other staples of Saturday morning fare resulted solely from network pandering to children. However, children *wanted* to see *Space Ghost;* they *wanted* to watch *G.I. Joe,* they *chose* to watch *Super Friends* instead of watching *Talking with a Giant.* As we look back, we are actually surprised at the number of attempts by the networks to offer "quality" shows. We don't really remember many of them, partly because they were never syndicated but mostly because they were dull. The memorable "quality" shows—both bad and good—were largely those aired on public television on the weekdays or the ones like *Schoolhouse Rock* that aired in between the regular cartoons. If it had been a choice between *George of the Jungle* and *Sesame Street,* then the latter would have lost in our household—and, we gather, in most households.

Kids made their choices throughout the history of Saturday morning. And they rarely chose what the various adult advocates of "quality" wanted them to choose. We don't stand above this all. We both are pretty snobby ourselves when it comes to television or mass culture. It's not as if the networks have ever offered up a real smorgasbord of programming choices and let audiences choose freely what they liked best. If such a thing ever happened, it's entirely possible that large factions of television audiences—both adults and children—might well choose differently than they have to date. There certainly should be a place for quality programs which only very small proportions of the viewing audience enjoy.

But few of the people concerned about children's television have ever bothered to deal seriously with the fact that children have historically sought out and enjoyed the very programming that their elders have condemned. Critics have often been resigned to the fact, but have treated it as completely mysterious or have offered simpleminded explanations. For example, the 1980 panel convened by *TV Guide* which judged *Sesame Street* to be too entertaining also disparaged almost all commercial kidvid. With regard to Bugs Bunny cartoons, the panelists sniffed, "The only thing to say is that some kids love this formula of chase, collision and comeuppance." Discussing another show, the experts sneered, "[We] can't understand why kids watch this, but they do." The contempt many of these experts have for children is obvious. Who knows why kids do what they do? Certainly not people who have supposedly committed their lives to understanding the nature of childhood.

———

"Bugs Bunny is still the model of a lazy, irresponsible, selfish individual who outwits and frustrates the serious purposes of the adult world." —University of Hawaii psychiatrist Dr. John F. McDermott, 1969

———

It has always been easier to promote a vision of children which stresses their alleged innocence and their consequent bad taste, easier to blame the networks, the advertisers, or the evil Cathode God itself for seducing cute little tykes. As Paul Taff, a developer of educational television, once said, "Given a choice between *Bugs Bunny* and *Mister Rogers,* children will watch *Bugs Bunny.* They don't yet have the critical ability to make judgments about which shows are better." Taff simply couldn't deal with the fact that children were choosing to watch Bugs Bunny because Bugs Bunny cartoons were hugely superior to *Mister Rogers* not only in terms of entertainment, but also because their value system—centered on Bugs, a quintessentially American wiseass and all-around champion gender-bender—was massively preferable to Fred Rogers's goody-goody vision of the world.

"Of course you know this means war." —Bugs Bunny

We should make it clear that we would have preferred a better Saturday morning than what we got. Today's children have a much richer variety of good shows from which to choose. Moreover, almost all of our contemporaries recall much of Saturday morning with something less than pure pleasure. Animation fans have developed particularly acute feelings of contempt for Hanna-Barbera, Filmation, and Ruby-Spears, but most Saturday morning veterans concede that the majority of these studios' output was weak. In the aggregate, it was indeed repetitious, crudely produced, badly written, derivative, and frequently boring. It's difficult to praise the cheap and shoddy cartooning conducted in overseas sweatshops that was so common on Saturdays.

We still love the stuff. Certain kinds of lame Saturday morning shows have their own sublime quality, a certain kind of Zen badness. Very few pieces of popular culture are so bad as to be completely unloved. Some programs are so bad that it's hard not to like them. You might call it the *My Mother the Car* [MMTC] effect, in reference to the short-lived prime-time sitcom that featured a man whose dead mother spoke to him through his vintage car. You've got to love it for its premise alone. Some Saturday morning shows were just plain bad—*The Kwicky Koala Show* or *The Skatebirds,* for example—but there were others that achieved true MMTC badness.

Take, for example, *The Super Globetrotters.* Now, this show couldn't hold a candle to the delightfully and staggeringly awful live-action TV movie *The Harlem Globetrotters on Gilligan's Island* (which features Martin Landau in a performance he should be forced to watch if his ego swells again to 1995 Academy Award levels). But *The Super Globetrotters* was fun because of the sheer inanity of some of its central conceits, most notably a character whose superpower was his really huge Afro. Another classic example, cited by many Saturday morning veterans, is the guest-star episodes of *Scooby-Doo*. One memorable discussion on alt.society.generation-x revolved around determining which of these episodes was the worst. (There was no general consensus, but the episodes featuring Jerry Reed and Sandy Duncan ranked high on most lists.) However, when these sucked, they sucked in a memorably entertaining fashion. It's hard to forget watching a badly animated Sonny and Cher scamper around a haunted hotel with Fred, Velma, and the rest of those darn kids.

Some of the later Sid and Marty Krofft shows and characters like *Captain Kool and the Kongs, Far Out Space Nuts, Electra-Woman and Dynagirl, The Lost Saucer,* and *Dr. Shrinker* achieved the same kind of exalted state of high-camp crappiness. The Krofft shows were always cheesy, but these shows went way over the line. How can you not find it in your heart to like a character called the Dorse (a combination of a dog and a horse), played by some poor soul costumed in a badly fitting shag rug and a head that looked like it was ripped off of some kid's hobby horse? How can you not love a show featuring two female superheroes that makes Adam West's Batman program look like it was directed by Tim Burton and written by Shakespeare? How can you dismiss the insanely overripe overacting of Billy Barty as Dr. Shrinker's evil right-hand midget? How can you not dream affectionately of Chuck McCann yelling "Lunch, not *launch!*" in the opening sequence of *Far Out Space Nuts?*

Similarly, how can you not worship the immortal lines from the theme song of the badly animated Trans-Lux cartoon *Hercules:* "Iron in his thighs / Virtue in his heart / Fire in every part / Of the mighty

Hercules!" We're talking gibberish! We're talking dementia! We're talking totally unacknowledged weirdness. It was great! Take the cartoon in which the early Hanna-Barbera superhero Birdman sights a giant monster walking away from a hole in the side of a building. Birdman speculates aloud that the giant ape-ant (yeah, an ape-ant: don't ask) *might* have made the hole. He then actually flies into the building to investigate whether it was the ape-ant. Jeez, we knew that there were lots of monsters walking around these Hanna-Barbera cities, but can't you be pretty sure that a forty-foot monster walking away from a hole in the side of a building is the guilty party?

It's these sorts of MMTC moments, along with the various hokey shticks of characters like Shaggy, the Wonder Twins, and He-Man, that lie near the core of Saturday morning's value to those who experienced it. There were shows we loved, and there were shows we endured. And then there were shows that we still hold close to our hearts simply because we watched them, because we know them, because no adult casually glancing at such programs could hope to understand the secret dialogue between us and the television set that unfolded as we watched these shows.

Recall Peggy Charren opening a box of Frankenberry some fateful morning in the seventies and discovering that it "smells funny." Saturday morning was full of funny-smelling programs that we ate up with gusto precisely *because* adults turned up their noses at them. Saturday morning was—and still is—a garden of many pleasures, a lot of them admittedly weird. Like any garden, it has had its weeds. The shame of it is that for so long, a huge bunch of concerned adults who saw the garden by furtively peeking over the wall have been certain it was nothing but a radioactive wasteland. If they had abandoned their self-conscious presentation of themselves as "good parents" for even a moment and actually strolled the grounds of Saturday morning in the knowing company of their children, perhaps they might have had the opportunity to smell—and come to enjoy—a few Frankenberry-smelling flowers.

Monotony

Even before the superhero cartoons drew fire in the late sixties, critics were beginning to grow concerned with the concentration of children's programming on Saturday morning and the increasing domination of cartoons. Not only did this leave children with no options besides "adult" shows in the evenings, but it turned Saturday viewing into a much more concentrated and intense experience. By the mid-seventies, many commentators expressed increasingly intense concern that the new Saturday morning was a sort of ghetto of monotony, that children were being stuck with a repetitious mass of bland goo on Saturdays and then ignored the rest of the week.

This claim doesn't quite hold water. For one, children never confined their television watching to Saturdays. From the beginnings of television to the present day, young audiences have had a polymorphous sense of taste, wandering all over the dial in search of interesting programs. Kids found as much to satisfy them on television at other times of the day and on other days of the week, even if the shows were not expressly intended for them. Whether our youthful tastes tended to *The Six Million Dollar Man,* various soap operas, the latest National Geographic program, *All in the Family,* or *Hill Street Blues,* watching cartoons on Saturday was never more than one relatively small part of our total television consumption. This makes the possible monotony of Saturday morning less of a concern, unless you assume that children should have a lot of programming time strictly devoted to their needs. We can't see why this should be the case. Saturday morning had the advantage of being a parent-free zone, giving the kids a bit of time and space to call their own. (Many parents saw it the same way, though in reverse.) For the rest of the week, why shouldn't children and adults be watching programs together? There's plenty of programming that is legitimately of interest to both groups, and even much of the stuff that kids *aren't* supposed to watch is good for them. Only a kid with a perilously overdeveloped superego leaves the room when the television screen warns, "Viewer discretion is advised."

Concern over Saturday's alleged monotony stemmed from two basic sources: disinterested adult viewing of kidvid and a fundamental antipathy toward animation. Saturday morning wasn't all that monotonous. Hostile adults who watched it often found it so, but kids often made fine distinctions between ostensibly similar shows, thus producing among themselves a sense of variety that adult observers never noticed. For example, Tom Engelhardt's essay on Saturday morning, "The Shortcake Strategy," typically contends that kidvid was relentlessly repetitive, reducible to a minuscule number of themes and motifs. Engelhardt ignores distinctions between characters and genres that were important to many child viewers—insisting, for example, that the characters and situations involving He-Man, G.I. Joe, and the Incredible Hulk are basically the same.

In fact, the characters not only have substantially different cultural histories, but they also operate from different premises. The Hulk is basically a nuclear-era Wolfman, a person transformed periodically into a monster he cannot control. G.I. Joe is a contemporary military/spy fantasy with various big guns and other fetish objects prominently displayed. He-Man combines elements of the Superman–Clark Kent motif (shy or meek person whose alter ego is a noble crusader) with basic fantasy staples like the evil sorcerer menacing a kingdom of good. Engelhardt's article misses important distinctions and nuances. For example, in his rush to declare the Superfriends' latest incarnation totally derivative, he claims that the continuing villain Darkseid is simply a rip-off of Darth Vader. This assertion not only betrays his essential lack of interest in the superhero genre, given that Darkseid is in fact a rather different sort of evildoer than Darth Vader, it also is factually incorrect. Darkseid was created by Jack Kirby in 1970 for DC Comics, seven years before Darth Vader appeared.

It may sound like we're picking nits, but we're not. For a lot of the kids watching *Superfriends* and other shows in 1986, these kinds of small points were the basis for perceiving distinctions between shows, both in terms of genre and in terms of quality. We take Engelhardt to task because his Procrustean interpretation of Saturday morning as an unbroken sea of monotony is typical. When Engelhardt, like many others, offers to see Saturday morning from a kid's point of view, he welches on his own bet. From a kid's point of view, the Incredible Hulk, Superman, and the Transformers are different sorts of characters, each attracting their own aficionados and fans. From a kid's point of view, there's a notable difference between *Dungeons & Dragons* and *He-Man* or between *Scooby-Doo* and *The Real Ghostbusters*. Both *Voltron* and *Tranzor-Z* are Japanese cartoons about giant robots and their pilots, but *Tranzor-Z* featured memorably goofy female robots which fired rockets from their breasts. This is the sort of difference a Tom Engelhardt might miss but no kid would overlook. In a kid's imagination, the difference between He-Man and Thundarr may have been as large as was the difference between Davy Crockett and the Lone Ranger for a kid in the fifties.

Critics who perceive Saturday morning to be endlessly imitating itself aren't completely loony. Engelhardt and others were quite right to see certain motifs repeated and they were also quite right that television executives and producers, whether thinking about children or general audiences, act as if imitation were the sincerest form of profit making. Some programs—*G.I. Joe* is a good example—basically rehashed the same sequence of individual scenes and overall plots in the same mechanical way that hard-core pornography cycles through sexual positions. Many themes flowed over Saturday morning like waves, from the sixties superheroes to eighties arcade-game-based cartoons. Nobody applauds this kind of dreary cannibalization.

There's a weirder logic at play here, though. Some of the observers who have charged Saturday morning with monotony think animation is inherently a Bad Thing. From our perspective, of all of the persistent arguments and themes to crop up in the history of kidvid, this one is the oddest. *TV Guide's* Richard Doan, for example, gloated openly in his column whenever a live-action kids' show did well in the ratings—in one instance, he hailed the ratings victory of *Land of the Lost* in 1974 as a "decisive breakthrough." We liked *Land of the Lost,* but we're puzzled by a sensibility that sees the decidedly low-rent goings-on in that show as intrinsically superior to an animated program. A more peculiar example of this hang-up was the hostility of some experts to *Schoolhouse Rock.* Admittedly, many of the usual suspects liked *Schoolhouse Rock* a lot, and those who didn't have tended to revise their opinions as a strongly favorable consensus about the educational shorts has developed over time. When the shorts appeared, a vocal minority shared the sentiments of one critic who commented, "Puppets would be better. They have believable character, real-world motion, and three dimensions."

What motivated this hostility? For one, we take it to be another clear sign of the nostalgic imperialism of many older baby boomers, since an attack on animation almost invariably accompanied a call for more live-action programming for children, "just like in the old days." There is something subtler at play here, however. Some of the critics of animation operated from a presumption that animation was inherently bad for children because its lack of realism was intrinsically subversive. Animation wasn't just unreal, it was antireal. This viewpoint suggests a painfully naive and simplistic understanding of how cinematic and televisual "realism" achieves its effects. A show like *Sky King* or *Mister Rogers* is no more intrinsically real than *Smurfs.* A photograph involves artificiality and confection, just like an artist's sketch. As author James Morrow commented in a 1982 article about children's television, "It's not our children who have trouble reconciling the fantastic with the factual, the pretend with the true. The grown-ups are the ones with the fantasy problem."

This kind of cultural illiteracy used to be nothing more than an annoyance, a weird hang-up. As we look forward to the next several decades, however, such an attitude seems a lot more dangerous, espe-

In a Battle to the Death, Who'd Win?

Birdman or Space Ghost?

Captain Kangaroo or Mr. Rogers?

Papa Smurf or Ernest Hemingway?

Zero the Hero or Naughty Number Nine?

Jem and the Holograms or Josie and the Pussycats?

Speed Buggy or Wheelie?

Rock Bottom or Riff Raff?

Batfink or Super Chicken?

Skeletor or Venjor?

The Galaxy Trio or the Fantastic Four?

Hector Heathcote or Mr. Peabody?

Captain Caveman or Korg?

Hair Bear or Yogi Bear?

Fangface or Yukk?

The Funky Phantom or Slimer?

The Cosby Kids or the Wee Pals?

Gleek or Blip?

cially since such critics believe that children cannot distinguish animated violence from real-world violence. Our generation is probably going to press for more animated entertainment at the same time that technological advances are rapidly making it possible to blur the lines between animation and live action in wholly new and exciting ways. A critic operating from the assumption that live-action "realism" is manifestly superior for children (and adults?) is going to be baffled by the kinds of computer-generated images appearing in movies and television programs like *Toy Story, Jurassic Park,* or *Babylon 5.* And such a critic, having emphasized false distinctions between animation and live action, is going to be even more clueless when confronted by the sort of artistic manipulation that seemingly darkened O. J. Simpson's skin on the cover of *Time* magazine or put Forrest Gump in the same movie frame as President Kennedy. Perhaps Saturday morning veterans should form an organization of Concerned People to help educate clueless boomers about how to watch television.

Animation did not intrinsically make Saturday morning monotonous, any more than prime-time programming is automatically boring simply because it's almost all live action. And though shows like *Goober and the Ghost Chasers, The Funky Phantom,* and *Scooby-Doo, Where Are You?* might all appear to the untrained eye to be evidence of monotony, the Saturday morning veteran knows that there's a world of difference between Scooby's early adventures and the retread capers of the ghostly Goober and his pals. Even though they used some of the exact same animated footage, the original Ralph Bakshi *Spider-Man* was quite distinct from the later syndicated program *Rocket Robin Hood.* Just as in the case of accusations of poor quality, lofty disdain for the cultural perspective of children among many adult critics kept them from seeing how Saturday morning looked when you watched it regularly.

Passivity

In the last four decades of the nineteenth century, medical science developed an increasingly strong interest in diseases and disorders linked to the body's energy. The definition and diagnosis of these disorders—and the medical specialists most interested in them—look pretty damn weird from a contemporary perspective. Doctors talked about diseases like neurasthenia, defined simultaneously as a form of chronic exhaustion, as nervous lassitude, as a failure of will, as an imbalance of mental energy over physical labor, as melancholy. As a clinical condition, neurasthenia disappeared from medical terminology early in the twentieth century. However, while neurasthenia itself may well have disappeared, the figure of the neurasthenic—a passive youth with a deficient will, gaunt, pale, and twitchy—remains with us. One of the neurasthenic's most interesting reappearances is in reference to children's television, in condemnations of its allegedly pacifying nature.

Passivity, like neurasthenia, was really a Rorschach blot whose alleged menace was open to nearly infinite interpretation. A lot of concern about passivity sounds in retrospect like it is just one small step away from worrying about Communists stealing our precious bodily fluids. Perhaps the strongest attack on television along these lines is Marie Winn's 1978 polemic *The Plug-In Drug*. In it, the author argues that television is inherently damaging to children, regardless of its content. Television retards the development of children both physiologically and psychologically. Winn writes:

> The television experience helps to perpetuate dependency. The child needs to acquire fundamental skills in communication. . . . The television experience does not further his verbal development because it does not require any verbal participation on his part, merely passive intake. . . . The child's need for fantasy is gratified far better by his own make-believe activities than by the adult-made fantasies he is offered on television. The young child's need for intellectual stimulation is met infinitely better when he can learn by manipulating, touching, doing, than by merely watching passively. And finally, the television experience must be considered in relation to the child's need to develop family skills he will need in order to become a successful parent himself some day.

We quote at length because we feel this passage perfectly exemplifies the hidden subtexts at play with this issue.

Much of Winn's book is based on generalizations and anecdotal evidence, on appeals to common sense. Winn argues that one need only ask any mother in order to discover that television makes "zombies" of children. None of the middle-class parents she interviewed sees evidence of an active mental relationship between television and children, and hence, none could possibly exist. For Winn, it is axiomatic that only "real" play produces healthy adults who can fulfill all the responsibilities of adulthood. The generations that have grown up since the advent of television are said to be prone to drug addiction, lazy and undisciplined, unable to communicate with each other or perform well in tests of intellectual ability.

Certainly anyone who falls within the age range deemed "Generation X" will recognize these noxious stereotypes. Embedded within Winn's vision (and the vision of like-minded critics such as pediatrician T. Berry Brazelton) is advocacy for particular middle-class and generational values, presented as a "scientific" finding about the development of children and the physiological and psychological impact of television. At the turn of the century, concerns about middle-class propriety, racial hierarchy, and industrial labor motivated public-health campaigns against neurasthenia and anxiety in like fashion.

Whenever issues which are fundamentally cultural in nature get laundered through the machinery of public health, be afraid. Be very afraid. Public wailing and gnashing of teeth over the passive child wasting away in front of the television set is a game of three-card monte, an act of misdirection. Notions that are anything but self-evident—say, that children must be socialized into certain patterns of "activity," or must prepare for their own impending parenthood—are taken as natural or axiomatic.

Reading Winn's book and similar polemics, we wonder when it was in history that children all made their own fantasies, when exactly it was that children were intellectually stimulated and verbally challenged, what halcyon era it was when children were not depen-

Verb: That's What's Happening

The Smurfs had an unfortunate and narcissistic habit of using their own name as all-purpose verbs. The more we think about it, though, the more it seems to us that other Saturday morning characters' names could be used to enrich the English language. A few suggested neologisms:

acme. To misuse or incorrectly assemble cheap or deceptively marketed merchandise.

bannon. To throw a barrel at a target, particularly a sinister Oriental mastermind or giant monster.

birdman. To yell one's own name.

bugaloo. To be unduly cheerful.

fleegle. To recall an obscure name or reference. (Fleegling is particularly useful when discussing Saturday morning.)

goliath. To hear voices in one's head, particularly that of a deity or divine spirit; see also **schizophrenia.**

luthor. To accomplish an unexpected escape or exit. See also **destro.**

marvin. (1) To be taken hostage; see also **jan;** (2) to obstruct, frustrate, or annoy; see also **orko.**

monchhichi. To coat oneself in sugar or syrup.

muttley. To snicker.

scooby. (1) To eat a Hostess snack food or other high-calorie treat while under threat of pursuit by a phantom, specter, or other supernatural entity; (2) to convert most consonants to the letter *r* while speaking; see also **astro.**

sleestak. To miss badly when firing a projectile at a target; see also **cobra.**

wildmon. To condemn or criticize a film, television show, or work of art that one has not seen; see also **dole.**

dent upon forms of entertainment controlled by adults. According to Winn, the 1930s and 1940s were a time when appropriate models of modern parenthood flourished, when the family was allegedly a strong institution. This claim is a favorite fantasy among the "family values" crowd, but *The Waltons* notwithstanding, it is very far from the complex historical reality of the United States during the Great Depression and World War II. This was in fact a time in which significant numbers of women and children worked outside the home. Broken families of various kinds were more common than the myth would have us believe. Children were not universally raised with rock-hard moral certitude by parents who were paragons of every virtue.

Even if this was a golden age of parenting, then we wonder exactly why anyone would think that earlier generations are better adults than we television-addled youngsters are. The general population of fine, upstanding adults who were weaned on radio and stern parental discipline contrived in many cases to either overlook or actively perpetuate vicious racial discrimination well into the 1970s. These honest citizens didn't just tolerate the hysteria and rabid persecution made possible by McCarthyism, but often cheerfully participated in it. So we're not sure why people like Winn see us as a bunch of passive, degenerate louts zombified by TV. So far our ethical and social track record is pretty good compared to the radio and pulp novel bunch. We'd certainly have to go a long way to be worse citizens than they.

Television didn't make us passive. We're doing just fine in society and in the workplace. And hey, if things start to go wrong, we can always rip off some Prozac from our parents' cabinets.

Violence

Fred Rogers once said of *Dastardly and Muttley* and *The Perils of Penelope Pitstop* that "the message that comes across is that big people are incompetent and go after little people for no good reason—and if this is the adult world, why should we make an effort to join it?" In spite of its many merits, *The Perils of Penelope Pitstop* was hardly a stinging critique of the adult world. However, suppose Fred Rogers was right. Obviously he thinks this would be a reprehensible message to give to kids. We, on the other hand, think it's a pretty fair one. If American children, teens, and twenty-somethings saw the adult world in 1970 as predatory, arbitrary, and nonsensical, they hit the nail right on the head.

And if (if!) kids have learned via television to see the world as a violent place, why does Fred Rogers think that's so wrong? The amazing thing was that adults in the seventies deluded themselves into imagining that their world—a world which had experienced in the previous forty years a massively destructive world war, extraordinary acts of genocide, numerous colonial and neocolonial conflicts, as well as a surplus of everyday violence—had been otherwise. One 1984 study by psychologists found that four- to nine-year-olds who viewed television frequently were more likely to see the world as a "mean, scary place." Well, good for TV, because the world sure as hell is a mean, scary place—and has been for most of this century. Those heavy TV viewers are going into life with their eyes open.

Moreover, the life of a young child—any child, whether she lives in a leafy suburb or the inner city—has its own particular forms of conflict, intimidation, and implicit violence within it. Power struggles with Mom and Dad may not necessarily be violent physically, but they certainly involve moments in which the wishes and desires of a child are denied through a show of force, whether it be banishment to one's room or a cussing out. In the volatile testing grounds of preschool and kindergarten, kids fight a thousand silent battles every day. This is not, by the way, a criticism of such parental and peer "violence": it's socially necessary and socially good and we'll do it to our own kids, if and when we have any. And no, none of this is in any way comparable to the risk of being shot in a crossfire between armed teenagers that a four-year-old kid in the inner city faces. That's a wholly different kind of violence.

Once again, though, the critique of violence in kidvid merely shows the odd durability of that peculiar Victorian invention: the innocent child. The same old moony rose-tinted fantasizing about some past golden age is at play again; whenever people moan about how kids are more and more violent these days, they're usually hallucinating about the lost world of peaceful nuclear families living happily in suburbs. Never mind that the era immediately preceding the introduction of television—the Great Depression—was one of the peak periods for violent crime in twentieth-century America. Never mind, as James Morrow points out, that "the night before he shot Lincoln, John Wilkes Booth had not been watching television."

Moaning about violence has been synonymous with bitching about them crazy young kids and their weird habits. Conformist adults in the late sixties and early seventies were terrified by the rise of dissent and discontent on college campuses, so they blamed kidvid for promoting this "violence." Bob Keeshan (alias Captain Kangaroo) said in 1970 that violent cartoons "have immunized children to violence. Today on the campus, for example we see a violent solution to almost every question." His fellow traveler on this issue, Spiro Agnew, suggested something similar by condemning television for producing "a fascination among young people with demonstrations as a means of communication." A producer for *Mister Rogers' Neighborhood* concluded that while television could decrease prejudice and "increase wonder," it was also, through the trivialization of adulthood, leading kids to protest and use drugs and other unwholesome things.

Of course, all these criticisms should have meant that the shows they were *really* condemning weren't the mid-sixties superheroes or the core programs of the seventies, but things like *Howdy Doody* and *The Lone Ranger.* No one pinned the pathological behavior of the cops in Chicago in 1968 on radio episodes of *The Shadow* or on pulp magazines from the 1930s. No one fretted that Robert McNamara must have been watching *Space Ghost* on the sly with his kids prior to the Tonkin Gulf incident. No one pointed with indignation at *Jonny Quest* for inspiring youthful National Guard troops to open fire at Kent State.

Whether it was Agnew, Keeshan, or some other untrustworthy person over thirty, the basic message was the same in the late sixties and early seventies: Blame television and you get an unlimited license to condescend. Then you don't have to explain exactly why it was bad that kids were in the streets protesting against war or why exactly dropping out and turning on was a terrible thing. The wheel keeps on turning: in the mid-seventies television got blamed for making you passive, and then once again in the eighties, it was creating violence. It's the excuse that keeps on giving. Amazing thing, television: it can make you passive and aggressive at the same time. If you don't like whatever it is that young people are doing, it must be television that's to blame.

———

"I think Saturday morning has had some fine shows and some awful ones, and certainly I've contributed to both." —David DePatie, quoted in Gary Grossman's *Saturday Morning TV*

———

Neither the nature of the violence within a program itself nor the interpretation of that violence have mattered to most critics, particularly not to various experts. Examined closely, virtually all expert definitions of "violence" in relation to kidvid, from Bandura's to Singer's, are too facile. Tautologies practically seep off the pages. One of our favorites is in George Comstock's *Television and the American Child,* which takes note of research that has shown that television consumption among youngsters is higher in households where the "centrality of television" is high, and among those "who perceive no other activity as more necessary or rewarding than watching television." Say it ain't so! Television consumption by children is higher in households where television is considered central! Now, we're not scientists, but—if we may be so bold—we will venture the hypothesis that television consumption by children is lower in households that don't have televisions. More studies are clearly required. We hearby offer a standing grant of five dollars to the first person who wants to give it a shot.

Almost none of the experts who have beaten the drums over the years about kidvid violence have displayed much aptitude for the actual *interpretation* of culture and almost none of them have conceded even for a moment that culture can—and in fact invariably does—mean more than one thing. What expert studies of violence and television have almost always offered instead is profoundly simpleminded bean counting, in which the researcher mechanically sums up "incidents" of violence within cartoons and pronounces the cartoons "saturated" with violent content. After such "violent" programs have been shown to a bunch of ~~lab rats~~ kids, researchers ask them to whale on Bobo the Clown. Because the kids who saw the supposedly violent cartoons popped balloons or smacked Bobo upside the head at a slightly accelerated rate, we are supposed to infer that watching *Tom and Jerry* may lead tots to butcher and eat Grandma.

Later researchers have acknowledged the weaknesses of these earlier experiments, conceding that they were not accurate measurements of aggression and that children were often visibly prompted to give certain responses. As a result, in research from the seventies and early eighties, children exposed to "violent" television were measured for allegedly natural responses. These may have been more sophisticated experimental models, but they suffered from some of the same weaknesses as earlier experiments. In many ways, this research was a precursor to the expert manipulation of children's memories that accompanied the moral panic over child abuse in the eighties, manipulation that ultimately revealed that many children can analyze the needs of adult researchers with surprising sophistication and will fabricate memories and testimonies (including detailed descriptions of sexual acts and bizarre perversities) to satisfy the needs of researchers.

Some specialists in child psychology have still not come to grips with this fact. Robert Liebert and Joyce Sprafkin say bluntly in the latest edition of their classic work, *The Early Window: Effects of Television on Children and Youth,* that it is not plausible that "children ferret out the subtle, unstated expectations of researchers whose aim is to avoid biasing them." Of course it's plausible. Children, even very young children, are often adept at interpreting and manipulating adults. They have to be. By the age of five or six, many children, if subjected to watching cartoons and then being asked whether they would hit someone back or go get an adult if a fight started, know fairly well what the researcher is getting at. By the time a television viewer is six years old, he or she has almost certainly overheard his parents discussing whether television is too violent— or war toys, or something similar. He or she has probably encountered the same concern among other adults, and has probably overheard television itself giving voice to similar worries. (This was even more acutely the case between 1965 and 1990, when American culture as a whole was saturated with concern over the violence of Saturday morning.) Faced with buttons labeled "hurt" or "help," or a multiple-choice card, a child was not robotically reflecting the influence of television: he or she was very possibly deliberately, and probably mischievously in many cases, choosing whether to do the "right" thing or to fulfill the researcher's expectation and do the "wrong" thing.

Some observers have other complaints about kidvid violence. For example, many intellectuals on the left have persistently charged that cartoon violence, and the advertisements for violent toys which have accompanied cartoons, represent a form of cultural training for war. Eric Barnouw comments in *Tube of Plenty* that "a visitor from another planet watching United States television for a week during the Vietnam escalation period might have concluded that viewers were being brainwashed by a cunning conspiracy determined to harness the nation—with special attention to the young." We're sympathetic, but we think this analysis is too simplistic. Like a lot of thinking on the left, it ultimately rests on a conspiracy theory. We think the making of popular culture is a lot messier than sinister decisions by a few powerful guys smoking cigars in some darkened star chamber, Oliver Stone's delusions notwithstanding. If war toys and violent cartoons have any connection to U.S. military power, then it's a complicated and indirect sort of connection, and not necessarily one that works to shore up U.S. military misadventures.

We have rather less sympathy for other political perspectives on kidvid violence, particularly the views of right-wing loonies like Donald Wildmon and Ralph Reed, who have always been relatively uninterested in the issue of violence within the bounds of their own ridiculously intolerant universe. (Remember, according to Bob Dole, the ultraviolent movie *True Lies* is a good family picture.) Concern over violence in kidvid for these folks tends to be accompanied by concern for hidden satanic messages and suchlike, which pretty much disqualifies their arguments from the Sanity Sweepstakes. In any event, almost all crusaders against kidvid violence have seemed almost pathologically incapable of dealing with the specific content of most of Saturday morning.

For example, take *Space Ghost* and *The Herculoids*. Both shows—and other superhero cartoons—were repeatedly cited by late-sixties critics as being "saturated" with violence. Various surveys and reviews claimed that most episodes of the shows were piling up the corpses of "monster people," robots, and the like at the rate of about one per minute. This statistic is a delusion. As network executives used to point out, these characters don't *die* and some of them aren't even *alive* in the first place.[2] When various Space Ghost and Herculoid antagonists got zapped by Space Ghost's power-bands or by Zok's eye beams, they generally just staggered and disappeared off the frame. If they were robots, they probably blew up. Some clueless adult obsessed with "weirdo superheroes" might suppose the bad buys had just been killed, but any kid schooled even minimally in the visual grammar of the comic-book genre knew full well that the antagonists had just been stunned or defeated. When Superman punched some guy through a wall and you didn't see him again, you didn't assume that the bad guy was a red pulpy mass stuck to a piece of masonry. You assumed the police would come along in good time and pick up the unconscious perpetrator. That is, unless you were a minion of the PTA trying to interpret a show you neither understood nor liked.[3]

These accusations had a visible—and generally negative—impact on seventies action-adventure shows airing on Saturday mornings. All of them more or less downplayed conflict, particularly the ones being vetted by expert consultants. Shazam and Isis spent most of their time being so understanding and mellow that any bad guys surrendered just so they could go back to jail. The 1975 cartoon version of *Planet of the Apes* didn't have human characters running from cruel ape overlords—instead, it had some human and ape kids deal-

---

2. We're well aware that this last point is a famous dodge in comic-book and science-fiction writing generally. In the comics, Superman had a code against killing but he could blow away robots—even sentient robots—because they weren't "alive." Captain Kirk had his Prime Directive, but let a sentient computer cross his path, and he'd fry it with a scintillating display of illogic. It's a loophole in antikilling rules, because if there were such a thing as a sentient machine, it would basically be a life form by proxy.
3. While we're on the subject, we also might note that the Star Wars films are widely considered to be completely appropriate for young children, even though they are veritable charnel houses with body counts in the tens of thousands. It's not just a question of whether bad guys get killed, but how they get killed, who exactly they are, and what genre the killing occurs in.

When I Awoke in the Morning, I Had Become a Cartoon

Over the years, many real-life people were converted into Saturday morning cartoons, either as themselves, or as characters they played in a live-action medium. Some people made the trip intact, while others were horribly disfigured.

SURVIVORS

Martin Short (as Ed Grimley)

The cast of *Star Trek*

Kevin Tighe and Randolph Mantooth on *Emergency +4*

The Globetrotters

John Candy

The Beatles

Mister T (he was kind of a cartoon already, anyway)

CASUALTIES

Hulk Hogan

Muhammad Ali

M C Hammer

The Globetrotters (in their *Super Globetrotters* incarnation)

Robin Williams (as an animated Mork)

ing with weird weather conditions and alien topography. Even *Emergency +4* took some heat from critics for what one might think was an inoffensive portrayal of kids actively assisting the adult paramedics in various rescues, according to author George Woolery. Later on, at least, adventure heroes got to fight again, although their creators always carefully stressed that no deaths or injuries had actually occurred. Thundarr the Barbarian had his fabulous Sun Sword, but the cartoon's creators were *very* careful to show viewers *explicitly* that Thundarr simply knocked over his enemies rather than killed them. The same was pretty much true of other eighties action-adventure series like *Blackstar, He-Man,* and *Pirates of Dark Water.*

This domestication of adventure and action is certainly far less irksome than the ugly lobotomy that many Warner Brothers cartoons have been subjected to as a result of the campaign against violent kid-vid. The cartoons which some of us saw uncut and intact in the seventies have frequently been slashed to ribbons by boneheaded censors in the eighties and nineties. One of the more prominent examples we've come across concerns the Bugs Bunny cartoon "Long-Haired Hare." In it, Bugs takes on an unpleasant opera singer who won't allow Bugs to play a banjo because it interferes with singing practice. After the singer smashes Bugs's banjo for the second time, Bugs turns to the viewers and offers his usual observation under these circumstances: "Of course you know, this means war." Bugs then impersonates the conductor "Leopold" during a concert and mercilessly torments the banjo-destroying singer. In one bowdlerized version, the original confrontation between Bugs and the singer is edited out, possibly because the banjo-smashing is considered "too violent."

In the course of our research, we have found nothing that angers Saturday morning veterans more than the contemporary censorship of classic Warner Brothers cartoons. For us, there has been no greater irritant while researching this book than our repeated encounters with the views of experts like George Gerbner and Dorothy Singer, who argue with great confidence that young children simply cannot understand the fictional rules of conflict in these cartoons. Our contemporaries have insisted repeatedly that *as children,* they *clearly* understood that the "violence" involved when Bugs blows up Yosemite Sam or Wile E. Coyote's latest Acme device launches him off a cliff takes place within a fictional universe with its own very particular rules. Such violence had little or no relationship with what we understood as violence in our own lives. Interviewed by *TV Guide* in 1970, one group of six- to eight-year-old kids were typically clear about this point. Asked if seeing people hit each other on television made children want to hit people, one child replied that violence in kidvid was just a "TV trick." A child added, "They pretend. They don't really hurt them." Another boy observed, "When you see a thing on television that's almost impossible, you're not supposed to believe it."

As many commentators have pointed out, the universe of the Warner Brothers cartoons was also a deeply moral one, something that was achieved without any psychologist hanging around telling Chuck Jones, Friz Freleng, Tex Avery, and their companions what the prosocial message of the day was. Bugs Bunny does not attack people for the hell of it, and he doesn't win out in the end because he's got the biggest gun. Bugs minds his own business until someone—Elmer Fudd, Yosemite Sam, Daffy Duck, Marvin the Martian—molests him. He outwits his antagonist: he's the trickster, he's Brer Rabbit. Wile E. Coyote and Sylvester always fail because, ultimately, they want something they really shouldn't have (the Road Runner or Tweety Bird).[4] The kids always understood all of this, even if the researchers never did. The cuts not only destroy the artistic integrity of

---

4. On the other hand, we'd pay good money to see a new Road Runner cartoon where the Coyote finally catches the Road Runner, beats the crap out of him, and eats him with relish. Tweety at least was witty and seemed to have some affection for Sylvester. The Road Runner is sort of a smug bastard who somehow seems to cheat in his duel with the Coyote. Chuck Jones made one Road Runner cartoon which dealt with these feelings. In it, several children are shown watching the television while the Road Runner is on. Among other things, they observe that the Coyote needs to see a "p-sigh-chiatrist."

some of the best cartoons ever made but they also can transform highly moral characters like Bugs Bunny into amoral psychotics. Take the example of "Long-Haired Hare" mentioned previously. When the original provocation by the opera singer is removed, smashed banjo and all, Bugs doesn't appear to be retaliating when he literally brings down the house on top of the singer; instead, it just looks like he's decided to go off and hassle the guy for the heck of it.

Some commentators complained that Warner Brothers cartoons and other similar programs did not teach children the "consequences" of violence, implying instead that hitting someone with a frying pan results in nothing worse than the victim's head taking on the shape of the frying pan. As we've already noted, this fear says more about the stupidity of some critics than the ignorance of kids, but it also begs the question of whether such critics would like to see kidvid actually show the consequences of violence. Probably not. We suspect that most kidvid critics think the best way to demonstrate the consequences of violence is to have Goliath tell Davey that God wants him to turn the other cheek.

"Now you know, and knowing is half the battle." —Typical saying from *G.I. Joe*

A serious demonstration of the consequences of violence would be something rather different, something never seen on children's television. For it to be meaningful, it couldn't involve the usual cringing compromises that self-consciously educational television typically pursues: it would have to be hard, unpleasant, and painful. Perhaps it might be an unsparing depiction of what happens when a six-year-old boy finds his father's gun and accidentally shoots his baby brother. Or maybe it could be the unedited brutalization of a child by a parent. Or it might show kids in great detail what the corpse of a soldier shot by an automatic weapon really looks like. We suspect that those who complain about the lack of consequences in Road Runner cartoons are somewhat less than sincere in their desire to remedy that situation in this manner.

We have dismissed many expert studies of television, violence, and kidvid because they fail to see individual cartoons as complex texts, because they assume far too much, because they refuse to respect the critical intelligence of most children. But in the end, we could ignore all of these problems and still find ourselves doubting the experts. For the sake of argument, we could allow that studies between 1960 and 1995 somehow demonstrate a relationship between Daffy Duck getting his beak blown off and "aggression" among children. Though we reject absolutely the crude presumptions of many kidvid critics from Senator Paul Simon to Donald Wildmon that cultural representation of certain actions produces particular behaviors modeled directly on those actions, we're also not enamored of the equally impoverished "it's just a show, you should really just relax" school. Popular culture, including kidvid, *has* provided much of the raw material through which we all make sense of the world; it *does* shape social reality. So we cannot entirely ignore relationships between some problematic violent actions and the representation of violence on television. Indeed, we accept that a diffuse relationship almost certainly exists.

However, we note that even the most comprehensive reviews of the scholarly literature on television and violence cannot offer with any degree of specificity an assessment of the relative importance of television as a factor in social violence, what Liebert and Sprafkin call "effect size." This is an important issue. If someone is stupid enough to light a trailer on fire after watching *Beavis and Butt-head,* or a kid is dumb enough to jump off the roof after watching *Superman,* then they are just an accident waiting to happen anyway. If a kid is already messed up in the head and inclined to destructively violent acts, then it's not clear why it matters if he or she gets an extra little push from watching Space Ghost kick Zorak's ass one more time. If children are already abandoned by our society and some car-

toon makes them even slightly more aware of the violent circumstances under which they are forced to live, then isn't the real problem the social conditions and not the cartoon? It's a cliché, but parents have a thousand times more influence on children than cartoons do, and if parents forsake that responsibility, they have no business expecting Saturday morning to do it for them.

The experts are generally silent when it comes to describing just why the vaguely defined idea "aggression" (or its even vaguer partner, "antisocial behavior") is a bad thing. Experts lack precision not only in their labeling of particular cartoon incidents as violent, but also in their presumptions about aggression, particularly among preschoolers. Even if we were to concede the "violence" of Saturday morning to the experts (and we don't), we still think that they—and their political allies—have persistently failed to explain *exactly* what worries them about its consequences, *exactly* what is wrong with "aggression" or "antisocial behavior," or for that matter, *exactly* what violence is. They don't because they can't. They don't, because to do so is to expose the arbitrary way that they exclude (and thus sanctify) some forms of "legitimate" violence.

Take for example the discussion in Newton Minow and Craig Lamay's 1995 book *Abandoned in the Wasteland.* Minow and Lamay assert that "the meaning of violence can be and has been adequately defined hundreds of times narrowly enough to exclude the many obvious instances (football games or the evening news) in which it is either unavoidable or serves a legitimate purpose." When we look to the footnote, we find definitions from the Centers for Disease Control, the American Psychological Association, and the National Research Council of Britain. Take one of these definitions, from the APA: violence is "behavior by persons against persons that threatens, attempts, or completes intentional infliction of physical or psychological harm." Minow and Lamay confidently declare that this definition obviously excludes football games, which only makes clear that they haven't ever watched football. Close scrutiny of the claims of kidvid critics almost always calls into question their swaggering confidence in the "scientific" basis of their arguments.

Violence and aggression have—at least potentially—creative and socially constructive sides. Understanding and interpreting violence is a crucial objective for any child. If Saturday morning has shown children something about the uses and prevalence of violence in daily life, then that is a mark in its favor rather than an indictment against it. Most of those we've criticized in this book probably also accept and support some social uses of violence—war, imprisonment, and self-defense, for starters. They just can't admit this fact, and instead construct a straw man of "cartoon violence" (or more broadly, televisual violence).

No matter how you add it up, we're in favor of more cartoon violence, not less.

There's probably no better summary commentary on violence in kidvid than the episode of *The Simpsons* in which Marge Simpson goes into a very ACT-like mode and campaigns for the pacification of Itchy and Scratchy, the ultraviolent Tom and Jerry dopplegängers that the Simpson kids love to watch. Itchy and Scratchy are transformed by Marge's campaign into best friends who sit around doing favors for each other. The kids grow bored and then all motherly desires are fulfilled: children go outside to play, they read books, they enrich themselves, and above all, they leave the television behind. But then Itchy and Scratchy go back to disemboweling each other and the kids are once again enthralled. In one stroke, the writers of *The Simpsons* parodied both the producers of cartoons and their leading critics, while also accepting the home truth: cartoon violence is much beloved by children. Deal with it.

Racism and Sexism

Let's get something out of the way at the outset. We're about to be politically correct. There has been an immense load of right-wing blubbering and sulking about the alleged menace of "political correctness," so it behooves us to set the record straight from the start. "PC" was something that activists used in the mid-eighties as a sardonic term for the occasional prissy creep who showed up to meetings and disciplined everyone else's terminology without actually participating in any other way. Somehow an in-joke concerned with a rare annoyance mutated into a bizarre general caricature that demagogues used crudely to bludgeon anyone they don't like. It has gotten to the point where the moment anyone begins to offer even the most modest sort of complaint, some stunted whiner will cry, "Political correctness, political correctness! You're a fascist who is taking away my right to enjoy Naked Female Slave Auction Mud Wrestling!"

While we freely concede that there have been some notorious cases where people have gone to ridiculous lengths to change terminology and nomenclature in order to avoid giving offense to anyone, we think there's nothing wrong with making a concerted effort to reinvent the way that Americans talk about race, gender, sexual preference, and other matters of identity. Television can shape our lives, it does provide raw material for constructing the world and the people in it, and it shores up ideologies and actions—both good and bad. You can overstate this influence, like the critics of kidvid violence do. But it is still there and it is still worth talking about.

Along these lines, with regard to race and gender, Saturday morning has inarguably been a failure over most of its history. In its earliest years, it was often overtly racist and sexist, and at the very least, almost always exclusionary. Kidvid producers and prosocial consultants later suggested condescendingly cosmetic changes that were often as bad as the distortions they sought to address. In an early article about the goals and outlook of ACT, Peggy Charren briefly deviated from a discussion of the evils of commercialism to observe with some amazement, "The other day I saw the 'Banana Splits' on UHF. There were black natives grabbing white blondes. It's incredible to get that kind of racial stereotype in this day and age." Charren's observation later led ACT to make common cause with African American lobbyists trying to improve the representation of blacks on television. Before ever reading Charren's quote, we ourselves had the same experience while watching *The Banana Splits* on the Cartoon Network. Charren was referring to the live-action serial *Danger Island,* which appeared on the program along with the Splits themselves and short cartoon adventures of the Three Musketeers and other characters. While we both remembered the Splits themselves, neither of us had recalled *Danger Island* until we watched that afternoon. We were as amazed as Charren had been back in 1970. Besides being astoundingly crudely made, *Danger Island* did indeed prominently feature, in almost every episode, various dark-skinned characters leering and pawing at a blond teenage girl.

Kidvid from the sixties and early seventies was rarely this blatant, of course. *The Adventures of Jonny Quest* had a tendency to pit its heroes against Fu Manchu types and racialized thugs of various sorts. A more notorious example occurred in one of Dick Tracy's animated incarnations, in which Tracy would introduce several other detective characters, including Go-Go Gomez, a lazy Mexican detective who solved crimes without moving from his hammock, and Ju-Jitsu, a caricatured Japanese sleuth. Similar ethnic stereotypes were a significant reason for the cancellation of the *Dr. Doolittle* cartoon in 1972. The Go-Go Gophers, who appeared in the wake of the superhero banishment, were American Indian characters whose stereotyping might make Tonto blush. Perhaps more subtly poisonous but to our minds equally nasty were some of the segments from "History Rock," the portion of *Schoolhouse Rock* devoted to American history. The one that really stands out in this respect featured a bunch of white colonists and frontiersmen happily singing, "Elbow room! Elbow room!" as they expand across the continent—with only a rubber-tipped arrow through the hat of one frontiersman reminding viewers of the existence of Native Americans. Setting Manifest Destiny to a lighthearted musical tune isn't exactly a good piece of pedagogy—unless one is trying to offer a DIY guide for imperialism.

What was more typical, however, was Saturday morning's almost unbroken sea of whiteness. From Scooby-Doo's gang to the Superfriends, nearly all of the early-seventies characters were as white as the driven snow. The network answer to criticisms of this sort was the same one that is still given today in mass culture, which is to add token characters whose only reason for being is the color of their skin.

———

"We have our entertainment networks everywhere but Africa. And we're talking about going into Africa with *Tom and Jerry* because Africans like cartoons too. Trouble is, most of them don't have television sets or electricity." —Ted Turner, 1995

———

This toothless form of "multiculturalism" doesn't change the central narrative in any fashion, doesn't tell stories any differently, doesn't actually alter the core perspective. It just adds on a dark face someplace. Some of the added characters in Saturday morning were nothing more than blond Caucasians whose skin and hair were recolored. A more typical model was the addition of characters to *Superfriends:* Black Vulcan, Apache Chief, and Samurai. (A Hispanic character, El Dorado, appeared in a single episode.) The characters existed for no other reason than to provide some kind of diversity: they were ciphers whose real superpower was the color of their skin. They might as well have been called "Generic Negro Guy" and "Generic Injun Guy." No kid was going to watch *Superfriends* and think to himself, "Man, I like that cool superhero, *Black Vulcan.*"

This sort of pointlessly empty gesture of "inclusion" has remained a surprisingly consistent feature of kidvid up to the present. J. Michael Straczynski, recalling his work on the mid-eighties show *The Real Ghostbusters,* noted that various consultants pressured the show's creators to "clarify" the role of a black character by making him the driver—i.e., chauffeur—for the white characters. The contemporary syndicated program *Captain Planet and the Planeteers* features this sort of empty multiculturalism: each of the Planeteers represents a different geographical area and racial group, but underneath it all they're all basically the same, white North Americans wearing ethnic drag, doing cute little shuffles to establish their authenticity.

The one nonwhite character in various group cartoons was generally included to prove that America was really all tolerant now, that everyone not only should be but already was equal. As Benjamin De-Mott commented in his book *The Trouble with Friendship,* this "ideology of sameness" has dominated television generally for the past two decades, and cartoons have been no exception. As in the case of violence, we have no problem with the proposition that cartoons can and should show more of the ambiguous reality of race in America to children. One of the minor reasons that contemporary young adults seem bewildered by the intractable nature of race is that they were told repeatedly by prosocial children's television programs that racial prejudice is nothing more than bad manners between individuals, that all we need is cooperation and racial difference will melt away like a bad memory, that discrimination is in our past and racism is practiced only by sneering villains. But just as in the case of violence, we rather doubt that the usual pack of critics has ever been interested in children's programming that would deal honestly with race and ethnicity in America. Such programming, by its very nature, would be deeply troubling to the kind of unctuous middle-class liberalism that lies behind most hostility to kidvid.

There were a few interesting exceptions to bland official multiculturalism in the seventies and eighties. The most notable and successful of these programs was Bill Cosby's *Fat Albert and the Cosby Kids.* Cosby's show worked because the characters weren't cookie-cutter figures off of some assembly line for good ethnic stereotypes. Instead, they were aggressively weird and individualistic. Another and slightly more complicated effort along these lines was the show *Kid Power,* based on the comic strip *Wee Pals,* that appeared in 1972 and was produced by Rankin-Bass. Each of the eleven main characters represented a specific different ethnic group, and the show rarely overcame this kid of simpleminded compartmentalization in its short run. But at the very least, *Kid Power* didn't simply add colored faces as afterthoughts to an essentially white universe.

At the same time, as we've argued throughout this book, the children who actually watched Saturday morning were often able to subvert the content of programs to fit their own needs, adding material to fill up the silences. Many views of the children raised on Saturday morning (and of "Generation X" generally) see them as monolithically white—for example, on the cover image of the tribute album *Saturday Morning* (as well as the interspersed bits of the album's videos featuring Drew Barrymore and fellow white couch potatoes). Viewing Saturday morning was not a white privilege. The cartoons themselves may have been totally white or blandly multicultural, but this doesn't mean that African American, Latino, and Asian audiences were completely unable to find characters and themes which they could appreciate and appropriate. Just as Bart Simpson and Batman have been remade at times as "black" on T-shirts and other fannish ephemera, other white characters in cartoons could also be reclaimed, though not without considerable creative labor on the part of audiences. We don't mean to suggest that the absence of genuinely evocative characters from a range of racial and ethnic backgrounds was not in and of itself troubling, but that absence has complex implications for understanding the Saturday morning phenomenon.

———

"Who or what is Godzilla? On first viewing the show, I speculated that he represented the primitive natural forces that we have at our disposal to see us through our current crises. As such Godzilla would be a very positive force. But I have since made a more pessimistic identification. Godzilla seems more like a symbol of corporate power, of the industrial complex." —Celia Catlett Anderson, "The Saturday Morning Survival Kit"

———

The same holds equally true for gender as well as for race. Racial difference was subjected to stereotyping or tokenism in most of Saturday morning, or was simply submerged beneath whiteness. Gender was treated similarly shabbily, but in a rather different manner. Female characters were relatively common in Saturday shows, but they were subject to very particular patterns of (mis)representation that were echoed in popular culture in general. In her book *Where the Girls Are: Growing Up Female with the Mass Media,* Susan Douglas describes the world of fifties and sixties kidvid as offering two simultaneous messages, "sales pitches that reaffirmed that, as a girl, I had indeed been born into the very best of times" and "retrograde messages about traditional femininity." Watching Saturday morning cartoons with her daughter, Douglas concludes that not only has this not changed, but that the situation has actually worsened. In contemporary kidvid, she argues, girls are still taught to make themselves "desirable commodities" for male consumption, still told to hate themselves and their bodies.

We can't really disagree with Douglas in her characterization of past and present kidvid. In the broadest terms, she's absolutely correct. At the same time, she seems unable to trust that her daughter will achieve her own form of self-awareness about television. What we like about Douglas's book is that she allows that audiences have deeply contradictory feelings about television and its stereotypes. Oddly, though, Douglas doesn't concede fully that more recent televisual kidvid must have its own guilty pleasures, even on the matter of its representation of gender.

Saturday morning has had its own very particular archetypal gender figures, particularly in the core decade of the seventies. Possibly the most iconic female duo in cartoons to emerge from this era was Velma and Daphne on *Scooby-Doo*. Many women who discussed their memories of Saturday morning with us focused on these two characters. Velma was the brainy woman, often given the role of explaining the mystery at the conclusion of the episode—usually with some help from Fred and Shaggy. Bespectacled and perpetually clad in an orange sweater that made her look like a pumpkin (several of our respondents commented that they remembered Velma being fat and were surprised to find out that she wasn't), Velma represented a distillation of virtually every noxious stereotype about intelligent women that one could find. Small wonder that Saturday morning veterans have joked about Velma being a lesbian: it was the only stereotype left (explicitly) untapped. Daphne, on the other hand, had perhaps the most exaggerated figure on the whole of Saturday morning: calling it an hourglass is underestimating it. She wasn't quite stereotypically airheaded, but her role in the Scooby gang's adventures was significantly decorative. Of course, one could say the same about Fred, with his blond bodybuilder figure, or his spiritual twin Alan on *Josie and the Pussycats*—but both Fred and Alan were invariably central to the solution of their group's various dilemmas.

There were some female characters with some potential sassiness and independence in seventies kidvid. Three out of the four women on *Josie and the Pussycats* were at least somewhat interesting, though the group also had its resident blond ditz, Melodie. In particular, Alexandra, in the resident bitch role, could be refreshing, though she was hardly intended to be. Josie and Valerie, the two competent Pussycats, were relatively bland and boring. As a result, Alexandra, with her unrequited lust for Alan and her cynicism, at least provided a rather different sort of female character for Saturday morning audiences to view. In fact, the mix on *Josie and the Pussycats* was pretty much typical of all-girl teams both in the cartoons and on prime time—rather akin to the mix of brainy, ditsy, and bland that one found in *Charlie's Angels* or their cartoon doppelgängers, the Teen Angels.

Sabrina on *The Groovie Goolies,* on the other hand, was an independent, take-charge character, though she was also essentially walking on ground prepared by prime-time magic women Jeannie and Samantha. Another magical woman, Isis, appeared prominently in many of the reminiscences that our contemporaries shared with us. Particularly by women, Isis is remembered as a strong and well-rounded female character, though her adventures were not terribly memorable. Other Saturday morning veterans cited the Krofft characters Electra-Woman and Dynagirl, but conceded that the characters were not only goofy, but highly derivative of Batman and Robin. A later character who stands out for many former viewers and even for some critics was She-Ra. Though clearly a female doppelgänger of He-Man, and hobbled by certain kinds of gendered restrictions in her portrayal, she was nevertheless an unusual character—a female action hero designed to be at the center of her own program, kicking (mildly and politely) some butt in the course of her adventures.

What is equally interesting is to consider instances where women were missing altogether. For example, as we've noted, Race Bannon and Dr. Quest were one of the most attractively portrayed gay couples to appear in American televisual history—at least until Ted Turner's minions ridiculously rewrote the series to claim that Mrs. Quest had been around all the time and we'd just never seen her before. The implication that Jonny, Race, Dr. Quest, and Hadji were running around having thousands of adventures while Mrs. Quest baked cupcakes at home is more offensive than the total absence of women from the cartoon. In other shows, implied or subversively insinuated relationships between men and women were less offensive and more intriguing. Very few were explicitly intended to have romantic overtones: married couples on Saturday morning included Mr. Fantastic and the Invisible Woman on *The Fantastic Four,* Zandor and Tara of *The Herculoids,* and the married couples on *The Flintstones* and *The Jetsons.* There were also male-female pairs more or less explicitly defined as a couple—Lori and Gator on *Inch High, Private Eye,* Pebbles and Bamm Bamm on *Pebbles and Bamm Bamm,* Boris and Natasha on *Rocky and His Friends.*

There were other kinds of implied relationships. We've already mentioned, for example, the widespread assumption that Fred and Daphne of *Scooby-Doo* were making the beast with two backs on a regular basis: other assumed or even overt unmarried heterosexual couples on Saturday morning included Thundarr and Princess Ariel on *Thundarr the Barbarian* and Speed Racer and Trixie (though they seem a bit nauseatingly prepubescent for that sort of thing) on *Speed Racer.* Even more kinky possible relationships include, as we've previously discussed, Smurfette servicing an entire village of male Smurfs, Penelope Pitstop and the Ant Hill Mob, Alan with anywhere from one to four Pussycats (though we doubt he was getting it on with Alexandra), Nancy and Chuck on *Shazzan!,* and the potential ménage à trois between the three human characters on *The Funky Phantom* and *Speed Buggy* (unless the Phantom and Speed Buggy were in on these relationships as well, which is too kinky even for us). Some implied relationships were more overt and more annoying in their use of stereotypes than others. As Susan Douglas points out, Betty and Veronica on *The Archies* could never escape their stupid characterization as Archie's harem, perpetually locked in combat for his affections.

Saturday morning was certainly no better and frequently much worse than the general span of American popular culture when it came to depicting female characters and the relationship between the

Be sure to use a No. 2 pencil and fill in the bubbles completely.

1) Sleestak: Deceptikon as Legion of Doom:

    a) Smurf

    b) Cobra

    c) Zarn

    d) Donald Wildmon

2) Complete this sequence: Boo Berry, Count Chocula, Franken Berry, and

    a) Corpse Crunchies

    b) Texas Chainsaw Massacre Flakes

    c) Fruit Brute

    d) Mummy Muesli

3) If Penelope Pitstop, Dick Dastardly, and the Ant Hill Mob all leave Cleveland at 8:30 P.M., driving at 60 miles per hour toward Cincinnati, and Peter Perfect, Blubber Bear, and Professor Pat Pending leave Cincinnati at 9 P.M. and drive toward Cleveland at 45 miles per hour, at what time will Dick Dastardly's car explode because he tries to cheat?

    a) 8:30 P.M.

    b) 10 P.M.

    c) It depends on whether he's using Acme car parts.

    d) Whenever Rufus Ruffcut leaves Pittsburgh.

4) Which of the following bands of the sixties was not made into a Saturday morning cartoon?

a) The Partridge Family

b) The Osmonds

c) The Monkees

d) The Jackson Five

e) All of the above

5) Match the grammatically appropriate *Schoolhouse Rock* song with the cartoon phrase "Jane, stop this crazy thing!"

a) "Conjunction Junction"

b) "The Good Eleven"

c) "Rufus Xavier Sarsaparilla"

d) "Interjections!"

sexes. More often than not, it showed us all a world in which girls fretted about being pretty, deferred to boys, and otherwise fit neatly into a world where they were second-class citizens. Cartoons from the late seventies and the eighties tried to make up for these early deficiencies by rigorous gender-neutrality or bland prosocial messages. But just as in the case of race, such a portrayal had the net effect of denying the existence of deep-rooted conflicts which were otherwise very visible and of immediate importance to children.

To criticize such representations—whether overtly racist and sexist or merely bland—is no big deal. If cartoons really explored the anxieties and ambiguities of American society regarding race, ethnicity, gender, or sexuality, things would not change all that much. Precisely because we think that moving kidvid to a more honest and interesting (if uncomfortable) engagement with such issues is a relatively modest step, we think that it ought to be easy to make that step, just like it ought to be easy to avoid ethnic slurs and to stop calling women "girls."

One of the most corrupt and hypocritical aspects of right-wing bellowing is the repeated claim that leftists and liberals have injected politics into domains where it doesn't belong—such as popular culture. In the end, most right-wingers actually share the assumptions of the most extreme of their foes, namely, that popular culture is not merely a significant influence on social behavior but a nearly all-powerful one. From Bob Dole to Ralph Reed, the cry goes up that popular culture—whether it's kidvid or *Kids*—actually creates immorality and criminality out of nothing. That is most emphatically not a view that assumes the neutrality of culture *until* it is politicized by "politically correct" fanatics. Most cultural conservatives are not against politicizing something like cartoons, they simply want the politics to be *theirs.* It all comes down to a question of content and values. Kidvid cannot help but be politicized. The question is what its politics should be, along with a proportionate sense of what such politics can and cannot accomplish. Even though the answer is "not much," it's still worth addressing the issue.

Commercialism

For every G.I. Joe with Action King-Fu Grip, there's a bunch of dead Sea Monkeys in a fish bowl. Every cool toy that lingers lovingly in the memory is matched by a toy that disappointed, a toy that was advertised misleadingly or deceptively. And though Count Chocula and Freakies were really cool cereals, they certainly helped some of this generation head toward premature obesity. It's hard to view the graspingly commercial nature of Saturday morning with anything better than ambivalence. Nevertheless, on closer examination, the whole issue is a lot messier than groups like ACT saw it.

A basic purpose of Saturday morning was to sell products to children, or more accurately, to get children to beg their parents to buy products. There's no need to obscure this elemental fact. Kidvid migrated to Saturdays because there were no other audiences who might watch at such a time and because affluent families had money to spend on toys and other luxuries for their children. Television executives were not doing us a favor out of the goodness of their hearts. The consequences of this foundation of avarice, however, are not as sinister as many critics would have it. Advertisers and television executives developed a much deeper and more authentic appreciation of the critical intelligence of children than did the critics of kidvid. They consistently saw children as capable of independent thought about their likes and dislikes in programming. As Ellen Seiter points out in *Sold Separately,* though this presentation of children was in part a PR strategy, it also confirmed that "advertising researchers have come to understand children's experience of television better than the well-intentioned effects researchers."

Inasmuch as we're inclined to see commercialism as a peculiarly negative aspect of the history of children's television (as opposed to a much more generally negative aspect of our culture as a whole), the main issue is the way that a commercial imperative forced the relentless economizing of cartoon production in the seventies and early eighties. Producers and executives may have claimed to respect the intelligence and good judgment of children, but they evinced relatively little of that respect during the evolution of Saturday morning. High volume and low cost drove the production of children's television more than any desire to find cartoons which most appealed to children.

Commercial interests understood what the children's advocates and experts did not: that the tastes of children would not always or even often tend toward shows that were self-consciously educational or prosocial. This insight did not necessarily lead them to produce good cartoons. Ultimately, the best children's programs of the seventies were either those which had been produced for theatrical release in an earlier era or those that had some kind of other incarnation elsewhere in popular culture, like *Star Trek, Super Friends, Tarzan,* and *Dungeons & Dragons.*

"And on shows like Hot Wheels they say not to smoke because some kids have died from smoking and other drugs, so I know not to do it. Commercials help with things not to do. I won't take aspirin except when my mother tells me to. So many kids under 12 have taken dope and kids over 12 have taken dope. But I'm under 12 and I don't take it. And I hope I don't begin taking it like people taking dope." —Seven-year-old Randy Hall, quoted in *TV Guide*, 1970

What is so striking about the renaissance of kidvid in the late eighties and the nineties is that television producers seem to have finally grasped the idea, albeit tenuously, that the commercial staying power of a well-produced children's program—something like *Gargoyles, Reboot,* or *The Tick*—is considerably higher than that of a piece of industrially produced dreck. In a strange way, the nadir of commercial kidvid—the mid-eighties pit of toy-related cartoons—was what paved the way for a richer synergy between commercialism and children's entertainment in the nineties. In the first rush to duplicate the unexpected success of He-Man, many producers assumed that one merely had to have a program and some toys in order to make money. But the resulting glut on the marketplace proved that both the toys *and* the program itself needed to offer quality entertainment. The commercial potential of the wonderfully animated and sleekly plotted new *Batman* series is many times that of the old cheap Filmation *Batman* series.

Assessing advertising's relationship to kidvid is not just a matter of studying its impact on programming. There are also the advertisements themselves as well as the toys, cereals, games, and other products being advertised. Both the ads and the products are major subjects in and of themselves, independent of Saturday morning, but each warrants some discussion here. As we noted in chapter 4, many Saturday morning veterans are as prone to describe their favorite commercials and their favorite products as they are to discuss particular programs. For us, the issue of whether the Rabbit should have Trix was as interesting as anything which actually happened on the programs themselves. The characters on ads for Cap'n Crunch or Freakies cereal were just about as intriguing as Scooby-Doo or Batman. The blissful explosion of lustful desire brought on by a commercial for some new cool toy was a pleasurable part of childhood.

This blissful sensation had its downside. Few toys could live up to their televisual coolness in real life, and some of the coolest toys were ones you discovered with friends that weren't really advertised on television. More importantly, you couldn't always have what you wanted, and desire often gave way to envy and melancholy longing. We grew up under conditions of privilege, so we imagine that the occasional frustration we felt of not getting or finding the toys we wanted and had seen on television was only the palest echo of the habitual frustration felt by most children. Given that a consumer-driven economy requires people to feel perpetual dissatisfaction, we have to acknowledge the role of Saturday morning in making kids feel that way early in their lives.

Commercialism also played a key role in creating the characteristic mix of affection and cynicism that most Saturday morning veterans employ when wallowing in nostalgia about their childhood television experiences. Our collective awareness that cartoons were designed to sell us things—an awareness sharpened a hundredfold in the eighties, when the cartoons themselves became extended advertisements for particular toys—led many of us to regard kidvid with suspicion. On balance, we think that such cynicism is not a bad thing, but it is to some extent connected to corollary feelings of alienation and helplessness among many of our contemporaries.

None of the above analysis contradicts the standard liberal attack on commercial television. We agree that commercialism tends to dull the edges of popular culture relentlessly, to make it so much less than it could be. But we seriously question whether commercialism has had any peculiarly negative impact on children or on children's television. The whole issue is like the schizoid attitude that surrounds teenage sexuality in public service announcements. In them, sex is portrayed as dreary, unpleasant, and pathological. But everywhere else, sex is shown as fun, fun, fun. Children aren't stupid and they know adults are hypocrites. Lying to them about sex is the worst possible way to discourage teenage pregnancy or dangerously unprotected sex. Likewise, trying to shield children from commercialism and then dropping them unprotected into its maelstrom at age eighteen is about the worst possible strategy imaginable for creating informed and critical perspectives among a media-literate adult public.

Nor are noncommercial alternatives for financing kidvid viable. Unless the whole of television were transformed by such a plan, noncommercial financing would simply be another instance of foolishly trying to protect children from the adult world. More importantly, though commercialism may inhibit the spread of excellence in television programming, it is by no means certain that noncommercial alternatives would be better. The various funding schemes advanced by ACT and other groups over the years usually require a vastly increased role for the federal government in monitoring and even providing programs. Putting the federal government in the driver's seat of kidvid would inevitably lead to a plague of bland and sanctimonious programs. We feel certain that the U.S. government is not up to the task—they're incapable of ignoring the legions of prosocial experts, concerned parents, and right-wing fundamentalist goon squads that would doubtless cluster like flies around government-funded children's television. If ACT or groups like it were in charge, kidvid would almost certainly be stultifying, phony, and alienating. To make good television, kidvid or otherwise, you must understand that you cannot please everybody all of the time.

This consideration is putting aside the fact that in the political climate of the late nineties, the prospect of extensive government expenditures on television production is about as likely as Michael Jackson becoming the anchor of the ABC nightly news. The profusion of children's programs created by commercial television over the past forty years—good, bad, and indifferent—strikes us as a better alternative for now. Given the relative fecundity of commercial television to date, any alternative to advertising would have to be far more compelling and bolder than anything yet proposed or imagined. We doubt it would be worth the trouble. Judging from the programs airing in 1996, commercial television is doing okay by kids for the moment.

The Pleasures and Uses of Nostalgia

Nostalgia gets a bum rap from a lot of people, including our contemporaries. That's partly because the members of Generation X are accustomed to the baby boomers and the so-called Silents running around acting like they're the last group of people on Earth to have experienced anything meaningful, like Garrison Keillor in a moronic 1996 *New York Times* article in which he moaned that future generations will "miss that time in the past—it really did exist—when kids used to mess around outdoors. Go off and just *do stuff*. Build forts, have wars, die, hang out." Newsflash, Garrison: kids still do that. Come back down from Planet Wobegon and join us in the real world, pal.

Nostalgia is too often a completely fraudulent distortion of the past, used to justify nonsensical political or social agendas in the present. An obsession with nostalgia can blind you to what is new and interesting, to the forward motion of history. We're not shilling for that kind of nostalgia. We're not pleading for our take on Saturday morning because we want to make sure that all the generations of kids that come after us know we were the coolest people ever. We're not trying to take over the culture.

But there are reasons why Saturday morning veterans turn to each other in a frenzy of remembrance every time the subject of our youthful television habits comes up, reasons why we ask each other about baby superheroes and hissing lizardmen, reasons why we all laugh with pleasure when the theme song to *Josie and the Pussycats* begins to play. This kind of nostalgia, with all of its characteristic Generation X guardedness and double meanings, is about nothing more and nothing less than confirming that you are alive and that other people lived at the same moment in time that you did. It's a way of grasping the tangible *fact* of generational identity. We discover in Saturday morning that we share our childhood memories with strangers, that others sat in front of their televisions and thought the same things we did. It's a glorious discovery. No wonder everyone babbles excitedly at the outset of such a conversation.

"Exit, stage right." —Snagglepuss

What frustrates us, after years of reading what everyone else has had to say about the institution of Saturday morning, is not just the absence of our own productive nostalgia from the debate, but the active denial that any such sense could or should exist. We do not ask that our stories about Saturday morning be the only allowable stories. Few of us, old or young, are fortunate enough to see ourselves authentically reflected in pop culture's mirror, after all. In the end, all we really ask is that we be permitted to become the active custodians of our own memories.

Bibliography

Books and Articles from Journals and Anthologies

Adler, Richard P. *The Effects of Television Advertising on Children: Review and Recommendations.* Lexington, Mass: D.C. Heath, 1980.

Anderson, Celia Catlett. "The Saturday Morning Survival Kit." *Journal of Popular Culture* 17, no. 4 (spring 1984): 155–161.

Barbera, Joseph. *My Life in Toons: From Flatbush to Bedrock in Under a Century.* Atlanta: Turner Publishing Company, 1994.

Barnouw, Erik. *Tube of Plenty: The Evolution of American Television.* New York: Oxford University Press, 1981.

Beck, Jerry, and Will Friedwald. *Looney Tunes and Merrie Melodies.* New York: Henry Holt and Company, 1989.

Brown, Ray, ed. *Children and Television.* Beverly Hills: Sage Publications, 1976.

Bruce, Scott, and Bill Crawford. *Cerealizing America: The Unsweetened Story of American Breakfast Cereal.* Boston: Faber and Faber, 1993.

Cater, Douglass, and Stephen Strickland. *TV Violence and the Child: The Evolution and Fate of the Surgeon General's Report.* New York: Russell Sage Foundation, 1975.

Chen, Milton. "Six Myths About Television and Children." *Media Studies Journal* 4 (fall 1994): 105–113.

Comstock, George. *Television and the American Child.* New York: Academic Press, 1991.

Coupland, Douglas. *Microserfs.* New York: Regan Books, 1995.

Crawford, Ben. "Saturday Morning Fever." In *The Illusion of Life,* edited by Alan Cholodenko. Sydney, Australia: Power Publications, 1991.

Davis, Stephen. *Say Kids! What Time Is It? Notes from the Peanut Gallery.* Boston: Little, Brown, and Company, 1987.

DeMott, Benjamin. *The Trouble with Friendship: Why Americans Can't Think Straight About Race.* New York: Atlantic Monthly Press, 1995.

Doty, Alexander. *Making Things Perfectly Queer: Interpreting Mass Culture.* Minneapolis: University of Minneapolis Press, 1993.

Elliott, William Y. *Television's Impact on American Culture.* East Lansing, Mich.: Michigan State University Press, 1956.

Engelhardt, Tom. "Children's Television: The Shortcake Strategy." In *Watching Television,* edited by Todd Gitlin. New York: Pantheon Books, 1986.

Fiske, John. *Reading the Popular.* Boston: Unwin Hyman, 1989.

———. *Television Culture.* New York: Routledge, 1987.

Gitlin, Todd. *Inside Prime Time.* New York: Pantheon Books, 1983.

Gorman, Paul R. *Left Intellectuals and Popular Culture in Twentieth-Century America.* Chapel Hill: University of North Carolina Press, 1996.

Grossman, Gary H. *Saturday Morning TV.* New York: Dell Publishing, 1981.

Hanna, Bill. *A Cast of Friends.* Dallas: Taylor Publishing Company, 1996.

Himmelweit, Hilde T., et al. *Television and the Child: An Empirical Study of the Effect of Television on the Young.* London: Oxford University Press, 1958.

Howe, Neil, and Bill Strauss. *13th Gen: Abort, Retry, Ignore, Fail?* New York: Vintage Books, 1993.

Huston, Aletha C., et al. *Big World, Small Screen: The Role of Television in American Society.* Lincoln, Nebr.: University of Nebraska Press, 1992.

Javna, John. *Cult TV: A Viewer's Guide to the Shows America Can't Live Without!!* New York: St. Martin's Press, 1985.

Jenkins, Henry. *Textual Poachers: Television Fans and Participatory Culture.* New York: Routledge, 1992.

Kaye, Evelyn. *The ACT Guide to Children's Television.* Boston: Beacon Press, 1979.

Kinder, Marsha. *Playing with Power in Movies, Television, and Video Games.* Berkeley: University of California Press, 1991.

Korkis, Jim, and John Cawley. *Cartoon Confidential.* Westlake Village, Calif.: Malibu Graphics Publishing Group, 1991.

Lazere, Donald, ed. *American Media and Mass Culture: Left Perspectives.* Berkeley: University of California Press, 1987.

Liebert, Robert M., and Joyce Sprafkin. *The Early Window: Effects of Television on Children and Youth.* 3rd ed. New York: Pergamon Press, 1988.

Maltin, Leonard. *Of Mice and Magic—A History of American Animated Cartoons.* New York: New American Library, 1980.

McNeil, Alex. *Total Television.* New York: Penguin Books, 1991.

Miller, Mark Crispin. *Boxed In: The Culture of TV.* Evanston, Ill.: Northwestern University Press, 1988.

Minow, Newton N., and Craig L. Lamay. *Abandoned in the Wasteland: Children, Television, and the First Amendment.* New York: Hill and Wang, 1995.

Owen, David. *The Man Who Invented Saturday Morning.* New York: Villard Books, 1988.

Palmer, Edward L. *Television and America's Children: A Crisis of Neglect.* New York: Oxford University Press, 1988.

Parisi, Peter. "'Black Bart' Simpson: Appropriation and Revitalization in Commodity Culture." *Journal of Popular Culture* 27, no. 1 (summer 1993): 125–142.

Phillips, Phil. *The Truth About Power Rangers.* Lancaster, Pa.: Starburst Publishers, 1995.

Ritchie, Karen. *Marketing to Generation X.* New York: Lexington Books, 1995.

Rudd, David. "Children and Television: A Critical Note on Theory and Method." *Media, Culture and Society* 14 (1992): 313–320.

Schramm, Wilbur, et al. *Television in the Lives of Our Children.* Stanford, Calif.: Stanford University Press, 1961.

Seiter, Ellen. *Sold Separately: Parents and Children in Consumer Culture.* New Brunswick, N.J.: Rutgers University Press, 1995.

Shapiro, Mitchell E. *Television Network Weekend Programming, 1959–1990.* Jefferson, N.C.: McFarland and Company, 1992.

Smoodin, Eric, ed. *Disney Discourse: Producing the Magic Kingdom.* New York: Routledge, 1994.

Spigel, Lynn. *Make Room for TV: Television and the Family Ideal in Postwar America.* Chicago: University of Chicago Press, 1992.

Tichi, Cecelia. *Electronic Hearth: Creating an American Television Culture.* New York: Oxford University Press, 1991.

Ulrich, Charles. "Bullwinkle Briefs." *Frostbite Falls Far-Flung Flier* 10, no. 1 (September 1995).

U.S. Congress. *Children's Television Act of 1990.* Washington, D.C.: United States Government Printing Office, 1990.

U.S. Federal Communications Commission. "Children's Television Programs: Report and Policy Statement." *Federal Register* 39 (November 6, 1974): 215.

Winn, Marie. *The Plug-In Drug.* New York: Viking Press, 1977.

Woolery, George M. *Children's Television: The First Thirty-five Years, 1946–1981.* Volumes 1 and 2. Metuchen, N.J.: Scarecrow Press, 1983.

Yohe, Tom, and George Newall. *The Official Guide to Schoolhouse Rock.* New York: Hyperion, 1996.

Newspaper and Magazine Articles

We made general reference to a wide range of articles relating to children's television, particularly from the *New York Times* and *TV Guide,* while researching this book. Specific articles that we found particularly relevant are listed below.

Andrews, Edmund L. "A Bitter Feud Fouls Lines at the F.C.C.: Children's TV Is Just the Beginning." *New York Times,* November 20, 1995.

Anton, Glenn. "Joe Barbera Speaks His Mind." *Animato* 34 (spring 1996): 40–43.

Barclay, Dorothy. "A Decade Since 'Howdy Doody.'" *New York Times,* September 21, 1958.

Barthel, Joan. "Boston Mothers Against Kidvid." *New York Times Magazine,* January 5, 1975.

Blum, Sam. "De-Escalating the Violence on TV." *New York Times Magazine,* December 8, 1968.

Boyer, Peter J. "CBS Plans 'Noids' Cartoon Series." *New York Times,* January 25, 1988.

"Bullwinkle vs. NBC." *TV Guide,* August 11, 1962.

Carlsson-Paige, Nancy. "Saturday Morning Pushers: The Toy Industry Takes Over Children's Television." *Utne Reader,* January-February 1992.

Charlton, Linda. "FCC's Johnson Accuses TV of Molesting Children's Minds." *New York Times,* March 23, 1972.

Charlton-Perrin, G. "How Not to Sell to Children on TV." *New York Times,* August 22, 1972.

Corry, John. "Cartoons or Commercials?" *New York Times,* October 30, 1983.

Culhane, John. "The Men Behind Dastardly & Muttley." *New York Times Magazine,* November 23, 1969.

Daley, Eliot. "What Produced Those Pot-Smoking, Rebellious, Demonstrating Kids? Television!" *TV Guide,* November 7, 1970.

Denison, D. C. "Children Have a Voice in Peggy Charren." *New York Times Magazine,* June 5, 1983.

Doan, Richard. "Ratings Upset: Live Kid Shows Beat Cartoons." *TV Guide,* November 16, 1974.

———. "Seek to Rout Cartoon Monsters." *TV Guide,* March 10, 1968.

———. "Where Did All the People Go? Saturday Morning's World Is Populated by Curious Creatures Direct from the Inkwell." *TV Guide,* February 11, 1967.

Efron, Edith. "The Battle Again Rages." *TV Guide,* November 8, 1969.

———. "The Children's Crusade That Failed." *TV Guide,* April 7, 1973.

———. "The Man in the Eye of the Hurricane." *TV Guide,* November 15, 1969.

———. "The Real Reason for the Saturday Morning Catastrophe." *TV Guide,* April 21, 1973.

———. "Television as a Teacher." *TV Guide,* October 25, 1969.

———. "Witless, Heartless, Charmless, Tasteless, and Artless." *TV Guide,* April 14, 1973.

———. "You Can Take Your Choice." *TV Guide,* November 1, 1969.

Gould, Jack. "Children's Television: Pinky Lee Makes Some Valid Observations." *New York Times,* October 13, 1958.

———. "State of Children's TV Shows." *New York Times,* November 6, 1960.

———. "TV: Fathers Know Best." *New York Times,* September 23, 1961.

Gross, Leonard. "Television Under Pressure." *TV Guide,* February 22, 1975.

Handler, David. "TV Bookshelf: *Saturday Morning TV* by Gary Grossman." *TV Guide,* December 5, 1981.

Harvey, James Neal. "In Defense of Children's TV." *New York Times,* January 14, 1973.

Hickey, Neil. "'I Would Like a Program with Daffy Duck and Bowling.'" *TV Guide,* June 27, 1970.

———. "The Key Word Is Entertainment." *TV Guide,* October 18, 1969.

———. "Skipper Chuck and Buckskin Bill Are Not Feeling Very Jolly." *TV Guide,* June 2, 1973.

———. "What Is TV Doing to Them?" *TV Guide,* October 11, 1969.

———. "What Television Should Be Doing to Safeguard Our Greatest Natural Resource—Our Children." *TV Guide,* November 29, 1969.

Higgins, Robert. "Mickey Mouse, Where Are You?" *TV Guide,* March 23, 1968.

Horn, Miriam. "Salvaging Saturday Morning Prime Time." *U.S. News & World Report,* March 4, 1991.

Jacobs, Theodore J. "What's Wrong with Children's Television." *New York Times,* December 27, 1970.

Jahn, Mike. "The Archies Are Fictional, but Their Success Is Not." *New York Times,* November 5, 1969.

Keillor, Garrison. "The Future of Nostalgia." *New York Times Magazine,* September 29, 1996.

Leonard, John. "Why Not Use TV for a Head Start Program?" *New York Times Magazine,* July 14, 1968.

McDermott, John F. "The Violent Bugs Bunny et al." *New York Times Magazine,* September 28, 1969.

Mifflin, Lawrie. "Can the Flintstones Fly in Fiji?" *New York Times,* November 27, 1995.

Morrow, James. "TV Didn't Turn Us into Lemmings and Vikings." *TV Guide,* October 9, 1982.

Safran, Claire. "Children's TV: Is It Getting Any Better?" *TV Guide,* October 20, 1979.

———. "*Sesame Street?* 'Too Frenetic.' *Captain Kangaroo?* 'A Baby Sitter.'" *TV Guide,* August 16, 1980.

Sarson, Evelyn. "A Day in the Life of an ACTivist Mom." *New York Times,* August 15, 1971.

———. "We as Parents Accuse You of the Five Deadly Sins." *New York Times,* February 27, 1972.

Saudek, Robert. "Must It Be 'Kookie' and 'Ka-Pow'?" *New York Times,* March 25, 1962.

Schumach, Murray. "Animated, Yes—Frantic, No." *New York Times,* August 28, 1960.

Wolff, Craig. "Mighty Mouse Flying High on Flowers?" *New York Times,* July 26, 1988.

Internet Resources

Usenet Newsgroups

alt.animation
alt.society.generation-x
rec.arts.animation
rec.arts.sf.tv
rec.arts.tv
soc.culture.us.1970s

Web Sites and FAQs

Cartoon Ring Homepage. http://pubpages.unh.edu/~mpc1/scooby.html
The 80s Server. http://www.80s.com
Hanna-Barbera Studios. http://www.animationusa.com/hb.html
Hype! The Nostalgic Wave. http://www.hype.com/nostalgia/
Ultimate TV List. http://www.ultimatetv.com/
The World Famous Scooby Homepage. http://www.oxy.edu/~scooby/home.html
The Zone: Television. http://www.thezone.pair.com/tv/
Alpha_Trion. *Official Cartoons of the 80s Homepage.* http://www.geocities.com/TelevisionCity/1984/
Arlington, Dave. "The Jonny Quest Episode Guide." ftp://src.doc.ic.ac.uk/public/media/tv/collections/tardis/us/drama/JonnyQuest
Astro. *The Ultimate Web Smurf Club.* http://websmurfclub.arcos.org/
Barnhill, Mark. "The Flintstones FAQ." http://www.powerup.com.au/~ves/faq.html
Bono Estente. *Wacky Races.* http://www.bono-estente.demon.co.uk/section2/wacky/
Chambers, Chris. *80s Cartoons Homepage.* http://home.rogerswave.ca/3cpo/80s.htm
Chimielecki, Mike. *Scooby-Doo, What Happened to You?* http://pubpages.unh.edu/~mpc1/scooby.html
Cluff, Chad. *Official Anti-Smurf Page.* http://www.utw.com/~cluff/smurf.html
Coyote. *The Scooby Zone.* http://www.microserve.com/~coyote/frames13.htm
Cringer. *He-Man and She-Ra Page.* http://www.west.ga.net/~eternia/index.html
Eva. *Eva's Scooby Page.* http://www.geocities.com/EnchantedForest/1250/scooby.htm
Fein, Doug. *The Superfriends Archive.* http://fantasia.ncsa.uiuc.edu/Doug/superhtml/
Ferenczy, *Officially Anti-Smurf Page.* http://www.enol.com/~ferenczy/smurf.html
Graphica Daroma. *Rocket Robin Hood Page.* http://centaurcorp.com/rocketrobinhood/

Grasshopper. *The He-Man Universe.* http://www2.fwi.com/~grasshopper/enter.html

Hill, Richard. *The Unofficial Guide to Classic Jonny Quest.* http://www.illuminatus.com/quest

Dr. Jekyll. *The Dark Side of Scooby-Doo.* http://www.cdc.net/~drjekyll/negscooby/main.htm

Johnson, Hal, and Mike Stutzman. "Towards a Hanna-Barbera Taxonomy." http://web.syr.edu/~ctgueret/toon.html

Kurer, Ron. *Toon Tracker Home Page.* http://www2.wi.net/~rkurer/index.htm

Lloyd. *Completely Voltron Home Page.* http://www.inch.com/~pbalch/toon.html

Martins, Daniel Luis Pires. *Cartoons of the 1970s.* http://www.geocities.com/Hollywood/Hills/4862/cartoons.html

Meece, Darrell W. *Sleestak!* http://www.auburn.edu/~meecedw/sleestack.html

Munding, Kurt. *The Original Space Ghost Web Site.* http://iquest.com/~cshuffle/sghost/

Noyes, R. *Spatch's Own Stupid Homepage.* http://pupil.retina.net/~spatula/stupid/index.shtml

Pace, Jeremy. "Transformer Chronology." http://www4.ncsu.edu/eos/users/j/jhpace1/WWW/Files/Transformer_Chronology

Paulson, Sheila. *The Real Ghostbusters Home Page.* http://users.aol.com/venkie/rgb/rgb.htm

Popomatic. *The Unofficial Sid and Marty Krofft Home Page.* http://www.west.net/~popomatic/Krofft.html

Schubach, Erik. *Cartoon World.* http://www.cet.com/~rascal/

Tina. *Scooby-Doo, Where Are You?* http://www.call-us.demon.co.uk/scooby.html

Tyner, Adam. *The He-Man and the Masters of the Universe Homepage.* http://www.awod.com/gallery/rwav/ctyner/he-man.html

Ulrich, Charles. *Frostbite Falls Page.* http://home.iSTAR.ca/~culrich/index.html

V-X. *My Hearthrob, Velma.* http://www.ungh.com/vx/coolness/velma.html

Veselovsky, Cassie-Chamberlain. *Hanna-Barbera Shows.* http://www.powerup.com.au/~ves/hbshows.htm

Wetherholt, David. *DMW Scooby-Doo Homepage.* http://devserve.cebaf.gov/~wether/scoob.html

Worth, Steven. *Ralph Bakshi's Mighty Mouse The New Adventures.* http://www.vintageip.com/bakshi.html

Saturday Morning Sightings

Before he was Gopher on *The Love Boat,* before he was a member of the U.S. House of Representatives, Fred Grandy achieved true fame on the live-action Saturday morning show *Monster Squad.*

Bet you thought Bill Laimbeer just had basketball as his main claim to fame. That pales beside his major thespian achievement: Laimbeer, like a number of USC basketball players, was a Sleestak on *Land of the Lost.*

Walter Koenig, who played Chekov on *Star Trek,* and more recently, the villainous Bester on *Babylon 5,* wrote the episode of *Land of the Lost* that introduced Enik, the wise Sleestak from the distant past.

Keye Luke, who played Number One Son in ten Charlie Chan movies, finally got to do the voice for Charlie Chan himself in the Hanna-Barbera cartoon *The Amazing Chan and the Chan Clan.*

Index

Index

Index   **245**